UNDERSTANDING THE JEWISH AGENCY
A HANDBOOK

REVISED EDITION

UNDERSTANDING THE JEWISH AGENCY

A HANDBOOK

Edited by: Daniel J. Elazar
and Alysa M. Dortort

Jerusalem Center for Public Affairs

The Jerusalem Center for Public Affairs
21 Arlozorov Street, Jerusalem, 92181, ISRAEL
Center for Jewish Community Studies
1017 Gladfelter Hall, Temple University
Philadelphia, 19122, USA
Printed in Israel

Cover by Avi Shapira

ISBN 965-218-005-X

CONTENTS

INTRODUCTION

Daniel J. Elazar

The most important institutional task facing the Jewish people today is creating a proper structure and process of governance for the emergent world Jewish polity. As the major institutional link between the State of Israel and the diaspora communities, the reconstituted Jewish Agency stands at the nexus of this effort. That is why it has been subject to so much controversy in recent years, even if not always for the right reasons.

The Agency is unique not only in the Jewish world but in the world as a whole. It was established as a government-like instrumentality in international law, yet it carries out functions often defined as philanthropic. It originally was designed to build a state-in-the-making, and has now become a key institution for worldwide action on behalf of the Jewish people in both the state and the diaspora.

The Jewish Agency for Palestine was established in 1929 under the terms of the League of Nations mandate for Palestine and pursuant to international law as the operative arm of world Jewry in building the Jewish national home. In the years immediately following the establishment of the State of Israel, it was widely assumed that the Jewish Agency would wither away. Its principal functions, virtually all of its leadership, and much of its bureaucracy were transferred to the new state, which, in the first flush of sovereignty, looked down upon the institutions of pre-state Zionism as obsolete and irrelevant.

Nevertheless, the Jewish Agency survived as the arm of the World Zionist Organization (WZO) within Israel, principally because there was a need for a way to channel diaspora philanthropic contributions, particularly those from the United States, to appropriate programs in Israel which were defined as non-governmental and, hence, eligible for tax-exempt aid. Consequently, in the early 1950s a covenant between the State and the WZO was drawn up and ratified, defining a limited role for the Jewish Agency, renamed the Jewish Agency for Israel (JAFI).

While the Jewish Agency survived, it sank further and further into desuetude, coming under almost the complete domination of the Israeli Government. Then, in the late 1960s, for reasons described in the following pages, the late Louis Pincus, then Chairman of the Jewish Agency Executive, in conjunction with Max M. Fisher, the dominant figure in the United Jewish Appeal (UJA), spearheaded the reconstitution of the Jewish Agency to broaden its base. The reconstituted Jewish Agency included 'non-Zionists' — that is to say, leaders of the community federations and their equivalents in the diaspora who were responsible for raising most of the funds which provided the Jewish Agency with its budget — as equal partners. In part, this was a response to the necessity of giving the American Jewish contributors greater control over the disposition of their funds to accommodate the United States Internal Revenue Service requirements and also to meet the then still limited but rising criticism of the way in which the monies were spent in Israel.

The reconstitution in 1971 not only breathed new life into JAFI but, more important, created a new world arena for Jewish public affairs. During the 1970s, under the continued leadership of Max Fisher as Chairman of the Board of Governors and Arye Leon Dulzin as Chairman of the Jewish Agency Executive, that arena became very real for the most influential leaders of diaspora Jewry who previously had viewed their Israeli connections as a matter of philanthropy and had accepted Israel's right to unilaterally dispose of their contributions. In the course of the decade, the reconstitution was implemented, not as rapidly as some might have liked, but consistently and inexorably, forging a sometimes difficult but still real partnership between the so-called 'fund-raisers' and the WZO. At the same time, those who had been exclusively fund-raisers increasingly gave way to those who were also representatives of the diaspora community umbrella organizations, thereby making the latter's segment of the partnership even more representative.

With the inauguration of Project Renewal in 1977, these trends were accelerated. The links between Israel and the diaspora which had, up until then, represented two separate pyramids lightly touching at their tips, began to be transformed into a network of connections, a matrix, as it were, as people in second and third echelon leadership positions in diaspora communities and even beyond developed their own connections with their Project Renewal neighborhoods, and with those Israeli officials involved in implementing the Project. This, in turn, further strengthened the new arena established by the reconstituted Jewish Agency. It is a sign of the importance of Project Renewal that Jerold C. Hoffberger, the first Chairman of the Board of Governors Project Renewal Committee, who led the way in forging the partnership, was elected to succeed Max Fisher as Chairman of the Board of Governors in June 1983.

The inauguration of the Caesarea Process in February 1981 provided an additional impetus for this transformation. The process was born out of the frustrations of the community representatives with what they had encountered in the first years of the reconstituted Jewish Agency — budgets that were not budgets, meetings that had no operative dimension but merely consisted of being lectured at by Israelis, a sense of impotence and lack of control even when they were called upon to formally make decisions. While progress in all of these areas was being made, many thought that it was being made too slowly, that some catalyst was needed. Hence, the Board of Governors retreat at the Dan Caesarea Hotel which launched an internal review process designed to institute reforms or clarifications with regard to the Jewish Agency's goals and objectives, its major functions of education and aliyah, debt reduction, internal management, and, what was deemed most important of all, governance.

The Caesarea Process followed on the heels of the very successful review committee of the North American Council of Jewish Federations and, consciously or not, seemed to be a next step in the process of improving the institutions of Jewish governance in the major arenas of Jewish public life. At least so it was greeted by the diaspora members of the Board of Governors and the Jewish Agency Assembly and their constituents as they came to know about it. Hence, while the six Board of Governors commissions established to carry out the process originally worked behind closed doors, once they reached the recommendation stage, there were demands that they share their work with their larger constituency. These demands were intensified because of continuing dissatisfaction in some quarters with the Agency's performance in a variety of fields.

During 1983, the Caesarea Process was made public throughout the Jewish world and soon attracted the interest of key figures in the diaspora communities who had previously paid little if any attention to the Process or to the Agency as a whole. As a result, a greatly expanded constituency now exists that is concerned with the Jewish Agency and its workings. This constituency is new to JAFI and hence needs to learn about it.

The struggle going on around the governance and role of the Jewish Agency today has to do with the effort to reach a common understanding of the institution and its purposes. That struggle must be based on understanding if it is to be properly resolved. Perhaps the principal problem of understanding is that many, if not most, of the diaspora community leadership who have contact with the Jewish Agency see it as a philanthropic body in the way they saw their community federations or the equivalent thirty years ago, while that half of the Jewish Agency represented by the WZO, and most particularly the Israelis among them, see it as a political body first and foremost. This dichotomy has many operative consequences, influencing the entire gamut of Jewish Agency operations. For example, if it is a philanthropic body, JAFI should be led by volunteers and managed by a permanent staff of professionals in an efficient, non-partisan way. If it is a political body, it is properly governed by party coalitions and manned by the party faithful. This, indeed, is a major point of contention between the two groups.

More than that, conflict between the two groups has been exacerbated because it is so dichotomous. Thus, over the years, many in the WZO and Israeli party leadership came to see the political dimensions of the Agency not in their original ideological terms, which of necessity led to party divisions and coalitions, but in patronage terms. At the same time, the diaspora leadership has been pushed back to emphasize the Agency's philanthropic dimension far beyond what they would in their own federations where community planning replaced the philanthropic approach many years ago.

In fact, the Jewish Agency is a political instrumentality in the highest sense, that is to say, a government-like body which is one of the principal authorities, if not the principal authority, of the world Jewish polity. That needs to be understood by diaspora Jewry. At the same time, its purposes fall primarily in the social and educational realms. Therefore, Israeli Jews must understand that there has to be a limit to the party political dimension for those who are involved in its day-to-day governance.

The Jerusalem Center for Public Affairs has followed the work of the Jewish Agency and the process of its reconstitution since the establishment of the Center's predecessor in 1968. In our contacts with Jewish communities and their leaders throughout the world, we have discovered a great lack of specific knowledge about the Jewish Agency and its special character, based in great part on a dearth of information that is both concise and comprehensive. As a result of our experiences in trying to explain what was happening with the Agency, we concluded that it would be helpful in advancing that understanding if a handbook existed to introduce those concerned with Jewish public affairs to the Jewish Agency. The first edition of this handbook, published in June 1984, was the result.

The response to the first edition was extraordinarily gratifying. Within a year, the entire first edition was sold out, reflecting the interest of readers in all parts of the Jewish world and of all opinions and interests with regard to the Jewish Agency. Given this response, it was not difficult for us to decide that a second, revised edition was in order, one that would not only answer the continuing demand for the handbook, but correct the modest errors which had inadvertently crept into the first edition, respond to some suggestions made with regard to improving the book, and update the information contained within it.

This handbook consists of three parts and two appendixes. Part One, *The Jewish Agency: A Summary Overview,* is a brief presentation of the highlights of the history, structure, functions, and processes of the Jewish Agency designed to introduce the reader to JAFI as an institution. The importance of the Agency for the Jewish people and an evaluation of its present role is covered generally and specifically in Part Two, *The Jewish Agency and World Jewry.* Part Three, *The Reconstituted Jewish Agency: Cases and Documents,* includes the constitutional documents of the Jewish Agency with commentary by the Agency's legal advisor, two case studies by a Fellow of the Jerusalem Center and a veteran journalistic observer, and reports of the Caesarea Commissions as adopted by the governing bodies of the Agency. Appendix One presents highlights of the World Zionist Organization's structure and budget, and Appendix Two consists of a listing of the present members of the Board of Governors.

In the interim, the continued efforts of the Jerusalem Center in promoting analysis and understanding of the Jewish Agency have led to the publication of *A Common Agenda: The Reconstitution of the Jewish Agency for Israel,* by Zelig Chinitz, a book-length history of the reconstitution of the Agency and its subsequent development, prepared by one of the key figures in the process. The second in a series of studies of the Jewish Agency and its related institutions which the Jerusalem Center is presently undertaking, we strongly recommend it to our readers for a highly readable presentation of the subject. It should be viewed as a companion to this handbook.

As in the case of the first edition, this handbook was prepared entirely within the Jerusalem Center for Public Affairs, which is solely responsible for its contents. However, its preparation would not have been possible without the assistance of Irving Kessler, Executive Vice-Chairman of the United Israel Appeal; Zelig Chinitz, Director-General, and Neale Katz, Deputy Director-General, of the UIA Israel office; Harry Rosen, Secretary-General, and Eli Likhovski, Legal Counsel, of the Jewish Agency; and Chaim Zohar, Secretary-General, Dr. Aaron Zwergbaum, Legal Advisor, and Avraham Schenker, Head of Development and Services, of the World Zionist Organization. We are indebted to them for their comments and cooperation. The United Israel Appeal and Keren Hayesod have played vital roles in enabling us to cover the costs of publication through their bulk orders and assistance in distribution of the handbook.

Special acknowledgement is due the staff of Jerusalem Center Publications, particularly Colleen Siegel, for bringing this manuscript to publication.

PART I

Summary Overview

THE JEWISH AGENCY FOR ISRAEL: A CAPSULE HISTORY

In 1897, in a historic act, Theodore Herzl convened the First Zionist Congress in Basle, Switzerland. Its two major accomplishments were the formulation and adoption of the Basle Program and the creation of the World Zionist Organization (WZO). According to Herzl, the immediate aims of the Congress were "to close the Zionist ranks, bring about an understanding between all Zionists . . . to unify their endeavors," and to establish "the national assembly of the Jewish people." Its larger aim of Jewish restoration in Eretz Israel was embodied in the Basle Program, a four-point program outlining the goals of political Zionism. As Herzl put it, "The Congress will show what Zionism is and wants."

The WZO made its first goal the securing of international recognition of its efforts through a charter. Herzl died in 1904 while in pursuit of that charter. The Balfour Declaration, issued by the British Government in 1917, was considered by Zionists to be that charter. It stated that "His Majesty's Government views with favour the establishment in Palestine of a national home for the Jewish people."

In 1922, the League of Nations reaffirmed that charter and gave to Great Britain the Mandate for Palestine. As part of the Mandate it was stated that, to implement the Balfour Declaration, there should be established a "Jewish agency."

In August 1929, after several years of negotiations, the Jewish Agency for Palestine was established as a partnership between the WZO and non-Zionist Jewish leaders. It was the conviction of Chaim Weizmann, President of the WZO, that all Jews would want to share in the establishment of the "Jewish national home." The non-Zionists included such distinguished figures as Louis Marshall, Leon Blum, Albert Einstein, Felix Warburg, and members of the Rothschild family. Unfortunately, the development of this partnership was arrested almost from the first as a result of the death of Louis Marshall and the worldwide depression which began that autumn. For all intents and purposes, it ceased to exist after 1939.

Nevertheless, from 1929 until the establishment of the State of Israel on 15 May 1948, the Jewish Agency was the WZO's instrument for the upbuilding of the Jewish national home and the struggle for statehood in Palestine proper. It was also directly responsible for the health, welfare and educational institutions serving the Yishuv (the Jewish community in Palestine). Together with the Va'ad Leumi (National Council), the Jewish Agency represented Palestinian Jewry before the mandatory power. It was in this period that the infrastructure of the state-to-be was formed.

After the establishment of the State of Israel in 1948, most of the original functions of the Jewish Agency were transferred to the new government. In 1952, the official role of the Jewish Agency-WZO was defined through a covenant between the WZO and the State, embodied in the Knesset Law of Status which made the Jewish Agency/WZO responsible for the "ingathering of the exiles" and for their absorption in Israel.

In the interim, a limited partnership had developed between Jews of Israel and the diaspora around fundraising for the Yishuv and then the state. The founding of the United Jewish Appeal (UJA) in the United States in 1937 by the United Palestine Appeal (now the United Israel Appeal) and the Joint Distribution Committee, and the urging of the Council of Jewish Federations and Welfare Funds (now the Council of Jewish Federations), marked the turning point. From then on, the leadership of these organizations began to replace the diaspora Zionist leadership in the United States as Israel's principal partners. This trend was encouraged by David Ben-Gurion, especially after 1948.

The reaction of world Jewry to the threat to Israel preceding the Six-Day War and the subsequent results of the fundraising campaigns on behalf of Israel introduced a new dimension into the traditional partnership of Jewish communities throughout the world and Israel. To give this new dimension organizational expression, the WZO undertook negotiations with the United Israel Appeal (UIA) in the United States and the Keren Hayesod fundraising bodies throughout the world to assure direct participation of the world Jewish community in carrying out the responsibilities of the Jewish Agency. These negotiations culminated in the Agreement for the Reconstitution of the Jewish Agency, initialled in Jerusalem in August 1970 and formally ratified at the Founding Assembly in June 1971. The Agreement has been periodically amended. (See Agreement for the Reconstitution of the Jewish Agency for Israel in Part III.)

The Agreement for the Reconstitution of the Jewish Agency for Israel assigned to the WZO responsibility for "the fulfillment of Zionist programs and ideals" and to the Jewish Agency responsibility for immigration and absorption; welfare and health services in relation to absorption of immigrants; support of education and youth activities, particularly Youth Aliyah; absorption in agricultural settlements; and immigrant housing.

Under the reconstitution arrangement, the 'non-Zionists' are designated, in accordance with a specifically defined formula (see "Structure and Electoral Process of the Jewish Agency"), by the central fundraising organizations for Israel, these being the community bodies which have the broadest base of representation. In the United States, the designating body is the UIA; in the other countries of the diaspora, the designating bodies are the fundraising organizations affiliated with the Keren Hayesod. Israel is represented through the WZO.

In February 1981, the Caesarea Conference of the Jewish Agency Board of Governors was convened to review the ten-year period since the Agency was reconstituted. During the three-day conference, the topics under discussion included the functioning of the Agency since reconstitution; its goals and tasks for the next ten years; and the structure and governance of the Agency (see "The Caesarea Process: A Status Report").

THE JEWISH AGENCY: A CHRONOLOGY

1897	First Zionist Congress
1919	Idea for a 'Jewish agency' first suggested by Felix Frankfurter at the Versailles Conference
1922	League of Nations Mandate provides for a Jewish agency as a "public body under international law"
1929	Jewish Agency established. Zionists combine with non-Zionist notables from community relations sphere
1937	Enlarged Jewish Agency collapses over statehood issue; United Jewish Appeal established
1939	Failure of efforts to revive enlarged Jewish Agency
1940s	Ben-Gurion throws his support from Zionists to fundraisers in the United States (UJA/Federations)
1952	WZO Covenant and Law of Status
1959	JAFI, Inc., established (until 1966 when it became United Israel Appeal, Inc.)
1960s	Israeli Government tries and fails to bypass Jewish Agency/WZO through instrumentalities such as Mercaz Hatefutzot and Ministry of Absorption (1968)
1965	Louis Pincus becomes Chairman of the Jewish Agency Executive
1967	Six-Day War
1969	Conference on Human Needs leads to initiation of reconstitution process
1971	Jewish Agency reconstituted at initiative of the diaspora community leaders from fundraising/communal-welfare sphere; Founding Jewish Agency Assembly meets
1979	Signing of separate WZO and Jewish Agency covenants with Government
1981	Caesarea Process inaugurated
1983	Max Fisher retires as Chairman of the Board of Governors and Jerold Hoffberger succeeds him
1984	Summary Report of the Governance Commission adopted

STRUCTURE AND ELECTORAL PROCESS OF THE JEWISH AGENCY[1]

THE ASSEMBLY

The Assembly is the constituent body of the Jewish Agency and has 398 members. Fifty percent of the members are designated by the WZO (199); 30 percent by the United Israel Appeal (UIA) in the United States (119); and 20 percent by the fundraising bodies affiliated with Keren Hayesod (80). In the United States, the UIA Board of Directors takes the responsibility of designating its 119 members. It does so by requesting nominations from all large, most intermediate, and a rotating group of small city federations. Assignments are made after consultation with the individual federations.

All UIA Board members representing communities, including the current members of the Board of Governors, are automatically seated at the Assembly. While only members of the Assembly are entitled to vote, it is accepted practice that all attending, including alternates and observers, can participate fully in discussions.

The Reconstitution Agreement as amended provides that the Assembly's functions are:

> . . . to receive and review reports from the Board of Governors; make recommendations on major issues; determine basic policies and goals of the Agency; advise on major trends in the budget, including long-range perspectives; consider and act upon budgets submitted by the Board of Governors; adopt resolutions on the above; elect the Board of Governors.

In addition,

> . . . The officers elected by the Assembly from among its members shall be its Chairman, the Treasurer, and such additional officers as the Assembly may determine from time to time. A committee on nominations, composed in the same proportion as the Assembly, shall be appointed to recommend candidates for the office of Chairman, Treasurer, and such other offices as the Assembly may determine . . . . The Assembly shall establish its own rules of procedure.

THE BOARD OF GOVERNORS

The Reconstitution Agreement assigns to the Assembly the duty of electing members of the Board of Governors, the policy-making body of the Jewish Agency. The Governors play the crucial role in the governance of the Agency: setting priorities, overseeing budget and operations.

The Assembly elects the seventy-four members of the Board of Governors every four years according to the same formula used for the Assembly: 50 percent from among the members of the Assembly designated by the WZO (37 members)[2]; 30 percent from among the members of the Assembly designated by the UIA (22 members); and 20 percent from among the members of the Assembly designated by the Keren Hayesod affiliates (15 members).

The Agreement calls for the appointment of a nominating committee based on the accepted proportional representation as defined above. This committee receives recommendations from the three participating bodies, checks qualifications, and reports to the Assembly. There are no tenure provisions currently in effect.

The UIA has previously determined its

recommendations through a special committee appointed by the Chairman. Those elected have included top leadership of the Council of Jewish Federations (CJF) and United Jewish Appeal (UJA). Past experience has shown that the founders, as well as subsequent UIA Governors, represent the highest levels of American Jewry's community leaders. For example, the sitting presidents of CJF and UJA, the UJA National Campaign Chairman, the President of the Joint Distribution Committee (JDC), and the Chairman of the UJA, have always been Governors. So too have all past CJF, UJA and UIA presidents and chairmen who remain active. This group makes up over one-half of the twenty-two Board members designated by UIA. The others hold or have held key positions directly influenced by Board of Governors activity such as President of the Israel Education Fund or National Chairman of Project Renewal.

The Board of Governors' responsibilities are stated in the amended Reconstitution Agreement as:

> . . . determines the policy of the Jewish Agency for Israel and manages, supervises, controls and directs its operations and activities. All bodies (other than the Assembly), officers and officials of the Jewish Agency shall act within the policies set by the Assembly and Board of Governors and are accountable to the Board of Governors. Between meetings of the Assembly, the Board of Governors shall have full power to act for the Agency and may fix policy, provided that its acts and decisions are not inconsistent with previous decisions or instructions of the Assembly.

Also, the Board of Governors has the power to appoint a Standing Budget and Finance Committee, approves and determines the annual budget of the Jewish Agency, elects members of the Executive, and receives and considers reports of the Executive.

There are a number of standing committees which expedite the work of the Board, assure its continuity and allow the Board as a whole to carry out its functions to a greater extent, covering a broader range of issues. These are divided into the *Departmental Committees,* which include

Amigour—Housing, Immigration and Absorption, the Leadership Development Institute, Project Renewal, Rural Settlement, and Youth Aliyah; *Other Programmatic Committees,* which include Assembly Planning, Jewish Education, Joint Program for Jewish Education, Long-Range Planning, and the Pincus Fund; and the *Administrative Committees,* which include Assets and Liabilities, Budget and Finance, Comptroller's Reports, and Management. In addition, ad hoc committees are appointed as needed.

CHAIRMAN OF THE BOARD OF GOVERNORS

The Chairman of the Agency's most important governing entity, the Board of Governors, comes by agreement from the diaspora. More specifically, the Board elects its Chairman by majority vote at the first meeting after the Board of Governors has been designated by the Assembly. The Reconstitution Agreement states:

> The Board of Governors shall, at its first session held after the election of all its Members, elect its Chairman from among the Governors . . . A nominating committee selected by the Board of Governors for this purpose shall make recommendations for the office of the Chairman.

The Jewish Agency counsel has determined that nominations from the floor are not consonant with the Agreement. Also, Zionist leaders claim the same privilege of consent for this office which non-Zionists have used in the choice of Chairman of the Executive and heads of departments.

THE EXECUTIVE

The Executive currently consists of nineteen members and convenes monthly in order to facilitate involvement and greater oversight of the Agency's day-to-day operations. The pertinent articles of the amended Reconstitution Agreement read:

> The Executive shall administer the operations of the Jewish Agency, subject to

the control of the Board of Governors.

Policies adopted by the Assembly and the Board of Governors shall be implemented by the Executive and the Departments under the direction of the Chairman of the Executive.

The Executive shall act as a collective body with collective responsibility.

The Executive shall be composed of Members ex officio and of Members elected by the Board of Governors.

Members of the Executive shall serve as such only as long as they are Members of the Board of Governors.

The following holders of offices or positions shall be Members ex officio of the Executive while holding such offices or positions:—

(1) the Chairman of the Assembly, who shall also serve as Chairman of the Executive.
(2) the Chairman of the Board of Governors.
(3) the Founding Chairman of the Board of Governors, who shall serve as a life Member of the executive.
(4) the Treasurer.
(5) the Chairman of the Board of Governors Committee on Budget and Finance.
(6) the Chairman of the UIA, Inc.
(7) the National Chairman of the UJA.
(8) the Chairman of the Board of Trustees of the UJA.
(9) the President of the Council of Jewish Federations (U.S.A.).
(10) the Chairman of the Board of Trustees of Keren Hayesod.
(11) the World Chairman of Keren Hayesod.

The following Governors shall be Members ex officio of the Executive:—

(1) two Members, to be appointed by the WZO, from among the Governors referred to in Clause II.D.2(b)1.
(2) two Members to be appointed by Organizations other than the WZO and the UIA, and who serve as Appeal Trustees on the World Board of Trustees of Keren Hayesod.

The Chairman of the Assembly and the Treasurer shall serve for a period of four years, or until their successors are elected.

The Board of Governors shall elect to the Executive and as Heads of Departments:

(a) one Member, from among Members of the Assembly designated by the WZO, to serve as Head of the Immigration and Absorption Department.
(b) two Members, from among Members of the Assembly designated by the WZO, to serve as Co-Heads of the Agricultural Settlement Department.
(c) one Member, from among Members of the Assembly designated by the WZO, to serve as Head of the Youth Aliyah Department.

The Board of Governors has the option to appoint three more associate members to the Executive who have the right to attend all meetings, but do not have any voting rights.

CHAIRMAN OF THE EXECUTIVE

The Assembly elects its own Chairman who also serves as Chairman of the Executive. In accordance with a separate protocol appended to the Reconstitution Agreement, he also is the Chairman of the WZO Executive. By agreement, the Chairman of the Executive is an Israeli.

NOTES

1. The number of members of governing bodies in this article reflect the increase over the original numbers introduced through amendments to the Reconstitution Agreement. For the original numbers, see "The Reconstitution of the Jewish Agency: A Political Analysis" in Part III.

2. Members of the Zionist Executive constitute thirty-six of the thirty-seven members of the WZO component on the Board of Governors. At present, the thirty-seventh is the World Chairman of the Jewish National Fund.

TABLE 1: ORGANIZATION CHART OF THE JEWISH AGENCY FOR ISRAEL

THE JEWISH AGENCY ASSEMBLY - 398
WZO - 199 UIA - 119 KH - 80

BOARD OF GOVERNORS - 74
WZO - 37 UIA - 22 KH - 15

Office of the Comptroller

COMMITTEES OF THE BOARD OF GOVERNORS

Amigour-Housing Committee	Comptroller's Reports Committee	Long-Range Planning Committee	Rural Settlement Committee
Assembly Planning Committee	Immigration & Absorption Committee	Project Renewal Committee	Youth Services
Assets and Liabilities Committee	Management Committee	Pincus Fund Committee	
Budget and Finance Committee	Jewish Education Committee	Joint Program for Jewish Education Committee	
	Leadership Development Institute		

MEMBERS OF THE JEWISH AGENCY EXECUTIVE

Chairman of the Executive and Assembly	Chairman Board of Trustees UJA	Member-at-Large WZO	Co-Head Rural Settlement Department
Co-Head Rural Settlement Department	National Chairman UJA	Member-at-Large WZO	Head Youth Aliyah Department
Treasurer	President CJF (USA)	Chairman BOG	
Founding Chairman BOG	Chairman Board of Trustees KH	Member Board of Trustees KH	
Chairman UIA (USA)	Member Board of Trustees KH	Head Immigration & Absorption Department	
Chairman BOG Committee on Budget and Finance	World Chairman KH		

THE JEWISH AGENCY EXECUTIVE

DIRECTOR-GENERAL
SECRETARY-GENERAL
(Responsible also to the Chairman, Board of Governors)
PROJECT RENEWAL DEPARTMENT
PERSONNEL DEPARTMENT

Legal Counsel

KEY: BOG - Board of Governors
CJF - Council of Jewish Federations
JA - Jewish Agency
KH - Keren Hayesod
UIA - United Israel Appeal
UJA - United Jewish Appeal
WZO - World Zionist Organization

TABLE 2: STRUCTURE OF THE JEWISH AGENCY FOR ISRAEL AND THE WORLD ZIONIST ORGANIZATION

THE WORLD ZIONIST ORGANIZATION

- Territorial Zionist Federations
- Ideological Groupings
- International Jewish Bodies

→ Zionist Congress - 657 Delegates

USA 29%   Israel 38%
Other Countries 33%

→ Zionist Supreme Court
Attorney of the WZO

The Jewish National Fund

→ Zionist General Council 144 Members*

→ Presidium
Perm. Budget & Finance Comm.

The Comptroller

THE JEWISH AGENCY

- World Zionist Organization
- United Israel Appeal
- World Keren HaYesod

→ The Assembly - 398 Delegates

UIA 30%(USA) World Keren HaYesod 20%
WZO 50%

→ Board of Governors
74 Members

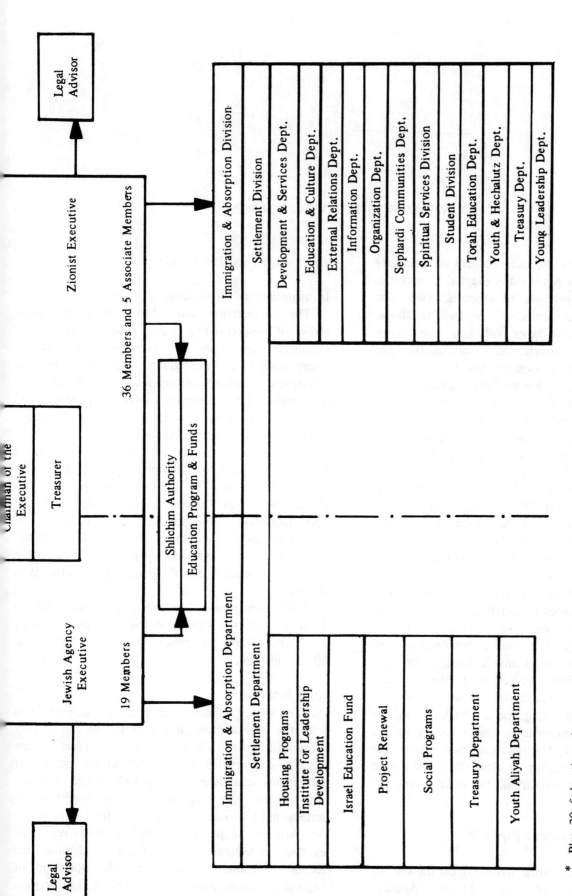

Legal Advisor

Zionist Executive

36 Members and 5 Associate Members

Chairman of the Executive

Treasurer

Jewish Agency Executive

19 Members

Legal Advisor

Shlichim Authority

Education Program & Funds

Immigration & Absorption Division

Settlement Division

Development & Services Dept.

Education & Culture Dept.

External Relations Dept.

Information Dept.

Organization Dept.

Sephardi Communities Dept.

Spiritual Services Division

Student Division

Torah Education Dept.

Youth & Hechalutz Dept.

Treasury Dept.

Young Leadership Dept.

Immigration & Absorption Department

Settlement Department

Housing Programs

Institute for Leadership Development

Israel Education Fund

Project Renewal

Social Programs

Treasury Department

Youth Aliyah Department

* Plus 20 federation chairmen from Zionist federations from countries having 3 or more delegates at the last Zionist Congress.

ACTIVITIES OF THE JEWISH AGENCY

In the years since the establishment of the State of Israel, the Jewish Agency has adapted its activities and methods of operation to changing needs and priorities within the limits of its available funds. Today, the Agency's tasks fall into two major categories: one, its historic role in immigration and absorption; and two, helping to close the social gap. In one way or another, Jewish Agency programs and services directly affect the lives of some 600,000 Jews in Israel — and indirectly many more.

Since the proclamation of Israel's statehood, the Jewish Agency has assisted in the absorption of more than 1,800,000 immigrants. Over five hundred agricultural settlements have been established containing some 150,000 settlers. More than 150,000 children and youth have been able to enter the mainstream of Israeli society through the programs of Youth Aliyah. Some 350,000 housing solutions have been provided.

The 1967 war marked a significant change in the nature of the Agency's activities as well as its budget. Since that year, the defense burden has required such a large proportion of Israel's resources, that the Agency had to assume a much larger share of those responsibilities directed at finishing the task of absorbing the hundreds of thousands of immigrants of earlier immigrations who lagged behind the rest of the population as Israel's society moved forward. Specifically, this meant a much greater role for the Agency in helping to close the social gap in Israel — in housing, education, and in improving the quality of life.

THE OPERATING DEPARTMENTS

The bulk of this work has been carried out by four departments of the Jewish Agency: Immigration and Absorption, Rural Settlement, Youth Aliyah and Project Renewal.

Immigration and Absorption

The Immigration and Absorption Department's areas of responsibility cover rescue efforts and assistance for Jews in countries of distress, transportation of immigrants and their personal belongings, initial absorption of immigrants, information and advocacy services, provision of temporary housing facilities, Hebrew language training, and short-term financial aid.

The department played a major role in Operation Moses — the airlift of Ethiopian Jewry to Israel. Its ongoing involvement in the social absorption of the Ethiopians is the most recent example of the interrelationship of the department's mandated responsibilities at their most important levels. Other priorities today include seeking more readily available housing solutions for all immigrants, particularly singles.

Total immigration for the years from 1981 to 1984 was 60,945, broken down as follows: 12,032 in 1981; 13,260 in 1982; 16,417 in 1983; and 19,236 in 1984.

Rural Settlement

The Agency's Rural Settlement Department deals with the establishment of new settlements in priority areas within Israel's pre-1967 borders (that is, not across the 'green line'); the care and development of settlements established with Jewish Agency aid and still in need of support; the consolidation of settlements ('weaning' a settlement from dependence on Agency support); absorption into new and existing settlements of new immigrant families and second generation settlers; and the operation of regional rural enterprise, water supply and other rural improvement projects.

Youth Aliyah

Traditionally the Youth Aliyah Department has been responsible for integrating children from distressed lands into Israeli society, including children brought to Palestine during the rise of the Nazis in Germany; refugee children after the war; those from Arab countries and totalitarian regimes in Eastern Europe during the 1950s and 1960s; children from Iran in the 1970s; and, most recently, children from Ethiopia.

While the services presently provided to those from Ethiopia attest to the continuation of the department's historic role, in reality the overall thrust of its activities have been altered to accommodate Israeli children from disadvantaged backgrounds. In fact, the bulk of its pupils are now drawn from this group.

The eighteen thousand children with whom Youth Aliyah will deal in 1985/1986 fall into the following categories: Israeli children from disadvantaged families; Israeli youth requiring special educational programs; immigrant youth without parents in Israel; and those from abroad on one- or two-year study programs in Israel.

Housing

Housing in one form or another has been provided through all of the aforementioned departmental frameworks. However, it was not until the creation of the Jewish Agency's Amigour Housing Management Company in 1972 that housing acquired a separate framework. Amigour is one result of the expansion in the Jewish Agency's field of community work that burgeoned after the Six-Day War.

Project Renewal

After the establishment of Amigour in 1972, other community-oriented programs were added, such as the Special Program for Disadvantaged Youth, the Community Leadership Training Program conducted in conjunction with the World Zionist Organization (WZO) Department of Sephardi Affairs, and a number of other special projects.

In 1977/78, the Jewish Agency joined with the Government of Israel in sponsoring Project Renewal, a program directed at the rehabilitation of 160 slum neighborhoods in which some 45,000 families

(300,000 persons) resided.

Project Renewal utilizes a comprehensive approach to distressed neighborhoods, emphasizing cultural, educational and social programs and the development of communal facilities and services as well as the improvement of housing and physical infrastructure. The Jewish Agency's share of the program is financed by contributions to Keren Hayesod and United Jewish Appeal (UJA) campaigns over and above the regular contributions. Thus far, eighty-two neighborhoods have been included in the program, most of them 'twinned' with communities in the United States and Keren Hayesod countries. The work in several of these neighborhoods is nearing completion.

JEWISH EDUCATION

Beginning in 1975, the Jewish Agency has become increasingly involved, in coordination with the relevant WZO departments, in Jewish education. The Louis A. Pincus Memorial Fund for Jewish Education is a foundation fund managed by the Jewish Agency, in association with the WZO, the American Joint Distribution Committee (JDC) and the Israeli Government. In 1979, there was established the Joint Committee on Jewish Education of the Jewish Agency the WZO, and the Ministry of Education. The Agency also makes grants to Israel's institutions of higher learning.

FUNDS

Since the establishment of the state, the Jewish Agency has spent approximately $7.6 billion, of which two thirds have come from world Jewry through the campaigns of the UJA and Keren Hayesod. The rest of the income has come from German reparations (until 1969/70), participation of the Israeli Government, loans, collection of debts, and other sources.

High points were in 1967/68 when campaign income reached $370 million and in 1973/74 with an all-time high of over $700 million. Both these years reflected the outpouring of concern and understanding of world Jewry in response to the threat to Israel's existence of the Six-Day War in 1967 and the Yom Kippur War in 1973.

In 1975, the Jewish Agency established a long-range planning committee. With the guidance of this committee and the assistance of teams from the Harvard Business School and others, the Agency undertook a review of its operations with a view to improving the utilization of its funds.

Over the years, the Agency has built up a debt of over $400 million, much of it in the early years of the state when immediate immigrant absorption needs far out paced campaign income. One immediate consequence of the Caesarea Process is the debt reduction program, first discussed and recommended in the Finance and Fiscal Policy Commission. The goal is to completely eliminate the Jewish Agency debt by 1990, with diaspora Jewry, particularly in North America, and the Jewish Agency sharing equally in the responsibility for implementation of the program.

Restrictions on Use of Funds

The nature and scope of the Jewish Agency's activities take into account restrictions imposed by the laws of certain countries in which funds are raised on behalf of the Agency. For example, the Reconstitution Agreement states:

> The functions, tasks and programs administered by the Agency or to which it may contribute funds shall be only such as may be carried out by tax-exempt organizations.

Therefore, the Agency does not undertake or support any activities which fall within the statutory responsibility of the Israeli Government, such as elementary and high school education. However, the Agency can and does support education in the pre-school years and in the institutions of higher learning.

The Jewish Agency carries the responsibility for immigration from lands of distress, while the WZO handles immigration from the free world countries. Furthermore, as previously mentioned, the Agency does not conduct any activities beyond the green line, the June 1967 borders. Such activity is in the hands of the Government of Israel and the WZO.

THE BUDGET OF THE JEWISH AGENCY

INTRODUCTION

The budget of the Jewish Agency reflects the two major tasks carried out by the Agency on behalf of the world Jewish polity: the ingathering of the Jewish people, namely immigration and absorption; and improvement of the quality of life for immigrants from previous years and the rest of Israel's citizens. The three line departments responsible for these functions are Immigration and Absorption, Rural Settlement, and Youth Aliyah. Project Renewal represents a special program for the revitalization of distressed neighborhods in Israel, jointly undertaken by the Government of Israel and the Jewish Agency. The Agency's expenditure on Project Renewal activities is not included as part of the regular income of the Jewish Agency budget, but is a separate supplementary income item.

The various programs and services included in the Agency's budget benefit over half a million people in Israel including the following categories:

New immigrants
Immigrants in absorption facilities
Handicapped or elderly persons
Immigrant students
Students from development towns
  and distressed neighborhoods
Residents of development towns
Youth Aliyah pupils
Youth in distress
Settlers
Residents in distressed neighborhoods

Since Operation Moses was launched, several thousand Ethiopian Jews have arrived in Israel. Given the unique circumstances of the Ethiopian immigrants and their need for special attention, additional funds were allocated to the 1985/86 budget for the Immigration and Absorption and Youth Aliyah budgets.

In addition, the Israel Government contributes to the Jewish Agency's budget in the form of a grant ($29.138 million in FY 1984/85).

This section contains materials related to the budget of the Jewish Agency for Israel. It has been broken down as follows[1]:

Description of Income Items
Table 3, Income from Appeals Flow Chart
Table 4, Process of Authorization
  of the Budget
Table 5, Itemization of the Annual Budget
  (includes proposed 1985/86 budget
  and comparison by years)
Table 6, Jewish Agency Expenditures
  since Reconstitution, 1971–1985

DESCRIPTION OF INCOME ITEMS

United Israel Appeal, Inc.

The United Israel Appeal (USA), Inc., (UIA) is accountable for the monies raised in the United States for Jewish Agency programs. The UIA receives its income from the United Jewish Appeal (UJA) and in recent years also from a special grant from the United States Government for the resettlement of immigrants from Eastern Europe in Israel. After payments for debts, services, and administrative expenses, the UIA transfers the balance of funds to Israel for implementation by the Jewish Agency.

Table 3 shows the distribution of funds raised by

the American Jewish communities. After the agreed upon deduction of income for local needs, the community federations transfer the balance to the national office of the UJA. National UJA distributes these funds (together with contributions directly received by the UJA) to its two constituents, the UIA and the Joint Distribution Committee (JDC), and also to NYANA — the New York Association for New Americans, and to HIAS — Hebrew Immigrant Aid Society. Thus, only part of the funds raised by American Jewish communal organizations are used to finance Jewish Agency activities. This figure includes UIA's debt repayment since all loans raised by the UIA are undertaken in coordination with the Jewish Agency and in order to finance Agency programs. The UIA is the recipient of funds granted by the United States Government in accordance with Refugee Resettlement Grant Agreements for the absorption of Jewish immigrants from Eastern Europe. These sums are designated for activities such as the maintenance of these immigrants in absorption centers, transit centers, and scholarships for immigrant students, but do not cover the full cost of these programs. In addition, rental income and income from the sale of apartments constructed with the aid of Resettlement Grant funds, are reallocated to these activities. Funds are allocated in accordance with the different Grant Agreements, which determine the overall level of United States Government funding for each program. Monies are only transferred on the basis of actual expenditure by the Jewish Agency.

Keren Hayesod

Keren Hayesod—UIA is the umbrella organization under whose aegis fundraising for Israel is carried out in the various Jewish communities throughout the world apart from the United States. The funds are usually transferred directly to the Jewish Agency by the national appeals, while the Head Office of Keren Hayesod coordinates the campaigns and provides services such as speakers, publications and staff. The Income Budget under the heading "Keren Hayesod" shows the estimated income which the Jewish Agency should receive after the deduction of administrative expenses both of the Keren Hayesod Head Office and the national appeals. It also presents

the amount required for debt payment on loans raised by Keren Hayesod organizations in order to finance Jewish Agency programs. In addition to its funding of the Jewish Agency, Keren Hayesod also allocates funds to the World Zionist Organization (WZO).

Israel Government Grant

The Israeli Government allocates funds to the Jewish Agency in order to assist the Agency to participate in activities in which the Israeli Government has an interest. The sum in the Income Budget represents the dollar equivalent of the budgeted allocation, which will be made in Israeli currency.

Other Receipts
Immigration Receipts

Most of the income under this heading represents allocations by the International Committee for European Migration — ICEM. These funds are granted on a per capita basis toward the travel and freight costs for East European immigrants. The level of income is thus dependent upon the number of these immigrants arriving in Israel. These funds are now part of the United States Government's Refugee Resettlement Grant for helping East European immigrants. In addition, this item includes income received from certain immigrants who participate in their transportation costs.

Youth Aliyah Receipts

Besides campaigns held by the UJA and Keren Hayesod, special campaigns are carried out for youth care and training by Youth Aliyah committees throughout the world. The Youth Aliyah Department is the only Jewish Agency department to operate a separate campaign, this campaign being based on a longstanding tradition. The Youth Aliyah campaign, some of whose income is for the Department's special projects, accounts for about 80 percent of the budget under this heading. The balance consists of parents' contributions toward the maintenance costs of pupils.

Debt Collections, Miscellaneous

Receipts from debt collections are mainly from

the repayment of loans given to new immigrants as part of the financial assistance they receive during the process of absorption and repayment by settlers of the resources invested in their settlement by the Jewish Agency once this property has been transferred to them.

This heading also covers income from various sources such as receipts from property managed by the Properties Division of the Jewish Agency's Treasury Department, the sale of used equipment, etc.

Amigour Income

Income from sale of apartments belonging to the UIA, Inc., and managed by Amigour.

Receipts for Israel Education Fund

The Israel Education Fund is a special fund established by the UJA for the construction of schools, libraries, cultural and social centers, pre-kindergartens and other community facilities. Donations for this fund are also received through Keren Hayesod. The Israel Education Fund is based

NOTE

1. The numerical notations for all expenditures in the tables refer to all categories for programs listed in the Jewish Agency for Israel Proposed Budget 1985/86.

on contributions of at least $100,000 which are over and above the contributor's donation to the regular campaign.

Special Campaign for Project Renewal

Project Renewal is a special program undertaken by the Jewish Agency, representing the Jewish communities abroad, in partnership with the Government of Israel. Its aim is to carry out a comprehensive renovation of distressed neighborhoods throughout Israel. The funds for the Jewish Agency's share of Project Renewal are raised in separate special campaigns by the UJA and Keren Hayesod, and are expended only within the framework of Project Renewal. The expenditure budget for Project Renewal is included in the budget proposal of the Jewish Agency but it is implemented as an independent program on the basis of the income included under this heading.

TABLE 3: INCOME FROM APPEALS
Flow Chart

TABLE 4: PROCESS OF AUTHORIZATION OF THE BUDGET

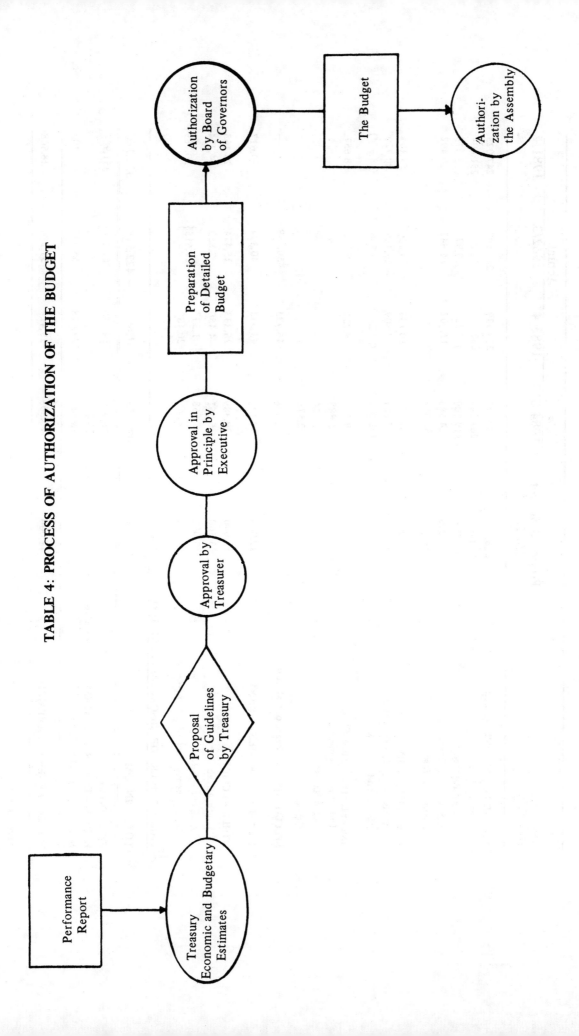

TABLE 5: ITEMIZATION OF THE ANNUAL BUDGET

INCOME ($ 1,000)	Proposed Budget 1985/6	1984/5 *	1983/4	Actual 1982/3	1981/2
UNITED ISRAEL APPEAL Inc.:	**306,000**	**302,942**	**259,539**	**267,808**	**247,023**
Contributions	268,000	261,248	263,973	271,844	251,604
Interest Payments	(–)17,000	(–) 19,000	(–)15,736	(–)19,978	(–)25,073
U.S. Government Grant	20,000	24,680	11,302	15,942	20,492
Operation Moses	35,000	36,014	–		
KEREN HAYESOD:	**68,000**	**61,416**	**60,104**	**66,686**	**59,104**
Allocation to Jewish Agency	42,000	35,801	27,809	29,380	20,720
Allocation to W.Z.O.	(26,000)	(25,615)	(32,295)	(37,306)	(38,384)
ISRAEL EDUCATION FUND:	**10,000**	**9,790**	**8,251**	**9,293**	**8,657**
United Israel Appeal Inc.		5,888			
Keren Hayesod		1,324			
Others		2,578			
SPECIAL APPEAL (Peace of Galilee):	–	9,996	16,731	50,169	–
ISRAEL GOVERNMENT GRANT:	**29,000**	**29,138**	**43,033**	**40,394**	**50,617**
OTHER RECEIPTS:	**14,000**	**20,389**	**26,333**	**25,474**	**25,163**
Youth Aliyah	3,500	6,861	4,450	3,859	4,374
Amigour – Sales	3,000	5,668	1,397	21,615 }	20,789 }
Miscelleneous (Including Rents)	7,500	7,860	20,486		
CARRIED OVER FOR ABSORBTION FROM 1984/5	13,000				
TOTAL INCOME	**414,000**	**408,056**	**381,696**	**422,518**	**352,180**
EXPENDITURE		376,910	354,078	367,176	351,984
EARMARKED FOR OPERATION MOSES IN 85/6		13,000			
SURPLUS/SHORTFALL**		18,146	27,618	55,342	196
PROJECT RENEWAL CAMPAIGN	48,000	28,508	29,424	31,386	28,668

* Provisional.

** Applied to changes in Debt Balances.

(TABLE 5 CONT.)

EXPENDITURE ($ 1.000)		Proposed Budget 1985/6	Budget 1984/5	Actual		
				1983/4	1982/3	1981/2
	TOTAL	414,000	425,000	354,078	367,176	351,984
310	IMMIGRATION AND ABSORPTION	50,000	95,380	56,157	47,077	60,059
	ADDITIONAL IMMIGRATION BUDGET	45,000	–	–	–	–
320	RURAL SETTLEMENT	67,000	70,289	55,240	60,431	59,532
330	YOUTH ALIYAH	50,000	58,090	50,732	50,052	47,209
	ADD. YOUTH ALIYAH	9,000	–	–	–	–
334	JEWISH EDUCATION	11,750	13,900	9,986	6,999	7,097
336	HIGHER EDUCATION	60,000	81,000	86,473	111,145	34,970
337-8	SOCIAL PROGRAMS	12,800	12,810	11,685	10,267	40,008
339	VOCATIONAL TRAINING	16,000	10,000	–	–	–
370	HOUSING – AMIGOUR	13,700	13,500	13,803	14,535	8,901
371-83	OTHER FUNCTIONS	10,500	18,431	25,178	11,595	19,879
384.10	INTEREST PAYMENTS	44,500	40,356	32,800	43,437	64,015
384.20	DEBT RETIREMENT	9,000	10,000	–	–	–
390-7	FINANCE & ADMINISTRATION	12,500	13,244	12,024	11,638	10,314
398	CONTINGENCY	2,250	–	–	–	–
	ANTICIPATED SAVINGS & CUTS		(–)12,000	–	–	–
	PROJECT RENEWAL	48,000	48,000	36,793	41,584	48,300

(TABLE 5 CONT.)

IMMIGRATION AND ABSORPTION		1984/5 $1000	1985/6 $100/M Shekel	%
310	TOTAL	95,380	95,000	100.0
310.10	PRE-IMMIGRATION PREPARATION	29,248	14,760	15.4
310.11	TRANSIT CENTERS	1,442	1,850	1.9
310.12	IMMIGRATION EXPENSES	5,000	5,000	5.3
310.20	FINANCIAL ASSISTANCE	1,075	810	0.9
310.30	ULPANIM	7,387	6,529	6.9
310.35	STUDENT AUTHORITY	4,058	4,000	4.2
310.40	HOSTELS AND ABSORPTION CENTERS	38,542	52,267	55.0
310.45	HOMES FOR THE ELDERLY	1,119	1,053	1.1
310.46	HOSTELS FOR THE ELDERLY	516	308	0.3
310.50	SUNDRY ACTIVITIES	1,347	1,321	1.4
310. 5	WELFARE SERVICES	3,408	5,367	5.7
310.84	RENT SUBSIDIES	175	25	—
310.90	HEAD OFFICE	2,063	1,800	1.9

EXPENDITURE – COMPARISON BY YEARS ($1000)

IMMIGRATION AND ABSORPTION		1983/4	1982/3	1981/2
310	TOTAL	56,157	47,077	60,059

RURAL SETTLEMENT		Comparison in $1,000		%
		1984/5	1985/6	
320	**TOTAL**	**70,289**	**67,000**	**100.0**
320.10	BASIC ACTIVITIES IN SETTLEMENTS	38,708	34,980	52.2
320.20	CONSOLIDATION OF SETTLEMENTS	15,055	14,000	20.9
320.50	SUNDRY ACTIVITIES	7,696	9,270	13.8
320.90	ADMINISTRATION	8,830	8,750	13.1

EXPENDITURE – COMPARISON BY YEARS ($1000)

RURAL SETTLEMENT		1983/4	1982/3	1981/2
320	**TOTAL**	55,240	60,431	59,532

(TABLE 5 CONT.)

YOUTH ALIYAH		1984/5 $1000	1985/6 $100/M Shekel	%
330	TOTAL	58,090	59,000	100.0
330.10	MAINTENANCE OF YOUTH	39,044	39,470	66.9
330.20	EDUCATIONAL SUPERVISION AND GUIDANCE	2,988	3,660	6.2
330.30	MEDICAL AND PSYCHOLOGICAL SERVICES	1,274	1,400	2.4
330.31	COUNSELING CENTERS FOR YOUTH	500	500	0.8
330.40	YOUTH IN DEPARTMENT INSTITUTIONS	7,410	7,200	12.2
330.45	YOUTH CENTERS	3,354	3,200	5.4
330.60	INFORMATION AND REPRESENTATIVES	820	870	1.5
330.90	HEAD OFFICE	2,700	2,700	4.6

EXPENDITURE – COMPARISON BY YEARS   ($1000)

YOUTH ALIYAH		1983/4	1982/3	1981/2
330	TOTAL	50,732	50,052	47,209

EDUCATION		1984/5 $1000	1985/6 $1000/M Shekel	%
334-6	TOTAL	94,900	71,750	100.0
334	**JEWISH EDUCATION**	13,900	11,750	16.4
334.62	SPECIAL PROGRAM FOR JEWISH EDUCATION	7,700	5,250	7.3
334.63	PROGRAMS FOR STUDENTS	2,000	2,000	2.8
334.64	EDUCATIONAL ACTIVITIES IN LATIN AMERICA	1,500	1,500	2.1
334.65	JEWISH EDUCATION IN FRANCE	1,500	1,500	2.1
334.67	INSTITUTE FOR LEADERSHIP TRAINING	350	320	0.4
334.68	EDUCATIONAL TELEVISION ABROAD	58	180	0.3
334.81	SCHOLARSHIP FOR OVERSEAS STUDENTS	492	500	0.7
334.84	AID FOR EDUCATIONAL INSTITUTIONS	300	500	0.7
336	**INSTITUTIONS OF HIGHER EDUCATION**	81,000	60,000	83.6

EXPENDITURE – COMPARISON BY YEARS ($1000)

EDUCATION		1983/4	1982/3	1981/2
334-6	TOTAL	96,459	118,144	42,067

(TABLE 5 CONT.)

SOCIAL PROGRAMS		1984/5	1985/6	%
		$1000	$100/M Shekel	
337-9	**TOTAL**	**22,810**	**28,800**	**100.0**
337.10	SPECIAL ACTIVITIES AMONG YOUTH	450	450	1.6
337.20	ADVANCEMENT OF COMMUNITY LEADERSHIP	1,200	1,200	4.2
337.30	SCHOLARSHIP FUNDS	100	150	0.5
338.35	ISRAELI EDUCATION FUND	10,000	10,000	34.7
338.50	DEVELOPMENT OF THE GALILEE	764	650	2.3
338.55	DEVELOPMENT OF THE ARAVA	296	350	1.2
339	**VOCATIONAL TRAINING**	**10,000**	**16,000**	**55.5**

EXPENDITURE – COMPARISON BY YEARS ($1000)

SOCIAL PROGRAMS		1983/4	1982/3	1981/2
337-8	**TOTAL**	**11,685**	**10,267**	**40,008**

HOUSING—AMIGOUR		1984/5 $1000	1985/6 $1000/M Shekel	%
370	**TOTAL**	**13,500**	**13,700**	**100.0**
370.05	REDEMPTION OF MORTGAGES	700	700	5.1
370.10	MAINTENANCE OF APARTMENTS	2,180	2,300	16.8
370.15	SALES EXPENDITURES	145	630	4.6
370.20	COMMUNITY WORK	829	820	6.0
370.30	ENLARGEMENTS AND RENOVATIONS	3,923	4,550	33.2
370.40	AREA DEVELOPMENT	553	200	1.5
370.50	SPECIAL PROJECTS	–	1,000	7.3
370.91	ADMINISTRATION	5,170	3,500	25.5

EXPENDITURE – COMPARISON BY YEARS ($1000)

HOUSING—AMIGOUR		1983/4	1982/3	1981/2
370	**TOTAL**	**13,803***	**14,535***	**8,901**

(TABLE 5 CONT.)

OTHER FUNCTIONS		1984/5 $1000	1985/6 $1000/M Shekel	%
371-82	TOTAL	18,431	10,500	100.0
371	COMPANIES AND AFFILIATED INSTITUTIONS	5,791	1,000	9.5
375	IDUD – ADMINISTRTION OF LOANS	1,640	1,500	14.3
380	ACTIVITIES THROUGH OTHER ORGANIZATIONS	2,812	2,747	26.2
381	ALLOCATIONS TO INSTITUTIONS	6,088	3,500	33.3
382	PENSIONS AND GRANTS	2,100	1,753	16.7
384.10	INTEREST PAYMENTS	40,356	44,500	
384.20	DEBT RETIREMENT	10,000	9,000	

EXPENDITURE – COMPARISON BY YEARS ($1000)

OTHER FUNCTIONS		1983/4	1982/3	1981/2
371-82	TOTAL	25,178	11,595	19,879

FINANCE & ADMINISTRATION		1984/5	1985/6	%
		$1000	$1000/M Shekel	
390-7	**TOTAL**	**13,244**	**12,500**	**100.0**
390	**OFFICE OF THE CHAIRMAN**	**2,326**	**1,957**	**15.7**
390.20	CHAIRMAN'S BUREAU	470	515	4.1
390.22	CHAIRMAN'S FUND	25	25	0.2
390.23	SPECIAL SERVICES	280	240	1.9
390.25	PRESS AND PUBLIC RELATIONS	230	220	1.8
390.26	JEWISH AGENCY ASSEMBLY	270	175	1.4
390.27	BOARD OF GOVERNORS	185	100	0.8
390.28	OFFICE OF THE SECRETARY GENERAL	190	190	1.5
390.30	COMPANIES AUTHORITY	176	187	1.5
390.34	COMPTROLLER'S REPORT UNIT	100	75	0.6
390.36	SPECIAL CAMPAIGN SECTION	120	–	–
390.38	VISITORS' RECEPTION AND SERVICES	280	230	1.9
393	**FINANCE DEPARTMENT**	**6,576**	**6,500**	**52.0**
394	**PROFESSIONAL SERVICES**	**817**	**820**	**6.6**
394.91	OFFICE OF THE LEGAL ADVISOR	817	820	6.6
395	**GENERAL ADMINISTRATION**	**2,325**	**2,223**	**17.7**
395.10	OFFICE OF THE DIRECTOR GENERAL	240	230	1.8
395.11	SECURITY DIVISION	275	250	2.0
395.12	PERSONNEL	870	840	6.7
395.13	OFFICE AND BUILDING MANAGEMENT	940	903	7.2
396	**COMPTROLLER'S OFFICE**	**1,200**	**1,000**	**8.0**

EXPENDITURE – COMPARISON BY YEARS   ($1000)

FINANCE & ADMINISTRATION		1983/4	1982/3	1981/2
390-7	**TOTAL**	12,024	11,638	10,314

TABLE 6: JEWISH AGENCY EXPENDITURE SINCE RECONSTITUTION: 1971 – 1985

(in $1,000)

	TOTAL	1971/72	1972/73	1973/74	1974/75	1975/76	1976/77	1977/78	1978/79	1979/80	1980/81	1981/82	1982/83	1983/84	1984/85 Budget
TOTAL	5,515,113	283,531	395,714	576,839	485,155	413,686	405,165	336,450	370,671	417,683	331,981	351,984	367,176	354,078*	425,000
IMMIGRATION AND ABSORPTION	925,284	28,161	46,251	76,258	80,417	70,575	61,732	58,699	64,388	111,424	68,706	60,059	47,077	56,157	95,380
SOCIAL WELFARE SERVICES	447,214	27,768	30,202	39,200	65,285	40,305	45,270	44,574	35,695	44,929	21,042	30,409	3,765	5,960	12,810
HEALTH SERVICES	100,336	15,348	30,746	9,397	14,000	8,902	10,856	8,816	2,271	—	—	—	—	—	—
EDUCATION (and IEF)	446,417	34,420	32,192	44,231	52,563	49,624	54,565	38,138	32,878	20,766	17,232	16,696	13,501	15,411	23,900
HIGHER EDUCATION	936,926	81,683	72,219	103,805	68,638	71,507	72,214	39,396	62,398	28,053	23,425	34,970	111,145	86,473	81,000
HOUSING	534,068	21,534	100,588	182,490	58,583	29,070	20,861	28,674	23,162	9,790	8,577	8,901	14,535	13,803	13,500
RURAL SETTLEMENT	720,598	26,448	30,422	43,965	55,946	60,059	54,396	37,559	42,533	59,644	64,134	59,532	60,431	55,240	70,289
YOUTH CARE & TRAINING	523,789	10,454	14,971	22,739	31,074	30,437	38,804	36,881	39,296	43,876	49,174	47,209	50,052	50,732	58,090
OTHER FUNCTIONS	236,860	34,741	6,924	9,812	12,732	11,846	11,423	11,249	13,173	40,327	9,550	19,879	11,595	25,178	18,431
DEBT SERVICE	554,903	—	28,271	41,410	40,741	37,272	30,218	27,650	48,950	49,845	59,938	64,015	43,437	32,800	50,356
GENERAL SERVICES/ ADMINISTRATION	94,791	2,974	2,928	3,532	5,176	4,089	4,826	4,814	—	9,029	10,203	10,314	11,638	12,024	13,244
RESERVE	5,927	—	—	—	—	—	—	—	5,927	—	—	—	—	—	—
ANTICIPATED SAVINGS AND CUTS	—	—	—	—	—	—	—	—	—	—	—	—	—	—	-12,000
PROJECT RENEWAL	—	—	—	(NOT	INCLUDED	IN	TOTALS)	—	40	6,130	6,453	48,300	41,584	36,793	48,000

*Excluding Special Emergency Fund

LEGAL STATUS OF THE WORLD ZIONIST ORGANIZATION AND THE JEWISH AGENCY FOR ISRAEL

Eli Likhovski

HISTORICAL BACKGROUND

The World Zionist Organization (WZO) was established by Dr. Theodore Herzl in 1897 at the First Zionist Congress in Basle, Switzerland. The Zionist program which was adopted in that Congress was to create for the Jewish people a home in Palestine, secured under public law (i.e., public international law).

What were the basic concepts of Dr. Herzl? How did he envision the implementation of this program? In his book, *The Jewish State,* published in 1896, he outlined his program:

1. To create a Jewish Society "which will be the administrator of the affairs of the Jewish people." This Jewish Society eventually became the WZO.
2. To establish a legal entity based on business lines to be known as the Jewish Company.
3. To ensure that the Jewish Company would secure a charter from the Ottoman Government which ruled Palestine at that time. Under this charter and pursuant to its provisions, the national homeland of the Jews in Palestine would develop. The charter was to be conceptually modeled on the charters under which the original American colonies were established in America (i.e., Massachusetts, Virginia, etc.)

In fact, Herzl never managed to establish his envisioned Jewish Company, but he did register the Jewish National Fund for the purchase of land in Palestine and the Jewish Colonial Trust Company (now the holding company of Bank Leumi).

Political events conspired against Herzl and no charter was granted by the Ottoman Government. He did, however, negotiate with the British Government for a charter in Cyprus and/or Sinai, territories in proximity to Palestine which were under British influence. The idea for the charter never died and became one of the basic concepts of Zionist policy.

In 1917, Dr. Chaim Weizmann secured, through Lord Rothschild, the Balfour Declaration, which was the first international recognition of the rights of the Jewish people to a homeland in Palestine.

In 1919, a Zionist delegation, headed by Dr. Weizmann and Justice Brandeis, negotiated with the Allied powers with regard to the implementation of the Balfour Declaration. Although the Treaty of Peace did not grant the Zionists a charter over Palestine, the Allied powers did agree to give a mandate to the British Government to administer Palestine for the purpose of establishing a Jewish national home in Palestine.

Article four of the Mandate for Palestine provided as follows:

An appropriate Jewish agency shall be recognized as a public body for the purpose of advising and cooperating with the Administration of Palestine in such economic, social and other matters as may affect the establishment of the Jewish national home and the interests of the Jewish population in Palestine, and, subject always to the control of the Administration, to assist and take part in the development of the country.

The Zionist organization, so long as its organization and constitution are in the opinion of the Mandatory appropriate, shall be recognized as such agency. It shall take steps in consultation with his Britannic Majesty's Government to secure the cooperation of all Jews who are willing to assist in the establishment of the Jewish national home.

It is to be noted that the Article provides for an appropriate Jewish agency* to be recognized by the mandatory power for the purpose of advising and cooperating with the British administration in carrying out the provisions of the Mandate for the establishment of a Jewish national home. It finally provides that until such time as an appropriate Jewish agency is established, the Zionist Organization, known today as the WZO, shall be that agency.

THE SIGNIFICANCE OF ARTICLE FOUR

This was the first time that the WZO was officially recognized in a legal instrument that was binding under international law as having a representative character of the Jewish people.

In 1929, an enlarged Jewish Agency came into being by agreement between Zionist and non-Zionist Jews on the basis of parity. Henceforth, two organizations were recognized as acting on behalf of the Jewish people in the implementation of the establishment of a national home in Palestine. In fact, owing to the course of Jewish history in the 1930s and early 1940s, the WZO assumed full control of the Jewish Agency, and they were, for all practical purposes, identical. The body known as the Jewish Agency Executive was recognized by the British Government, by the United States Government and by other states and international organizations, including the United Nations, as the representative body of the Jewish people both in Palestine and in the diaspora and as the shadow government of the Jews in Palestine.

---

* This name was suggested by Mr. F. Frankfurter, later Justice Frankfurter of the United States Supreme Court, who then acted as Legal Counsel to the Zionist Delegation to the Peace Conference.

THE ESTABLISHMENT OF THE STATE OF ISRAEL

The establishment of the State of Israel called for a clear separation between the democratically-elected Knesset and the Government of Israel and the political and philanthropic organizations which continued to act as the WZO and the Jewish Agency.

The Declaration of Independence of the State of Israel states that the State of Israel looks to the Jews in the diaspora to assist the people of Israel in the ingathering of the exiles (aliyah) and in the absorption of immigrants and the development of the country (settlement). This call was taken up by the 23d Zionist Congress which met in Jerusalem in 1951 and which assumed on behalf of the Jewish people these tasks. Obviously, such major tasks called for massive investment of monies and could only be carried out with the coordination and cooperation of the State. In order to achieve this end, the Knesset passed the Law of Status in 1952.

THE LAW OF STATUS OF THE WZO-JEWISH AGENCY, 1952

The Law of Status is the charter under which the WZO-Jewish Agency was to cooperate with the State of Israel in the organizing of Jewish coordination work in Israel. In introducing this law, the Prime Minister, the late Mr. David Ben-Gurion, said in the Knesset that he considered the law to be one of the most fundamental laws on the statute books of Israel. He considered the Law of Status as second only in importance to the Law of Return. Mr. Ben-Gurion stated that "the WZO came before the State, it stands above the State, it is the Jewish people in the diaspora."

GENERAL OUTLINE OF THE LAW OF STATUS

(a) The Declarative Part

The State of Israel is the creation of the whole Jewish people, and its gates are open to any Jew who wishes to come. The Law of Status declares that the WZO is the central movement which made it possible to establish the State.

(b) The Second Part

Under the law, the State recognizes the WZO-Jewish

Agency as an authorized agency which will continue to work in the State of Israel for the development and settlement of the land, for the absorption of immigrants, and for the coordination of the activities in Israel for Jewish institutions active in these areas.

The Law of Status calls upon the WZO to expand its basis and to include in its framework additional Jewish institutions and organizations willing to assist in aliyah and in the building of the country and to undertake such commitments.

(c) The Operative Part

This part deals with certain concrete legal matters needed to facilitate the activities of the WZO-Jewish Agency in Israel and outside. Facilities were created for the following purposes:

(i) for the spelling-out of the details of cooperation between the Government and the Executive of the WZO-Jewish Agency, the parties on the 26th of July 1954, entered into a Covenant pursuant to the provisions of Section F of the law;

(ii) the law provides for the setting-up of a coordinating committee between the Government and the WZO-Jewish Agency;

(iii) the law recognized and granted the WZO-Jewish Agency a legal personality;

(iv) the law grants the WZO-Jewish Agency exemption from certain taxes in order to facilitate its operation in Israel.

THE AGREEMENT FOR THE RECONSTITUTION OF THE JEWISH AGENCY, 21 JUNE 1971*

Since the establishment of the State, the WZO acted as the Jewish Agency and that body was elected and managed only by those Jews who were members of the WZO, while it received its income primarily from fundraising organizations in the diaspora, whose contributors were not in all cases members of the WZO. A case of "taxation without representation" could be made. Of even more importance, Jews who were willing to harness their abilities, expertise and talents in the cause of Israel did not possess a way of exercising their will in the councils of the WZO or of representing in an organized way the will of their communities. Taking this into consideration and with regard to Section 6 of the Law of Status, an agreement for the Reconstitution of the Jewish Agency was entered into on 21 June 1971.

Half of the membership of the newly reconstituted Jewish Agency was to be drawn from the WZO and the other half drawn from the fundraising organizations in the diaspora.

The newly reconstituted body was to have a separate and distinct legal personality and have its own governing boards: the General Assembly, the Board of Governors, and the Executive. The WZO was to continue to have its own governing bodies: the Congress, the Actions Committee, and its Executive. While the WZO was to continue as the political instrument of those Jews who are members of the organization, the Jewish Agency for Israel, under its Reconstitution Agreement, is a purely philanthropic body, helping needy and oppressed Jews settle in Israel and engaging primarily in these activities.

The creation of the newly reconstituted Jewish Agency called for an amendment of the Law of Status by the Knesset. The Law of Status (as amended on the 1st of June 1976, with retroactive effect to 21 June 1971, the date of the Reconstitution Agreement) now recognizes the distinct legal personality of these two organizations and defines clearly the philanthropic nature of the Jewish Agency. The new law called for the entering into of two new Covenants, one between the Government and the WZO and the other between the Government and the Jewish Agency. The Covenants were signed on 28 June 1979, with retroactive effect also to the date of the Reconstitution Agreement.

---

* See Part III for the Reconstitution Agreement and for the Covenant Between the Government of Israel and the Jewish Agency for Israel.

THE WORLD ZIONIST ORGANIZATION AND JEWISH AGENCY FOR ISRAEL (STATUS) LAW 5713-1952*

1. The State of Israel regards itself as the creation of the entire Jewish people, and its gates are open, in accordance with its laws, to every Jew wishing to immigrate to it.

2. The World Zionist Organization, from its foundation five decades ago, headed the movement and efforts of the Jewish people to realize the age-old vision of the return to the homeland and, with the assistance of other Jewish circles and bodies, carried the main responsibility for establishing the State of Israel.

2A. The Jewish Agency for Israel is an independent voluntary association consisting of the World Zionist Organization and other organizations and bodies. It operates in the State of Israel in fields chosen by it with the consent of the Government.

3. The World Zionist Organization and the Jewish Agency for Israel take care of immigration as before and direct absorption and settlement projects in the State.

4. The State of Israel recognizes the World Zionist Organization and the Jewish Agency for Israel as the authorized agencies which will continue to operate in the State of Israel for the development and settlement of the country, the absorption of immigrants from the Diaspora and the coordination of the activities in Israel of Jewish institutions and organizations active in those fields.

5. The mission of gathering in the exiles, which is the central task of the State of Israel and the Zionist Movement in our days, requires constant efforts by the Jewish people in the Diaspora; the State of Israel, therefore, expects the cooperation of all Jews, as individuals and groups, in building up the State and assisting the immigration to it of the masses of the people, and regards the unity of all sections of Jewry as necessary for this purpose.

6. The State of Israel expects efforts on the part of the World Zionist Organization for achieving this unity; if, to this end, the Zionist Organization, with the consent of the Government and the approval of the Knesset, should decide to broaden its basis, the enlarged body will enjoy the status conferred upon the World Zionist Organization in the State of Israel.

6A. The provisions of Sections 5 and 6 apply *mutatis mutandis* to the Jewish Agency for Israel.

7. Details of the status of the World Zionist Organization and the Jewish Agency for Israel and the form of their cooperation with the Government shall be determined by Covenants to be made in Israel between the Government and each of these two bodies.

8. (a) The Covenant with the World Zionist Organization shall be based on the declaration of the 23rd Zionist Congress in Jerusalem that the practical work of the World Zionist Organization and its various bodies for the fulfillment of their historic tasks in Eretz Israel requires full cooperation and coordination on its part with the State of Israel and its Government, in accordance with the laws of the State.

(b)The Covenant with the Jewish Agency for Israel shall provide for full cooperation and coordination on its part with the State of Israel and its Government, in accordance with the laws of the State.

9. Two committees shall be set up for the coordination of activities between the Government and the World Zionist Organization and the Jewish Agency for Israel in the spheres in which each of them is to operate according to the Covenant made with it. The tasks of the committees shall be determined by the Covenants.

10. The Covenants and any variation or amendment thereof made with the consent of the two parties shall be published in *Reshumot* and shall come into force on the day of publication, unless they provide for an earlier or later day for this purpose.

11. The World Zionist Organization and the Jewish Agency for Israel are juristic persons and may enter into contracts, acquire, hold and relinquish property and be parties to any legal or other proceeding.

12. The World Zionist Organization and the Jewish Agency for Israel and their respective funds and other institutions shall be exempt from taxes and other compulsory Government charges, subject to such restrictions and conditions as may be laid down by the Covenant; the exemption shall come into force on the coming into force of the Covenant.

(The amendments are in force as from the 28th Sivan 5731--21st of June 1971.)

---

* This is a consolidated translation (unofficial version) of the Hebrew version as it was amended in 1975. Only the Hebrew version is official legally.

THE CAESAREA PROCESS

Harry M. Rosen

The Caesarea Conference of the Jewish Agency Board of Governors, held in February 1981, was called to review the ten years of partnership between the World Zionist Organization (WZO) and the Jewish communities of the diaspora, as represented by the central fundraising bodies for Israel. The partnership was formed when the Jewish Agency was reconstituted in June 1971.

The issues discussed at the Conference included the centrality and primacy of Israel in the unity of the Jewish people; what the Jewish Agency should be doing in the next ten years; the Jerusalem Program of the WZO as a unifying basic platform for all those who call themselves Zionists (see Jerusalem Program immediately following this article).

Jewish education and aliyah emerged as top priority common tasks for the Jewish Agency and the WZO, in cooperation with the organized Jewish communities of the diaspora. Similarly, top priority was given to the need to find ways for the Jewish Agency, WZO and the communities to come closer and work together with maximum effectiveness in the pursuit of their common goals.

Following the Caesarea Conference, six commissions were appointed to bring back to the Board of Governors recommendations for the implementation of the findings of the Conference. These commissions are: Aliyah, Jewish Education, Finance and Fiscal Policy, Goals and Objectives, Governance and Management.

Following are highlights of the work of each commission.

GOALS AND OBJECTIVES

The Commission prepared a report on its findings based on its own discussions, the discussions in the last two Jewish Agency Assemblies and a questionnaire sent to participants in at least two of the last five Assemblies. The report was presented to the October 1982 meeting of the Board of Governors, and was adopted in principle, with one reservation, noted below. Following are the highlights of the report.

Principles — The primary task of the Jewish Agency is the upbuilding of the land of Israel. The Jerusalem Program expresses the links between Israel and the diaspora.

Priorities — Aliyah and rural settlement are integral to the functions of the Jewish Agency. The Commission recognizes the need for substantially increased concern with Jewish education. Programs to enhance the quality of life in Israel, like Project Renewal, should be on a time-limited basis.

Criteria — Jewish Agency activities should be undertaken in accordance with the above priorities. Programs must have specific achievement targets, including definition of time span.

When the Agency Board of Governors accepted these recommendations in principle, it made a specific reservation with regard to the definition of the role of Youth Aliyah, and a special committee was appointed to bring back recommendations.

GOVERNANCE

The work of the Commission touches directly upon the relationships and respective roles of the partners in the Jewish Agency, as well as internal structures. A modified summary version of the Commission's report was adopted by the Jewish Agency Assembly in June 1984. Major concerns covered thus far include:

Representativeness — The problem is twofold. One issue is that of rotation, to assure that there will be places for new people in the different governing bodies. The other aspect is the question of who appoints or elects which members, geographic considerations and other matters, all of which are internal to the designating bodies: WZO, United Israel Appeal (UIA), Keren Hayesod affiliates.

The Assembly — The Commission wishes to strengthen the Assembly by giving it a year-round function and giving more responsibility to the members, for example, as Agency spokespersons in their respective communities. There is also the issue of whether the Assembly should include members or observers from other organizations, not only the three 'partners'.

Executive and Board — The Reconstitution Agreement states that the Executive of the Jewish Agency is responsible to the Board of Governors. The issue is how to implement this: what should be the powers of the Executive, what should be the powers of the Chairman of the Executive, what role should be played by the Board committees.

FINANCE AND FISCAL POLICY

The Commission recommended and the Jewish Agency Board of Governors has already adopted a program for reducing the Jewish Agency accumulated debt and eliminating it by 1990. Responsibility for implementing this program is shared equally by the Jewish Agency in Israel and the fundraising communities, mostly in North America. The Commission is now working on ways of improving the Agency budget process.

ALIYAH

The essence of the Commission's proposals is the need to involve organized communities to the maximum in the promotion of aliyah and assistance to olim. It was agreed to concentrate first on the United States, beginning with a few demonstration communities. To assure success, top community leadership must be involved.

Other points include:

— creating a variety of program opportunities for potential olim of all age levels, such as summer education and other opportunities for study, specialized travel plans;
— upgrading aliyah on the agendas of all national organizations and local community federations;

— the closest coordination among all departments of the WZO and the Agency;
— a Government interministerial committee on aliyah.

JEWISH EDUCATION

It was agreed that the major emphasis of the Jewish education work of the WZO and Jewish Agency must be on Zionist-Israel aspects of Jewish education. Toward this end, the Commission recommends:

— Assuring effective intercommunication between Israel and the diaspora on Jewish-Zionist education goals and services, including involvement of top national and local leadership in the dialogue; taking into account differences in various countries; establishing a central mechanism to ensure effective intercommunication between Israel and the diaspora with regard to Jewish education.
— Setting sound priorities, taking into account which age groups should receive priority attention; types and quality of services appropriate for the respective diaspora communities; most effective use of financial and manpower resources.
— Enhancing organizational effectiveness; toward this end, it is essential that the WZO-Jewish Agency undertake periodic review of its organizational structure and functions for Jewish education.

MANAGEMENT

This Commission was the last to get started, and is still in the study and discussion process. Its mandate is to examine and make recommendations with regard to:

— Overall Agency management structure.
— Management and operational relations between the Agency and WZO and their departments.
— Communications among the partners and their constituents (Jewish Agency, WZO, fundraising bodies, communities).
— Role of the Executive and the Chairman of the Executive.

THE JERUSALEM PROGRAM

After the establishment of the State, the aims and tasks of the Zionist movement were redefined at the 23rd Congress, the first Congress held in Jerusalem. The first "Jerusalem Program," adopted at this Congress, pledged itself to the goals of "strengthening Israel, gathering the exiles in Eretz Israel and securing the unity of the Jewish people."

The 27th Zionist Congress, held in Jerusalem in 1968, adopted the second "Jerusalem Program" that reformulated the aims of the Zionist movement as follows:

- The unity of the Jewish people and the centrality of the State of Israel in Jewish life.
- The ingathering of the Jewish people in its historic homeland, Eretz Israel, through aliyah from all countries.
- The strengthening of the State of Israel which is based on the prophetic vision of justice and peace.
- The preservation of the identity of the Jewish people through the fostering of Jewish and Hebrew education and of Jewish spiritual and cultural values.
- The protection of Jewish rights everywhere.

The World Zionist Organization (WZO) organizes the Jewish people for actively supporting the Jerusalem Program. In a 'roll-call of members' organized in 1971 and in 1977 in the free countries of the diaspora, more than one million Jews declared themselves as members of the WZO.

PART II

The Jewish Agency
and
World Jewry

DANIEL J. ELAZAR

THE JEWISH AGENCY: AN INSTRUMENT OF THE WORLD JEWISH POLITY

The suggestion that it is possible to talk about a world Jewish polity is based upon a combination of factors. In part, it rests upon the reactivation of the sense of common fate among Jews all over the world as a result of the events of the past century, which has led to concrete efforts to work together to influence the shape of that fate wherever Jews have settled, particularly whenever they have required the assistance of their brethren. This, in turn, has led to the development of institutionalized frameworks for cooperation in a variety of contexts, increasingly revolving around the State of Israel for self-evident reasons. Finally, the entire effort has acquired a certain legitimacy in the eyes of the Jewish and non-Jewish worlds alike as a result of the emerging redefinition of what constitutes the proper context for political linkage and action, namely the recognition – in the Western world at least – that there are other forms of political relationships than those embraced within the nation-state, that polity is a far more complex condition than statehood, and that it can involve multiple relationships, not all of which are territorially based. In many respects, this represents a rediscovery of what had been an accepted phenomenon in the Western world until the modern era.[1]

In short, we are beginning to recognize that all polities are not states. The Greeks, as usual, had a word for it. The Hellenistic world coined the term *politeuma* to describe phenomena such as the worldwide Jewish polity of that age in which Jews simultaneously maintained strong political links, including citizenship, with their respective territorial polities, the Hellenistic cities, and with one another across lands and seas.[2]

FIRST STEPS TOWARD JEWISH POLITY IN MODERN TIMES

One of the primary characteristics of the Emancipation era was the effort of Jews in the Western world to redefine themselves politically as citizens of their respective states, albeit of a different religious persuasion. Connected with that was the effort on the part of many to detach themselves from the common fate of fellow Jews. This effort received its strongest formal expression in the formulations of the Napoleonic Sanhedrin where Jews, under some duress but not entirely so, specifically abjured any transnational ties. Nevertheless, it should be noted that the Jews were at the very least ambivalent about this dimension of their search for emancipation and citizenship as individuals. No longer comfortable about speaking of their brethren as members of a common nation, English-speaking Jews in the nineteenth century coined the term 'coreligionists', a philological barbarism designed to reflect the existence of ties but on a very limited and careful basis.[3]

A change in name did not change reality, however; the common interests of Jews the world over did not disappear and in fact were intensified in the course of the nineteenth century. Significantly, the attitude of the nation-states, new or old, did not really shift either, despite their demands that 'their' Jews become citizens or subjects on an individual basis. Thus, the Congress of Vienna in 1815 addressed itself to the Jewish question as part of its agenda, and since then hardly any significant international meeting has been without some Jewish issue in front of it.[4]

At first, the Jewish question was addressed without any immediate involvement of the Jews themselves. Obviously, this was not a position that the Jews could tolerate. Even under conditions of emancipation and denationalization, they were not prepared to allow others the exclusive right to determine their interests. Moreover, not all Jews, even among the most emancipated ones, had abandoned the sense of nationhood. In fact, it was precisely in the United Kingdom and the United States, where Jews were most free to become citizens on an individual basis, that many felt least constrained to abandon the sense that a Jewish nation existed. Moreover, it was not until the twentieth century that the term 'peoplehood' came into use to provide a more modest expression of that sentiment. Throughout the nineteenth century, among those who saw themselves as members of a Jewish body corporate that transcended their particular states of citizenship, the term 'nation' was the term they used to describe that body.

The first modern Jewish political responses (as distinct from philanthropic ones) to transnational Jewish problems were initiated early in the nineteenth century by individual notables working more or less quietly behind the scenes on behalf of Jewish interests — a revival in new form of the system of *shtadlanut*, which had once prevailed in late medieval Europe.[5] The greatest Jewish *shtadlan* of the nineteenth century was Sir Moses Montefiore, but he was by no means the only one. By and large, these *shtadlanim* were activated on behalf of their Jewish brethren in lands not yet touched by emancipation or where promises of emancipation were not fulfilled, essentially the lands of the East, both Eastern Europe and the Eastern Mediterranean, plus North Africa. As the Western European great powers became increasingly involved in the internal affairs of those lands, the Jewish notables were able to capitalize on their positions within their respective powers (particularly Austria, France, Great Britain and, later, Germany) to intervene on behalf of their brethren.

The first such intervention to attract worldwide attention came in 1840 as a result of the Damascus blood libel. It was undertaken strictly by individual *shtadlanim* but, significantly, the *shtadlanim* from the major Western European countries found it in their common interest to coordinate their work in what was perhaps the first modern transnational expression of Jewish political activity.

The construction of the first housing outside the walls of the old city of Jerusalem was a classic example of this new trend. Montefiore of Great Britain was entrusted with funds bequeathed by Judah Touro of the United States to utilize on behalf of the Jewish poor of the land of Israel. The result: Mishkenot Sha'ananim.

Between the 1840s and the 1870s the number of problems requiring such joint action grew, or at the very least the concern of the Western Jewish communities with those problems expanded. As involvement increased and a pattern of response emerged, the individual *shtadlanim* began to seek more institutionalized methods of handling the increased workload, which led to the creation of *shtadlanic* organizations, in the principal Western powers. The first of them, the Alliance Israelite Universelle, was established in 1860. It was followed by the Anglo-Jewish Association (1871), the Allianz Israelitische zu Wien (1873), and somewhat later, the Hilfsverein der Deutschen Juden (1901) and the American Jewish Committee (1906). Each of these organizations operated fully within the *shtadlanic* tradition, and consisted of self-selected Jewish notables who banded together to undertake common tasks more efficiently. Each was, at least in part, a representative of its sponsoring power as well as of the Jewish citizens of that power. At the same time, they found it advantageous to cooperate with one another, as did the individual *shtadlanim* earlier. Thus a kind of framework for the defense of Jewish interests worldwide began to emerge, first as an alliance of *shtadlanim* and then through an alliance of *shtadlanic* organizations. In this way, interventions were carried out in Russia, Rumania, the Ottoman Empire, and North Africa on a regular basis, and in other countries as needed.

Shtadlanut was able to hold its own as long as the large body of Jews was not awakened politically. The coming of the Zionist movement changed all that. Herzl's convening of the first Zionist Congress in 1897 marked a turning point in worldwide Jewish organization. Although he himself was a transitional figure, working in many respects as a *shtadlan*, he transformed the basis of his own activities, and more important, the character of the demands Jews made, by virtue of the establishment of the World Zionist Organization (WZO). One of the principles of the Basle Program was "the organization and uniting of the whole of Jewry by means of appropriate institutions, both local and international," thus serving notice that the Jews were prepared to act as a body, organized democratically on a worldwide basis to achieve their political goals.

For the rest of that generation, the struggle between the two approaches continued, culminating in the victory of the Zionists during World War I as a result of the struggle over the Balfour Declaration.[6] After the end of that war *shtadlanut,* even in its institutionalized form, essentially receded into the background and the field of worldwide Jewish activity was taken over by multi-country organizations with avowedly, if not exclusively, political goals. The basis for a worldwide Jewish polity was now in place.[7]

If we were to sum up the foci of transnational Jewish activity in the nineteenth century, we would see an evolution from activity to protect Jews during crises (the Damascus affair, the Mortara affair), to consistent efforts on the part of emancipated Jews to secure the emancipation of unemancipated communities (Rumania, Russia, North Africa), to a continuing, abiding, and unremitting concern for national revival. While the first two approaches already marked a tacit recognition of a Jewish interest that crossed national borders, it was the last that sought to redefine the Jewish people as a body politic once again. The victory of the Zionists, then, involved far more than the establishment of the Jewish State. It marked the reestablishment of a Jewish political consciousness, either willingly or reluctantly, and the reestablishment of the sense of Jewish peoplehood with all that this implied. The form of the Jewish polity today is the direct product of the Zionist victory; our responses to contemporary events are based upon the 'facts' which the Zionists established among the Jews themselves and within the non-Jewish world.

THE FORGING OF A NEW JEWISH POLITY IN THE TWENTIETH CENTURY

While the beginnings of an institutionalized structure for world Jewry were developing, massive demographic changes were taking place in the Jewish world. On one hand, the world Jewish population grew geometrically as the conditions under which Jews lived improved. From an estimated 2.5 million in 1800, the number of Jews in the world increased to 10.5 million a century later and to 16.5 million in 1939.[8]

At the same time, the Jews began to evacuate what had been the major centers of Jewish life in the Old World and to establish new centers in the New World of the great European frontier, namely North and South America, South Africa, Australia and, of course, the land of Israel, not to speak of Prussia, France and Great Britain, areas which had been utterly peripheral to Jewish life for centuries. This process, which had become a flood by the end of the nineteenth century, was given additional impetus by World War I and the Russian Revolution, and received its final dimensions as a result of the Holocaust, World War II and the establishment of the State of Israel.

By the time the dust cleared in the middle of the twentieth century, not a single Jewish area of settlement that had been prominent at the time of the American and French Revolutions remained in the forefront of Jewish life and hardly a single Jewish community remained undisturbed anywhere in the world. The number of Jews in the world declined to 10.5 million. The Eastern European Jewish centers were destroyed either physically or socially. Even in the Soviet Union, most Jews were no longer located in the areas of traditional Jewish settlement. The establishment of the State of Israel ended Jewish life in the Arab lands for all intents and purposes. Even the centers that had emerged in continental Europe in the nineteenth century were either physically destroyed or so reduced in numbers and morale as a result of the Holocaust that they were unable to play their earlier role. On the other hand, the United States had emerged as the largest Jewish community functioning as a unit under one government in all of Jewish history; a majority of the Jews of the world lived in English-speaking countries and had adopted English as their native language; and even such Yiddish and Ladino as did exist survived primarily in Latin America, Canada and (paradoxically enough) Israel rather than in the lands of their origin.

While this process was going on, new organizations had emerged to serve world Jewry.[9] The Americans contributed the Joint Distribution Committee (JDC), founded in 1914 through a union of the Orthodox socialist and landsmanshaft relief agencies established to provide assistance to Jews caught between the opposing armies on the eastern front in World War I. In 1922, the Jewish Agency was organized in the land of Israel to unite world Jewry, first through the Zionist Organization and then on a broader basis (1929), and in order to undertake the work of reconstruction in the Jewish homeland. Finally, in 1936, the World Jewish Congress (WJC) was organized, essentially by the Jewries of Europe, to try to protect Jewish rights in an age of growing Fascist anti-Semitism. From the very beginning, these organizations developed areas of functional specialization, the first two by design and the last by virtue of the situation in which it found itself. It is true that the WJC sought to become what its title implies, namely the all-embracing political forum for world Jewry (in their words: "a permanent address for the Jewish people"), at least for all matters in the diaspora, but at no point was it able to come close to such a goal. In its best years, it was essentially a European body and with the destruction of European Jewry its own power base was destroyed.

Crowning the creation of new centers and new organizations was the establishment of a new state, or more correctly, the renewal of independent Jewish national existence in the land of Israel within a politically sovereign state. By its very existence as a state, Israel transformed all previous relationships among Jewish communities. A state, possessing political sovereignty with both the powers and responsibilities that go with it, could not be treated simply as another Jewish community on the world scene. At the same time, since it had only a relatively small percentage of the total number of Jews in the world, and only in the 1970s became the second largest Jewish community (approximately half the size of the largest), it also could not become the sole voice of the Jewish people, either internally or externally, much as its leaders would have liked it to. Thus the blessings of statehood brought with them a new set of political problems for the Jewish

people; good problems, but problems nevertheless.

This entire transformation took place within essentially a single generation, from World War I to just beyond World War II. As a matter of course, the first generation of leaders to have to face these problems were products of the last generation of the nineteenth century when the struggle between the Zionists and the *shtadlanim* was at its height. Thus, the understanding and assumptions they brought with them were those of a much earlier age. The Ben-Gurion-Blaustein agreement reflects the efforts of two men of goodwill trying to come to grips with the new situation, but bound by their own experience of an earlier age to a certain intent and even phraseology.[10] Only now, as the first generation of Jewish statehood and post-war reconstitution comes to an end, is a generation of Jewish leaders likely to emerge whose formative experiences have taken place within the context of this new Jewish order and who are able and willing to directly face up to it and its implications.

What characterized the first two generations of the twentieth century, during which this new Jewish polity was being forged, was growing collective action of an overtly political nature on a wide variety of fronts, coupled with strenuous denials of its political character. The Ben-Gurion-Blaustein agreement is but one case in point. The Six-Day War and the Yom Kippur War six and a half years later did much to put an end to this dichotomy. If anything, the Jewish people in their numbers demonstrated how open they were to recognizing the political realities of the existence of the State of Israel and their attachment to it. Jews who in no overt way differed from their neighbors in their private lives were prepared to go out into the streets in frankly political demonstrations on behalf of Israel. Elsewhere I have suggested that this marked a reversal of the emancipationist dictum of Haskalah poet Y. L. Gordon: "Be a Jew in your home and a man in the street," as Jews who no longer knew how to be Jews in their homes and were simply men and women like all others, specifically went out into the streets to demonstrate their Jewish attachments.[11] Jewish leadership, naturally and necessarily cautious in its explicit description of what, indeed, it had been doing to foster the situation in the intervening years, then followed the lead of the people in acknowledging the emerging Jewish polity.

NEW STRUCTURES AND RELATIONSHIPS

The inter-war generation was primarily concerned with the creation of new structures for Jewish life. In a period of resettlement and national revival, this was inevitable. The concern for structures has persisted to no small extent, particularly where Jews have sought systematically to explore the possibilities for improving Israel-diaspora and inter-diaspora ties, but perhaps what was characteristic of the post-war generation was the turn away from an emphasis on structures to an emphasis on relationships.[12] This was a natural development based on two factors: first, the fact that certain basic structures had emerged by the end of the previous generation, which dictated the framework within which all relationships would be developed; and second, the practical difficulties that emerged in trying to extend structural arrangements any further. Our discussion here is based on the assumption that relationships are indeed of first importance, not to diminish the significance of proper structures but to emphasize that structures are designed to accommodate and foster relationships and not vice versa.

During and after World War II, other Israeli and American Jewish organizations and institutions also became involved on the world Jewish scene. The American Jewish Committee (AJC) undertook to develop an international program of some scope after World War II. The Bnai Brith expanded its operations outside the United States. The three American synagogue movements established worldwide associations to encourage the formation of synagogues with their respective trends beyond the confines of North America. Israel, in the meantime, was busy establishing branches or tributary organizations across the board to raise funds to assist in the rebuilding of the land or to provide support in other ways. Thus, in the years between 1945 and 1955, a whole network of worldwide organizations was developed, focusing either on the United States or Israel, but involving Jewries in many other countries as well. Table 6 catalogues the existing Jewish multi-country organizations.

The multiplication of organizations led to a new concern for restructuring the institutional framework of the emerging world Jewish polity to limit duplication and promote coordination. Some of the bodies, new and old, were indeed working at cross-purposes with one another, some in the pursuit of different goals, but many in pursuit of the same ones. In this respect, in a manner familiar to American Jews, the community relations organizations presented the biggest problem. The number of defenders of Jewish interests that came forward was such that, at times, the efforts at defense were themselves jeopardized.

So many Jewish agencies sought status as official non-governmental organizations before the United Nations that even they came to realize the necessity for working something out. As a result, two separate coordinating bodies were established to handle Jewish non-governmental representation at the UN — the Consultative Council of Jewish Organizations and the Coordinating Board of Jewish Organizations. Once the Jewish-Catholic rapprochement began, it became difficult for the Vatican to decide which among the many Jewish claimants to talk to, and again it was necessary to develop some means to speak with at least a coordinated set of voices, if not a single voice.

In the aid-to-Israel sphere, the multiplicity of organizations seeking to assist the Jewish State also led to demands for coordination. As Israel began to reach out to try to assist the diaspora in strengthening Jewish life, it initially did so in a manner that paid little attention to the established framework within the various diaspora communities. The Israelis were called to task and demands for coordination were raised.

A natural focal point for coordination might have been the WJC, but the Holocaust had destroyed whatever base it had by reducing the European Jewish communities to secondary or tertiary status on the Jewish map. Nahum Goldmann, the founder and leader of the WJC, remained the preeminent political figure in the diaspora and was successful in coordinating efforts to secure German reparations through the World Conference on Material Claims against Germany (1951). Among its other activities, the Conference entered into partnership with the JDC to assist in the rebuilding of Jewish life in Europe, and with the Agency to assist in the rebuilding of Israel. Goldmann, recognizing the new limits imposed on the WJC, took the lead in trying to stimulate a coordinating agency for those Jewish organizations involved in multi-country activities, out of which emerged the World Conference of Jewish Organizations (COJO) in 1958, a move welcomed by the Jewish Agency and the WZO, which had emerged as a major source of financial support for the WJC.[13] COJO lasted two decades but never fulfilled its promise and was finally disbanded.

At first, those advocating structural changes to reflect the new realities sought some overarching framework that would unite all bodies serving the Jewish people as a whole. This dream has never been abandoned in theory, but in practice the Jewish people has come to make do with a far looser structure, a number of separate 'authorities' with specialized areas of activity loosely tied together through coordinating councils. The Claims Conference, the JDC, and the Jewish Agency are good examples of such authorities, with the last having emerged in recent years as the most important.

This situation has developed pragmatically on a *de facto* basis. It has never been recognized as such or given any formal legitimacy on the part of either participants or commentators on the world Jewish scene. By now, however, it is fair to suggest that for the indefinite future world Jewry will be united only through these various functional authorities, linked to one another primarily through the formal mechanisms of coordinating councils and the more important informal mechanisms of overlapping leadership. Apparently the Jewish people does not seek a more comprehensive framework on a worldwide basis, particularly given the nature of contemporary Jewish life whereby most Jews are not even aware of the network that presently exists, even if they are very interested in Jewish survival, while Jewish leadership is extremely wary of anything that gives rise to thoughts of the "elders of Zion." Moreover, the religious and ideological differences that divide Jewry prevent unity on anything other than a loose confederate basis.

The authorities that do exist, and their coordinating organizations, are dominated by Israel and American Jewry, sometimes by the one, sometimes by the other, and sometimes on a shared

basis, depending on which authority is involved. At the same time, the structure of the authorities, as such, is that other Jewish communities are represented and even well represented, and the representatives of the stronger among them can play important roles.

Perhaps the major problem facing multi-country Jewish bodies other than the functional authorities is not how to better coordinate activities among themselves but how to link themselves with the realia of Jewish life in a world in which most Jewish activity is carried on locally in a large number of local Jewish communities. Even the country-wide organizations and institutions of most Jewries tend to be relatively weak and ineffectual except insofar as they confine their activities to limited purposes that require the concentration of some critical mass (e.g., representation before the government, support of a theological seminary, or a placement service providing assistance to localities seeking professional personnel) or serve, for all intents and purposes, one very large local community. If the country-wide bodies tend to be weak, the tendency is even greater for certain of the worldwide ones to be no more than forums where a certain segment of world Jewry, those who have become leaders in their respective communities, are able to meet together on a regular basis to exchange repeatedly the same views, almost totally outside of the awareness of the communities they purport to lead and with minimal, if any, effect on the activities of those communities or the quality of Jewish life within them.

CATEGORIES OF COMMUNITIES WITHIN THE POLITY

The first requisite for understanding the relationship within the emergent world Jewish polity is an understanding of who the actors are. Here a relatively simple classification may be of help. As an independent state with a Jewish majority, where Jewish culture (in some form) is dominant, Israel stands in a class by itself. Turning to the diaspora, there are over eighty organized country-wide Jewish communities in the world today and some 120 countries in which Jews reside as Jews.[14]

Among them American Jewry stands out, not only as the greatest, but as one in which sheer quantity has created a qualitative difference between itself and the others. American Jewry, along with Israel, is capable of functioning fully as a Jewish community, self-sufficient in its Jewish resources and, more than that, able to add significantly to the sum of the Jewish heritage within its own community and beyond. Without entering into the normative argument of Israel's centrality in Jewish life, empirically it must be understood that both Israel and the American Jewish community are strong centers of Jewish activity and existence today. There are those who would argue that twice as many Jews in the United States are not as culturally creative or as Jewishly aware as half their number in Israel, but nobody who knows the American Jewish community can deny that it plays a role in contemporary Jewish life and in Jewish history that goes far beyond simply sustaining Jewish existence.[15]

Ranking below Israel and American Jewry is a second category of diaspora communities, comprising those which can be said to be essentially self-sufficient Jewishly but whose power to add to the sum total of Jewish existence is limited to what they can do within their own borders except for the contributions of a few exceptional institutions or individuals. They can create and maintain their own institutions, even produce their own leaders, but their influence rarely extends beyond their own members. These self-sufficient communities include the Jewries of France, Great Britain, Canada and perhaps South Africa and Australia.[16] As self-sufficient communities, they are able to contribute actively to the overall work of world Jewry and to demand a place in the sun in matters affecting world Jewry as a body.

A third category consists of viable Jewish communities, those which, with a modicum of assistance from the outside (e.g., they usually have to import rabbis and Hebrew teachers), can maintain a viable Jewish life for their members. These are communities that may not be in danger of disappearing but that are also not likely to play significant roles on the world Jewish scene as communities. There are many such communities. Typical of them are Argentina, Brazil, and Switzerland. Communities like Argentina may be included in this category because a combination of local circumstances has made them less than self-sufficient.[17]

There is a fourth category of communities which consists of those with a small number of Jews that, despite their organizational integrity, are in constant danger of disappearing as communities through the assimilation of the local Jews. These communities possibly possess the wherewithal of the third category insofar as they are sufficiently well-organized to maintain their viability; but the combination of their small populations and the openness of their host environments works to reduce their chances of survival. The Scandinavian communities offer good examples of this type.[18]

Most recently there has grown up a fifth category of communities which may be termed protectorates of Israel and American Jewry. These are communities which contain their own internal institutions but which are dependent, or make themselves dependent, upon either one or both of the two great centers, not only for sustenance of their Jewish life but for direct guidance and even programmatic activity to sustain them. The first three categories of communities can be found throughout Jewish history. It is unclear whether this is a new category or whether it simply represents the emergence of a phenomenon that has existed at other times in the Jewish past. For our purposes, however, it can be treated as a new phenomenon, a product of twentieth century upheavals with hardly an echo before World War I.

Iran, before the Khomeini revolution, was a classic example of such a protectorate.[19] Then a Jewish community of some eighty thousand, it had the wherewithal, in principle, to be viable with a minimum amount of outside assistance. The particular character of Iranian Jewry, however, led them to rely heavily on the Israeli ambassador to guide their internal decision-making, on Israeli teachers to provide Jewish education in their schools and on the American JDC to maintain the schools and the community's social welfare institutions, and to provide organizational guidance for the community. In a very different way, Soviet Jewry is also a protectorate, unable to function legitimately as a community under Soviet rule. To the extent that there is any kind of organized Jewish life, it is dependent upon the work of Israeli and American

Jews in tandem with local activists, whether Zionists or Hassidism.

Protectorates are Jewish communities with indigenous populations but whose direction and principal activities have passed to the hands of outsiders from the major centers. Another category of community consists of colonies, communities actually planted by Jews from the major centers. Both Israeli and American Jewries have developed colonies in the post-war period. Israelis have done so primarily in Africa in connection with their missions for the Israeli Government or private companies, where sufficient numbers of them have gathered to create replicas of Israeli schools to serve their children's needs and other institutions on a modest scale to serve their own. American Jews have done so primarily in Asia as a result of American military activities overseas in the aftermath of World War II, where American forces have been stationed long enough to attract Jews connected with both military and civilian occupations and there to create communities. The Jewish communities in Japan, Okinawa and Thailand are good examples of this. Needless to say, these communities are very small, do not count for much on the world Jewish scene and are probably temporary in nature, as a number have already proved to be.

Finally, there is a category of communities in the process of dissolution, generally outside of the orbit of world Jewry for reasons peculiar to their internal situations, which are, at best, protected from time to time by other Jewries, almost in the manner of the nineteenth century, through sporadic intervention often via third parties. These are primarily the Jewish communities in Eastern Europe and the Arab countries.[20]

WORLD JEWISH COLLABORATION ON BEHALF OF LOCAL JEWRIES

What is characteristic of all these categories is that, where outside assistance or intervention is involved, it does not come simply from one center but almost invariably from several. We have already referred to Iran. There, even before the turn of the century, the Alliance Israelite Universelle established itself to provide basic education for the masses of Iranian Jewry. Its entry into the country was facilitated through negotiations by the *shtadlanic* institutions with the then rulers of Iran and only after the application of considerable pressure on the part of the Western powers triggered by the *shtadlanim*. The Alliance was dominant until World War II, when the Iranians perceived that French influence was on the decline in the world and American influence on the rise, at which point two American-sponsored institutions, the JDC and the Otzar ha-Torah (an organization established to build religiously-oriented schools for Jews in the Middle East), came into Iran to undertake social and educational activities. Both have been there ever since.

The Jewish Agency also arrived in Iran during the war and, with the establishment of the State of Israel, an Israeli presence was also established. The Israelis' first efforts were directed toward encouraging the mass migration of Iranian Jewry to Israel; but by the mid-1950s, when it became apparent that tens of thousands of Jews would stay in Iran, the Israelis changed their orientation to include an effort strongly to influence the Jewish community remaining in the direction of Zionism, aliyah, and financial support of the Jewish state. Later, I shall describe the tensions that developed between the American and Israeli institutions and leaders in the course of the intervening years. For our purposes here, it is sufficient to note that, whatever the antagonisms between them, they did develop patterns of cooperation in order to advance the common goal of strengthening the Jewish life of Iranian Jewry to the point where neither can function without the other.

Argentina is a good example of the intervention of both Israel and American Jewry. A community of perhaps 350,000 Jews, at one time it was at least self-sufficient, if not more. However, the combination of the breakdown of civil society in Argentina as a whole, coupled with the failures of the indigenous Jewish leadership to adjust to new world conditions, has forced the community to struggle for its very viability today. In that struggle, it has turned to the two great centers for support. It was encouraged to do so by the leaders of the two great centers themselves, who understood that the world's sixth or seventh largest concentration of Jews is an asset that cannot be abandoned to its own fate.

From the first days of Israel's independence, the Israeli role was actively welcomed and encouraged in Argentina. The original response of the Argentinian non-Jews was to recognize Israel as the *madre patria* (the mother fatherland) of Argentinian Jewry parallel to the mother fatherlands of Argentinians of Spanish, German, Italian and other extractions.[21] For Jews, this was a strong basing point for an identity, which was primarily secular in nature, in a community whose institutions were so dominated by Zionists that the very political parties that contested for control of them were part and parcel of the world Zionist party federations that included the Israeli political parties. As time went on, the Israeli ambassador became an increasingly important figure in the decision-making of Argentinian Jewry and Israeli assistance through the Jewish Agency in the form of *shlichim*, teachers, and rabbis became greater. When in the late 1960s a number of the communal institutions began to disintegrate, the Argentinian dependence upon Israel grew even more, almost as if Israel was called upon to replace a local lack of will as well as to fund certain communal functions and fulfill specific tasks.

Argentinian Jewry was less open in its welcome of American Jewish support, principally because of the endemic Latin American hostility to the big brother from the north. Nevertheless, shortly after World War II, the AJC opened up an office in Argentina to try to help the Argentinians deal with problems of anti-Semitism and to link them more closely with the rest of the Jewish world. Subsequently, the Conservative movement sent a rabbi to Argentina who, after considerable struggle, managed to create a very substantial movement based on congregations affiliated with the United Synagogue, a theological seminary, a Ramah camp, and a variety of educational programs. More recently, the National Jewish Welfare Board has provided technical assistance for local Jewish centers.

The principal point of sharing between Israel and American Jewry is to be found in the special assistance programs of the Jewish Agency, which were launched with the endorsement of the American representatives.

Europe remains a significant arena for Israeli and American Jewish efforts. Since World War I, American Jewish organizations, particularly the JDC, and Zionist agencies based initially on local forces but increasingly on emissaries from Israel, have been involved in the effort to encourage Jewish life on the continent. The respective efforts of the two often have been in different directions, although the gap between them has narrowed considerably in recent years.

Between World Wars I and II, the two were actually at loggerheads. The avowed purpose of the JDC was to strengthen Jewish life in the lands in which Jews were to be found on the emancipationist principle that it was the right and obligation of Jews to acquire equal rights in their countries of origin and to become good citizens of those countries even while maintaining their Jewish identity. To this end, the JDC poured millions of dollars into various schemes to strengthen the economic base and skills of the Jews in Poland, Russia and Rumania.[22] All the while, the avowed purpose of the Zionists was to encourage Jews to abandon their countries of origin in favor of aliyah to Israel. The clarity of this purpose became more evident as the Jewish Agency increasingly took over the Zionist activities from the hands of the local Zionist organizations, or at least became their senior partner.

The cross-purposes at which the principal representatives of the two major communities worked were to leave their scars well into the next generation, nor did the Holocaust entirely put an end to them. In the aftermath of World War II, the Jewish Agency and the JDC again found themselves working in the same field and at cross-purposes. By then, the ideological commitment of the JDC to discourage Jews from leaving their European lands of origin had disappeared. At the same time, the JDC leadership was strongly committed to the notion that those Jews who did want to resettle themselves in Europe should be assisted in doing so and those who did not wish to settle in Israel were entitled to seek other homes with the support of world Jewry. The Jewish Agency, on the other hand, was committed to convincing all the survivors to leave Europe for Israel and to actively discourage those who chose not to.

Matters were further complicated by the arrival on the scene of the American sponsored immigrant aid societies (the HIAS of today), whose avowed task it was to assist Jewish displaced persons in their efforts to emigrate to the United States. Particularly in the years between 1945 and 1947, when no Jewish state was immediately in the offing and the doors of Palestine were officially closed, the Americans felt a moral responsibility to assist Jews in their efforts to enter the United States. At the same time, the representatives of the Jewish Agency wanted all the DP's to stand fast in the camps so as to intensify the problem and stimulate world support for Jewish statehood. Nevertheless, the common interest of all parties in rescuing Jews and in helping them rebuild their lives brought them together into cooperative activity, albeit antagonistic cooperation.[23]

The issue was resolved, as we all know, by the establishment of the State and the migration of the great majority of the DP's to Israel. In the end, the JDC assisted in that migration and established its own institutions in Israel to assist those unable to become self-supporting there. At the same time, it continued with its efforts to assist the survivors who remained in Europe to rebuild Jewish life there. After a while, the Israelis reconciled themselves to the realities of the renewal of a European diaspora, albeit on a limited basis and they, too, began to work among European Jewry to tie them closely to Israel in commitment, if not through aliyah itself.

The Jewish Agency became the major vehicle for this effort. Its efforts have been especially important in the field of Jewish education. Agency *shlichim* make up the core of the teaching staffs in many, if not most, of the European Jewish communities and the Pincus Fund is a major catalyst for educational innovation on the continent.

The story of the role of the American Jewish community in the reconstitution of European Jewry in the post-war generation and in the development of new institutions to meet their needs has yet to be properly told. Suffice it to say that even France, the one European Jewish community that is now self-sufficient, was substantially shaped by the efforts of the JDC, while its present forms of communal organization are the product of JDC efforts in conjunction with the indigenous Jewish leadership.

Today the JDC's creation, the Fonds Social de Juifs Unis, also serves as the primary instrument for raising funds for Israel, thus closing the circle. In every country of Europe, the presence of the JDC has been felt proportionately. Moreover, such European-wide activities as have come into being also reflect the influence of the JDC. The Jewish Agency has also played a role in stimulating European-wide activities often in tandem with its American-sponsored counterpart.

The latest front, where American and Israeli efforts to serve the rest of the diaspora have come to the fore, is in the provision of rabbis for those communities unable to train their own. The American Jewish community began by taking a few students from Latin America, Europe, and even India into its seminaries during the immediate post-war period. Today, American rabbis are themselves going out to serve communities overseas. Mention has been made of Argentina. The chief rabbi of Sweden is a Philadelphian who is a graduate of the Jewish Theological Seminary of America.

Israel's role in this regard (which is of ancient vintage) is even greater and is growing in both ways. Students come from various parts of the world to study in Israeli *yeshivot* and then go back to serve their communities, while Israelis who train for the rabbinate in Israel go out to serve communities in the diaspora from East Africa to Chile. Here Israel has even developed mechanisms for cooperative activity with diaspora communities other than the United States. So, for example, the Indian Jewish community, which has no rabbi, has sent young men to study in Israel to learn to be at least *shochetim* and *mohelim*. Meanwhile, when the Jewish Agency had had a *shaliach* in Bombay in the 1960s and 1970s, he was from the Torah Education Department and served as a conduit for rabbinical matters, passing on requests for such things as divorce or conversion to the rabbinate in Israel, providing them with the relevant information as needed, and then executing their decisions. In matters of conversion of olim to Israel, a more complex procedure was developed. The local *shaliach* trained prospective converts and sent them off to Israel, via Turkey, with certification of their achievements. The chief rabbi of Turkey converted them before they arrived in Israel, thus avoiding any problem with the Israeli rabbinate of the kind that made the integration of Indian Jews particularly difficult in the 1950s.

The situation in Iran as it was reflected the end result — a world Jewish network in which the Jewish Agency is the fulcrum, but in which it must work in close cooperation with other bodies. The Israeli embassy in Iran functioned as a major point of influence in the Jewish community. The Jewish Agency conducted fundraising and aliyah campaigns and, whenever the Iranian Government permitted it, sent *shlichim* to work with Jewish youth. The Israeli Chief Rabbinate served as the court of last resort for the halachic problems of Iranian Jewry and the young rabbis in the community, insofar as there are any, have been trained in Israel.

The JDC still provides support for internal social and educational needs. In the case of education, the JDC works closely with the Otzar ha-Torah and Alliance. The professional leadership of the JDC, still an American organization, originally consisted of American and British Jews. Subsequently, Israelis made their appearance in Iran as part of the JDC's staff. The Alliance relies more heavily on local people, with an occasional French Jew. Otzar ha-Torah relies on local people, with Israelis filling the top professional positions. The Jewish schools, run directly by the Iranian Jewish community with the support of the JDC, made use of Israeli personnel whenever the government permitted them to do so, and they were then employed by the local schools themselves.

The intermixture created the beginning of what was, in fact, a worldwide Jewish civil service whose key people are drawn from several countries. Many of them have made career commitments to that civil service and not to any particular community within which they may be serving. (The first Israeli to serve with the JDC in Iran received his training and first work experience in the Jewish field in Jewish community centers in the United States. He went on to join the JDC staff in Geneva, to develop Jewish cultural programming for European Jewry. He subsequently returned to Israel and became a project manager in Project Renewal!)

This interlocking framework was developing at the same time that the tensions between the JDC and the Agency, which originally emerged in Europe

a generation earlier, were continuing on the old basis. The JDC was committed to strengthening Jewish life in Iran while the Agency wanted to encourage the Iranian Jews to leave. The cooperation between the two bodies had hints of antagonism below the surface, but the necessity to cooperate in order to achieve the common immediate objectives prevailed.

In France, a relatively large and strong Jewish community where local forces play a much more important role and the respective interests of the two outside centers can be better articulated on the ground, the cooperation between the JDC and the Agency is less clearly visible. But, as has already been indicated, the JDC's work in stimulating the creation of the Fonds Social has had direct payoff with regard to the improvement of fundraising for Israel. There the work of the JDC was carried out by a group of American Jewish social workers who spent their careers in Europe rebuilding European Jewish life, any number of whom have since retired or have been transferred to Israel.[24]

To date, this kind of coordination has developed on an ad hoc basis. This means that what has developed is real and in response to real needs and is not simply 'window dressing' to serve some external demands. In all of this, there has been a notable reluctance on the part of Israel to encourage American Jewish involvement in policies affecting it directly, even where American Jewish money is involved. Until recently, American Jews themselves were reluctant to press matters. Even in those areas where Israel demanded American Jewish mobilization within the United States on Israel's behalf, American Jewry was content to follow the Israeli lead on the grounds that Israeli vital interests are those most immediately affected. By the same token, American Jewry has strongly resisted Israeli efforts to intervene in its communal affairs for many of the same reasons, and while from time to time Israel has shown more interest in doing so, it generally has respected American Jewish wishes and pulled back when asked to do so.

For example, in the late 1950s the Jewish Agency, eager to promote day schools, decided to provide direct subsidies to Jewish day schools in at least one American Jewish community, which had been turned down for such subsidies by the local Jewish Welfare Federation, then rather firmly

TABLE 7:
JEWISH MULTICOUNTRY ASSOCIATIONS

Name of Association	Goals				
	Religious	Service		Political	
		Education Culture	Welfare Community Organization	Rights	Ideology
1. Agudas Israel World Organization	X*				Y*
2. Alliance Israelite Universelle[1]		X		Y	
3. B'nai B'rith International Council		Y	Y		
4. Conference on Jewish Material Claims Against Germany		X	X		
5. World Conference of Jewish Organizations (COJO)		Y		X	
6. Consultative Council of Jewish Organizations				X	
7. European Council of Jewish Community Services			X		
8. International Conference of Jewish Communal Service			Y		
9. Jewish Agency for Israel		X	X		
10. Jewish Colonization Association		X	X		
11. Maccabi World Union					
12. Memorial Foundation for Jewish Culture		X	X		
13. Mizrachi World Union	X				Y
14. ORT (World ORT Union)		X			
15. OSE (Oeuvre de Secours aux Enfants)[2]			X		
16. Women's International Zionist Organization		X	X		Y
17. World Conference on Soviet Jewry[3]				X	
18. World Council of Synagogues	X				
19. World Federation of YMHAs and Jewish Community Centers					
20. World Jewish Congress				X	
21. World Sephardi Federation					
22. World Union of Jewish Students					
23. World Union for Progressive Judaism	X				
24. World Zionist Organization					X
25. Zionist Youth Movements (Bnei Akiva, Habonim, etc.)					Y

* X = primary, Y = secondary.

[1] Although no longer multicountry by our criteria, the Alliance began its career in 1860 as the first "universal" Jewish association in modern times; it therefore deserves a place in this table.

[2] OSE is included because of its historic multicountry character; today, to all intents and purposes it is a French organization.

[3] This is an *ad hoc* association with a single purpose. Unlike the more permanent multipurpose political associations, it has been able to enlist across-the-board participation.

Goals			Structure and Membership				Mode of Operation		
Fraternal		Youth	Federative						
General	Special Interest	Sports	Roof Organization	New Body	Autonomous	Individual Membership	Operational	Consultative	Distributive
					X		**X**		
					X		**X**		
X			X				Y	X	
				X					X
			X					X	
			X					X	
			X					X	
X						X		X	
					X		X		
					X				X
		X	X				X		
				X					X
					X		X		
			X				X		
					X		X		
			X				X		
				X				X	
			X					X	
								X	
		X	X					X	
	X	X	X		X		Y	X	
	Y	X		X		X		Y	X
			X				Y	X	
			X				X	Y	
		X					X	Y	

From Ernest Stock, "Jewish Multicountry Associations," in *American Jewish Yearbook 1974-75,* vol. 75 (New York and Philadelphia: American Jewish Committee and Jewish Publication Society of America, 1974), 571-597.

opposed to the day schools as a communal solution to the problem of Jewish education. The leadership of the local Jewish Welfare Federation acted quickly and firmly to prevent the Agency from doing so, on the grounds that money collected through the Federation for use in Israel was not to be used to bypass Federation policies in their own community. The Agency reluctantly was forced to retreat.

Since then, the Agency has made certain cautious efforts to provide funds for specific projects in the United States with the consent of the local communities involved, but has generally refrained from trying to bypass them and certainly not to counteract local policies. At that, communities are very reluctant to see Agency money spent within the United States, understanding full well the implications of such a policy shift, even when the monies would be spent for mutually acceptable programs.

More recently, diaspora Jewish leaders have demanded a greater share in decision-making in matters that they see as affecting Jews as Jews, whether in Israel or elsewhere. At first, they openly challenged Israeli policy with regard to the resettlement of Russian Jewish emigres and then began to assert themselves actively within the Jewish Agency itself. This is both the cause and the effect of the reconstitution of the Jewish Agency in 1971.

NOTES

1. For an elaboration of this thesis, see Daniel J. Elazar, "The Reconstitution of Jewish Communities in the Postwar Era," *Jewish Journal of Sociology* XI, 2 (December 1969): 187-226, and "Jewish Political Studies as a Field of Inquiry," in *Proceedings of the Sixth World Congress of Jewish Studies* (Jerusalem, 1975), vol. 2. Both articles reprinted by the Center for Jewish Community Studies.

2. A *politeuma* was a substantially autonomous polity located within another polity but not federated with it. See Salo W. Baron, *The Jewish Community,* vol. 1, chap. 4 (Philadelphia: Jewish Publication Society, 1942). Baron suggests that a *politeuma* was "an organization of men of the same political status outside their native habitat" (p. 76) and that the term was also applied to the Greek, Idumean, Cretan, and Phrygian diaspora communities.

3. *The Oxford English Dictionary* indicates that this neologism was first used in 1842.

4. Mala Tabory and Charles S. Liebman, *The Study of International Jewish Activity: An Annotated Bibliography* (forthcoming).

5. It should be noted that the Board of Deputies of British Jews, founded in 1760, did make representations to the British and foreign governments regarding the situation of Jews in other lands but those representations were more symbolic than real until the *shtadlanim* began acting with the Board's blessing. Similarly, the Board of Deputies of American Israelites, founded in 1859, included among its purposes the defense of Jewish interests overseas. Nevertheless, even though it was the first country-wide Jewish body organized on democratic principles, its efforts were made meaningful (to the extent that they were) by quasi *shtadlanic* methods, in this case, the use of the good offices of the United States Government to obtain consular or ministerial appointments for American Jewish notables in countries where they had an interest in working for the improvement of the condition of local Jews. Thus armed with American governmental credentials, the notables could enhance their *shtadlanic* roles. For a superb case study of one such example, see Lloyd Gartner, "Roumania, America and World Jewry: Consul Peixotto in Bucharest, 1870-1876," *American Jewish Historical Quarterly* XVIII, 1 (September 1968): 25-117.

6. See, for example, Stuart Cohen, "The Conquest of a Community? The Zionists and the Board of Deputies in 1917," *Jewish Journal of Sociology* XIX, 2 (1977): 157-184.

7. It is worth noting that, in the interim, the first international Jewish fraternal organization had also emerged, significantly enough, an American Jewish creation. The Bnai Brith had been founded in New York in 1843 and had rapidly spread to every corner of the United States where Jews resided. In 1882, the first overseas lodge was founded in Germany and, by the turn of the century, even Palestine had a lodge. In the United States, Bnai Brith was a broad-based organization; in Europe and the Middle East it became an elite group. Until the end of the nineteenth century, its leaders also played roles as *shtadlanim,* but mostly locally. In some countries they still do. Subsequently, the international leadership became active in the world arena.

8. Estimates of Arthur Ruppin and the *American Jewish Year Book* as presented in Raphael Patai, *Tents of Jacob* (Englewood Cliffs, N.J.: Prentice Hall, Inc., 1971), 79.

9. The two best sources on multi-country Jewish organizations are Ernest Stock, "Jewish Multicountry Associations," *American Jewish Year Book, 1974-75* (New York and Philadelphia: American Jewish Committee and Jewish Publication Society, 1974), 75: 571-597, and Josef J. Lador-Lederer, "World Jewish Associations," *Encyclopedia Judaica Yearbook, 1973* (Jerusalem: Keter, 1973), 351-356.

10. See Charles S. Liebman, "Diaspora Influence on Israel: The Ben-Gurion-Blaustein 'Exchange' and its Aftermath," *Jewish Social Studies* 36 (July-October 1974):271-280. Reprinted by the Center for Jewish

Community Studies, 1978.

11. Daniel J. Elazar, "The United States," in *The Yom Kippur Kippur War, Israel and the Jewish People,* ed. Moshe Davis (New York: Arno Press, 1974).

12. For a running account of developments on this front, see the *American Jewish Year Book,* published annually by the American Jewish Committee and the Jewish Publication Society of America.

13. Nahum Goldmann, *The Autobiography of Nahum Goldmann,* trans. Helen Sebba (New York: Holt, Rinehart and Winston, 1969).

14. Elazar, "Reconstitution."

15. See Daniel J. Elazar, *Community and Polity: The Organizational Dynamics of American Jewry* (Philadelphia: Jewish Publication Society, 1976).

16. See Ilan Greilsammer, *The Democratization of a Community: The Case of French Jewry* (Jerusalem: Center for Jewish Community Studies, 1979); Marc Salzberg, *French Jewry and American Jewry* (Jerusalem: Center for Jewish Community Studies, 1971); Daniel J. Elazar and Harold Waller, eds., *The Governance of the Canadian Jewish Community* (forthcoming); and Daniel J. Elazar with Peter Medding, *Jewish Communities in Frontier Societies: Argentina, Australia and South Africa* (New York: Holmes and Meier, 1983).

17. Elazar with Medding, *Jewish Communities in Frontier Societies.*

18. See Daniel J. Elazar with Adina Weiss Liberles and Simcha Werner, *The Jewish Communities of Scandinavia: Sweden, Denmark, Norway and Finland* (Jerusalem: The Center for Jewish Community Studies; and Washington, D.C.: University Press of America, 1983).

19. See Daniel J. Elazar, "The Jewish Community of Iran " (Jerusalem: Center for Jewish Community Studies, 1975).

20. Daniel J. Elazar et al., *The Balkan Jewish Communities: Yugoslavia, Bulgaria, Greece and Turkey* (Jerusalem: The Center for Jewish Community Studies; and Washington, D.C.: University Press of America, 1984).

21. See Moshe Davis, "Centers of Jewry in the Western Hemisphere: A Comparative Approach," *The Jewish Journal of Sociology* 5 (June 1963): 4-26.

22. See Herbert Agar, *The Saving Remnant: An Account of Jewish Survival Since 1914* (London: R. Hart-Davis, 1960).

23. See Yehuda Bauer, *Flight and Rescue* (New York: Random House, 1970).

24. See Ilan Greilsammer, *The Jewish Community of France* (forthcoming).

THE GROWTH OF DIASPORA INFLUENCE

The principal purpose behind the reconstitution of the Jewish Agency in 1971 was to broaden its base as the principal instrumentality of the Jewish people in providing institutionalized assistance for the development of Israel. Its principal consequence was the expansion of diaspora influence in the workings of the Agency and in determining what would be done and how. Israel was eager for the former and much less eager for the latter.

The Israeli effort to limit diaspora Jewish involvement in its internal affairs is, in certain respects, more difficult to implement and in others, easier. It is more difficult because diaspora Jews are able to claim that the monies whose expenditure they want to influence, or at least participate in supervising, are indeed their own, raised by them for certain specific purposes in Israel and that they are entitled to assure themselves that the funds are being expended for those purposes, and efficiently at that. For American Jewry, this interest is all the stronger by virtue of the fact that their contributions are exempt from American taxes on the grounds that they are being used for specific humanitarian purposes and are being expended by instruments fully or substantially controlled by the American donors.

On the other hand, because Israel is an independent state with a certain status in the eyes of all diaspora Jews, including American Jewry, and because it is in a period of continued crisis which makes diaspora Jews less willing to press Israelis hard and thereby aggravate their problems, it makes it relatively easy for the Israeli Government to strongly limit even the modest American Jewish claims for influence or supervisory rights. To some extent, the Israelis themselves have had to accommodate the demands of American law to assure the continued tax exemption which is so important in assuring that large sums of money keep flowing from American Jewry. But that accommodation has been through the Jewish Agency.

Since the reconstitution, there has been a series of contests over the proper role of the diaspora communities. One of the first examples of this was the struggle over increasing the role of the Jewish Agency in supervising the expenditure of its funds by Israel's institutions of higher education. By the early 1970s, between three-fifths and two-thirds of the total budget of Israel's universities came from the Jewish people via the Jewish Agency, compared to less than 10 percent from the Government of Israel (the rest came from direct contributions and tuition). The Agency's funds have been channeled to the universities through a government body, the Council for Higher Education, in which the Agency has one representative, or essentially no voice. The diaspora leadership in the Agency, led by the Americans, decided that, since they were providing such a large proportion of the total, they should have a greater share in supervising the expenditure. They established a task force to look into the matter and appointed a very distinguished American Jewish leader, Dean William Haber of the University of Michigan, to undertake the appropriate study and negotiations to achieve their ends. Both the government representatives and those of the universities resisted and, after some effort at negotiation, the *status quo ante* was reaffirmed with

THE GROWTH OF DIASPORA INFLUENCE /61

minor changes. In response, the Agency reduced its share to 10 percent of the total higher education budget as the price for having only token representation and no control. The issue was buried and no diaspora voice was raised in protest, no doubt because the diaspora Jewish leaders were themselves ambivalent about the whole matter and did not consider it of first priority.

More visible and vital were the two contests for the chairmanship of the World Zionist Organization (WZO) and the Jewish Agency, the first of which took place after the sudden and unexpected death of Pinhas Sapir and the second after the May 1977 Israeli elections. After Sapir's death, Arye Leon Dulzin, Treasurer and senior Likud representative for both bodies, became Acting Chairman of both, as he had been once before after the equally sudden and unexpected death of Louis Pincus. Whereas on the previous occasion Dulzin had been more or less willing to accept the decision of the Labor Party to install Sapir and had not contested Sapir's election, when the Labor Party this time indicated that it was going to back Yosef Almogi for the two positions (a strong figure, but a man who had never had any significant association with the Agency or with diaspora Jewry), Dulzin decided to fight. His hopes were based on the response of diaspora Jewry, particularly American, with whom he had developed connections over the years, and much of his appeal was based on what he hoped would be a diaspora Jewish reluctance to accept an apparent *diktat* of the ruling Israel Labor Party. However, Dulzin was disappointed to find a sharp division in the ranks of diaspora leadership, with the foremost American leaders not particularly predisposed towards his candidacy, in part because of a reluctance to oppose the Israeli establishment, in part because they disagreed with Dulzin's stated opposition to the recent Israel-Egypt Sinai disengagement agreement. Thus, Dulzin failed to make the issue one of Israel versus diaspora and lost honorably in a political contest that saw Almogi win supporters and opponents from both groups.

Things took a different turn in 1977/78. It did not take long for those involved in the work of the Jewish Agency to realize that Almogi, whatever his other talents, was not suited for the chairmanship. His term was generally a disappointment and a strong

interest developed in replacing him. The Israeli Knesset elections of May 1977 provided the catalyst for change. The Likud victory meant that, according to the Zionist political tradition, Likud should name a new chairman of the WZO-Jewish Agency at the next opportunity. Almogi took advantage of this tradition to announce his resignation, despite a certain amount of pressure from segments of the Labor party leadership who urged him to remain so as to retain Labor control of at least that instrumentality.

Dulzin again announced his intention to stand for the chairmanship, this time with the backing of a party which would have the majority at the next World Zionist Congress. Once again certain elements of the Labor party, with their allies in the WZO, made an effort to build a coalition against him. This time, the non-Zionist diaspora Jewish leadership within the Agency made it clear that they would not condone any such arrangement and that they expected Dulzin to be elected by the WZO and then by the Jewish Agency as a matter of course. The Labor effort collapsed and Dulzin was duly elected at the Congress in February 1978.

The aftermath of the 1978 Congress led to another conflict which demonstrated the growing strength of the non-Zionist diaspora representatives. Part of the shift in party control after the May 1977 Knesset elections was manifested in the shifting of portfolios in the WZO and Jewish Agency Executives, several of which are held jointly by the same person for both bodies. The diaspora representatives' position has been that those joint portfolios should be given to the best person, without regard to party considerations. This is a position that is unheard of in Israel where every public office is handed out according to some party key. In the past, the diaspora representatives have had to concede to the realities of Israeli politics. This time, in part because of the change in party control and in part because of their own growing strength, they were able to take a stand. Thus, they insisted on the right to screen the party nominees who emerged out of the Zionist Congress, and behind the scenes in one or two cases even tried to influence the nominations. Thus, they pressured the Labor party to retain Raanan Weitz as head of the Settlement Department (ultimately divided into two as a compromise measure) in the face of Labor party choice, strictly on the basis of their assessment of their respective capabilities. They also insisted on screening the proposed candidates for Treasurer of the Jewish Agency nominated by the Zionist parties which led to the Board of Governors choosing Labor's Akiva Lewinsky over Likud's Yoram Aridor after the former responded more favorably in the interview process. Finally, they had a major hand in designating the new chairman of Keren Hayesod.

The Prime Minister took strong umbrage at this intervention, seeing it as a frustration of his party's success at the polls and a long and public fight ensued, which ended in a comprehensive compromise. What he and his colleagues in Herut failed to understand was that they had come to power at the end of an era, in a period of transition when the old rules were changing and new ones were being formulated. Their very rise to power was possible only because of the general changes taking place in Israeli politics but those changes meant that the new powerholders would not enjoy the fruits of victory in the same way as their predecessors. The end result demonstrated that a change had indeed occurred in the balance of power between Israel and the diaspora.

The new power of the diaspora communities was made even more manifest in 1983, when they succeeded in replacing Raphael Kotlowitz as head of the Aliyah Department. Kotlowitz, a long-time Herut activist, had suffered from bad relations with the community leadership for years. Their acquiescence to his election to head the department in 1978 came only after the intervention of Menachem Begin himself in the most forceful way. In the intervening years, Kotlowitz further alienated his diaspora associates and they insisted that he be replaced at the end of his term.

After a protracted struggle, which began prior to the 30th Zionist Congress in December 1982 and concluded at a special meeting of the Board of Governors in Atlanta in November 1983, Kotlowitz was formally rejected and Herut invited to submit a new nominee. The party responded by nominating Ariel Sharon and the community representatives geared themselves up to cast another veto. They were spared the necessity of doing so by the action of the Zionist General Council (ZGC) which has to

approve all party nominees before they are submitted to the Jewish Agency Board of Governors. In an unprecedented action, the ZGC rejected Sharon by a substantial vote holding that his controversiality in the diaspora rendered him inappropriate for the position. There is little doubt that its courageous step was a result of the new sense of the Jewish Agency fostered by the reconstitution and the Caesarea Process.

While the foregoing contests might have seemed at first glance to be strictly on an Israeli versus diaspora Jewry basis, it would be inaccurate to assume that this is the way the lines of conflict are inevitably drawn. On most issues there is no natural division between Israel and the diaspora but rather divisions which cut across both camps.

What is required, then, is not so much a means for diaspora Jewry, or even American Jewry, as a collectivity, to make its voice heard in Israeli policy matters, but means for appropriate access to and representation of those Jewries among those authorities in which they have some direct stake (whether because of a direct interest that is affected or through their contributions) operating within Israel as much as those operating outside of it. In some respects, the character of that access or representation will depend on the balance between the direct interests of diaspora Jewries and the direct interest of other groups, principally Israelis. It can be argued that at least the access exists today. It is hard to believe that any significant diaspora Jewish leader, particularly any American Jewish leader, could not speak to anybody in any ministry, not to mention the Jewish Agency, about any matter in which his constituency had a direct interest and express his or their opinions regarding that matter. In this respect, diaspora Jewish leaders have at least as much access as most Israelis, including most Israeli local government officials — the leaders most closely connected with Israel citizenry — for example. All Israeli first-line officeholders, not to speak of second and third echelon people, regularly appear before diaspora groups in Israel and abroad, and make themselves available for meetings with the diaspora leadership far more than they appear before Israeli groups or make themselves available on a regular basis to Israeli lower level leadership. Israelis perceive that it is easier for diaspora Jewish leaders, even of the second and third echelon, to see the Prime Minister than it is for any Israeli outside the Cabinet itself.

Whether or not the diaspora Jewish leaders have any influence as a result, is another matter. The fact that most of those appearances are one-way streets has to do as much with the situation as with the desires of the Israelis. The Israeli leadership may or may not be open to diaspora Jewish ideas in certain spheres, but it is equally true that most diaspora Jews are not sufficiently involved or well-informed to utilize the access they have. Significantly, when they are involved, informed, and do wish to utilize that access (as in the case with the "Who is a Jew?" issue, and more recently, decisions within the Jewish Agency) they do so, and it may even be said that they get results, depending of course on the whole constellation of factors influencing Israeli policy making on any given issue.

The initiation in 1978 of Project Renewal as an Israeli Government–Jewish Agency–diaspora–local community partnership to rehabilitate Israel's disadvantaged neighborhoods marked a new step in the development of a relationship based upon active diaspora involvement in Israel at the grass roots. This new project offered great potential for the development of a new matrix of relationships – local community to local community as well as between the representatives of larger arenas. The relationship was beset with certain difficulties at the beginning, as might have been expected, but at this writing it seems to have become one of real partnership so much so that the situation is not likely to return to the *status quo ante,* even after Project Renewal is completed.

Precisely because diaspora leaders are not around on a day-to-day basis and are not inside Israeli society – the very things that make them diaspora leaders, namely being in the diaspora and being inside other Jewish societies – means that their ability to utilize their access is limited. Clearly, there is no remedy for this by the very nature of the situation, nor indeed should there be. Perhaps in a few cases people can have their cake and eat it too, that is to say, be sufficiently inside both Israeli and some diaspora Jewish society to have influence in both (even in that case it is likely to be a fairly modest influence, simply because of the time and locational

factors involved), but this is not given to more than a handful and is probably temporary in any case.

As Charles Liebman has pointed out, the degree of influence on the part of the leaders or groups from one center on the internal life and activities of the other depends upon three factors: (1) how serious the desire for influence is; (2) how focused the effort is to bring influence to bear and perhaps how persistent as well; and (3) whether or not the particular group involved has strong allies within the other center. Thus American Orthodox Jews have had more influence on the Israeli definition of "Who is a Jew?" than perhaps any other American Jewish group in any other area because they meet all three conditions to a very substantial degree. The issue is of extreme importance to them, they are willing to make focused and persistent efforts to exert their influence, and thirdly they have very strong allies in the Israeli Government itself.[1]

By the same token, the concern of American Conservative and Reform Jews to gain official recognition in Israel has been of dubious seriousness in the sense that the 'heavyweights' in their respective movements have not thrown their weight behind the effort, the effort itself has been sporadic and diffused, and those leading it have no strong allies within Israel itself. Nevertheless, when changes were proposed in the laws defining who is a Jew that would have substantially affected Conservative and Reform conversions, the two groups did get together and made a very serious and focused attempt, for which they found allies in Israel, and succeeded in tabling the matter.

Similar examples can be found going in the other direction. Israeli efforts to influence Jewish education in the United States have been ambivalent, unfocused and sporadic. Moreover, the Israelis have developed no firm allies in the United States except on the level of glittering generalities, since they have made little effort to develop close links with American Jewish educators. Hence, their influence has been minimal. In the one or two areas where this is not so, it is precisely because in those very specific program areas serious, focused, and continuous efforts have been made in alliance with American Jewish counterparts. Cooperation in the field of summer camping is one example of this. The community *shaliach* and scholar-in-residence programs are others (it should be noted that the Jewish Agency's Youth and Hechalutz Department has most closely adhered to this rule of thumb).

On the other hand, in matters of fundraising, where they have sought to ensure that the greater share of funds collected by American Jewry goes to Israel, the Israelis have been extremely serious. Their efforts have been focused and undeniably persistent, and they have strong local allies. The results speak for themselves. From this, at least one point should be clear. Even under the best of circumstances, influence requires strong commitment, diligent work, and proper support. There is no avoiding that, no matter what frameworks are developed.

NOTES

1. See Charles S. Liebman, *Pressure Without Sanctions: The Influence of World Jewry on Israeli Policy* (Rutherford, N.J.: Fairleigh Dickenson University Press, 1977).

THE JEWISH AGENCY TODAY – MYTHS AND REALITIES

There is no more popular whipping boy in Israel and many diaspora Jewish circles these days than the Jewish Agency. The Israeli press, from the sensationalist *Koteret Rashit* to the respected *Ha'Aretz*, regularly calls for its abolition as a totally wasteful institution that could save half a billion dollars for Israel if it were only closed down. The Agency's presumed wastefulness, inefficiency, and political degeneracy are the subjects of this constant barrage of criticism. While no one would suggest that the Agency cannot be improved or should be immune from criticism, there is nothing so counterproductive as foolish criticism based upon ignorance or prejudice rather than sound analysis and understanding.

Seven areas of ignorance and confusion stand out. First of all, characteristic of almost all these criticisms is confusing the Jewish Agency with the World Zionist Organization (WZO). This is particularly true in Israel, where the general view is that the two organizations are one and the same.

Few Israelis are conscious of the reconstitution of the Jewish Agency which took place fifteen years ago and which separated the two bodies, transforming the WZO into a partner in the Jewish Agency, no longer conterminous with it. Those who are aware of the reconstitution tend to focus on the fact of the continuing links between the two, especially the personnel ties whereby the Chairman of the Executive of the Jewish Agency is also the Chairman of the WZO Executive and WZO department heads sit on the Jewish Agency Executive. They claim that the division was cosmetic only and that there is really no difference between the two bodies. In fact, there is a great deal of difference despite the continued links.

NOT AN ARM OF THE WZO

The Jewish Agency today is not an arm of the WZO. Under its present composition, half of the membership of its governing institutions are representatives of diaspora Jewish communities outside of the WZO, and these are the people who have increasingly assumed major roles in setting the broad policies of the Jewish Agency and overseeing its operations. None of this should minimize the continued role of the WZO, or those designated by the Israeli political parties through it, in the day-to-day operations of the Agency; but the extension of control by diaspora community leaders has meant that most of the truly partisan activities formerly associated with the Agency have been transferred to separate WZO departments, precisely in order to sharpen the separation between the two bodies in fact as well as in name. Ironically, almost all of the justified criticisms levied against the Jewish Agency are really criticisms of the activities conducted separately by WZO departments, many of which may be quite legitimate in that context. The critics simply have the wrong address and have not bothered to find out the right one.

RELATIONSHIP TO THE GOVERNMENT

Similarly, the critics assume that the Jewish Agency is merely a way for the political parties which dominate the Israeli Government to maintain a more or less unobtrusive slush fund. In fact, there too, there have been drastic changes in the past decade and a half. Just as it could be said that the WZO and the Jewish Agency were identical until the reconstitution, so too, throughout the 1950s and

1960s the Jewish Agency was a de facto subsidiary of the Israeli Government and could not operate independently except in marginal ways. Since the reconstitution, this has no longer been the case, either formally or, increasingly, in reality.

Anyone who has bothered to follow the activities of the Agency throughout the 1970s was witness to the battles which took place when then Prime Minister Begin tried to exercise what he honestly believed to be his prerogative to appoint people to key positions in the Agency, only to have them rejected by the appropriate Agency bodies dominated by representatives of the diaspora communities. First, there was the rejection of Yoram Aridor as Jewish Agency treasurer, after being interviewed by the committee appointed to review candidates for that office. Then there was the bitter fight over the late Raphael Kotlowitz which also culminated in an Agency victory. These two successes in the Agency proper so emboldened the WZO, the diaspora communities' partner, that the Zionist General Council rejected Ariel Sharon for the aliyah portfolio even before the nomination reached the Agency, something they never would have done had not the Agency established its own strength in such matters.

The new relationship between the Jewish Agency and the Israeli Government was concretized in connection with Project Renewal. When Project Renewal was launched, the Israeli Government sought to involve the Agency only in raising funds from the diaspora, but they were soon forced to establish a formal partnership with it in order to gain the consent of the diaspora communities to the whole enterprise. Again, it had been assumed that the partnership would remain a paper one, but the diaspora communities insisted and the Jewish Agency responded by gearing up to play a real role in the process. Within a short time, the Jewish Agency became the fulcrum of the whole enterprise, strongly influencing even the work of the government ministries in the various neighborhoods because of a trilateral alliance between the Agency, the Project Renewal neighborhoods, and the diaspora communities.

It is sometimes difficult to recall now that, until Project Renewal, Israeli law forbade the Agency from developing direct relationships with municipal governments of local entities in Israel. Any such ties had to be channeled through the state institutions. Today, not only are there direct relationships, but the Agency has become a third actor in the ongoing affairs of the localities. Moreover, this transformation has been a great success story, with the Agency on the side of the angels. Its response to Project Renewal and ability to forge the aforementioned trilateral alliance is what has made the project as successful as it has been — and it has been one of the most successful projects of its kind ever carried out anywhere. Had the Government been left to its own devices, there is every sign that the project would have been mired in the overcentralized, hierarchical approach complicated by inter-ministry rivalries which has been characteristic of so much government activity in Israel.

Today, the Jewish Agency has moved far down the road toward becoming the instrumentality of the Jewish people as a whole for work carried out in Israel, and in certain respects — education, for example — in the diaspora as well, not merely an arm of the Israeli Government designed to facilitate philanthropic contributions to Israel's development. This is related to the third confusion, namely, what can and cannot be done with diaspora contributions. Israeli critics look at the Jewish Agency as a convenient receptacle for the Government of Israel. What they do not seem to understand is that it is a necessary vehicle for North American Jewry, both in the United States and Canada — over half of the total diaspora, to be able to contribute to the Zionist enterprise. Contributions to the United Jewish Appeal (UJA) in the United States and the United Israel Appeal–Keren Hayesod in Canada are tax exempt under the laws of their respective countries provided that they are transferred only to nongovernmental bodies in Israel. Since there are many enemies of Israel looking over the shoulder of the UJA in the United States and United Israel Appeal in Canada, this is not a matter that can be compromised. Any deviations will be caught. Indeed, the United States Internal Revenue Service regularly sends staff inspectors to Israel to verify the situation on the ground. Thus, the Jewish Agency is more than a vehicle for transferring funds. It has to be an independent operating institution which actually expends the funds as well, in a way that is consistent with United States and Canadian tax laws as well as those of some other countries.

PHILANTHROPIC AND CIVIC

On the diaspora side, this in turn gives rise to a fourth set of misunderstandings regarding what is political and what is philanthropic. Many of the Jewish Agency's critics in the United States view their contributions as philanthropic ones in the strict sense of the term, that is to say, as charitable support for health, education, and welfare institutions. They do not have a sense of the way in which the funds, while used for those purposes, are part of a common Jewish effort at nation and state building in which diaspora Jewry must play its role, not merely support philanthropic projects in Israel that pull at the heartstrings of diaspora Jews.

The Jewish Agency is a unique institution designed, on one hand, to be a nongovernmental body, but on the other, to be a public one, to be able to channel funds and develop programs that will assist in rebuilding the Jewish nation and strengthen its state, both in such a way that the whole Jewish people can be involved irrespective of their different citizenships. In fact, the Jewish Agency was established as a public body in international law in the original League of Nations Mandate for Palestine back in 1922 as a unique institution to reflect the needs of a unique people in a unique situation. The Agency remains a one-of-a-kind organization as befits the Jewish people; however, now it is being truly transformed into an instrumentality of the people as a whole, the nexus or fulcrum of the world Jewish polity in the making.

As a result of the foregoing situation, the WZO receives no American or Canadian *magbit* funds. Its budget comes from the collections of the other Keren Hayesod countries, which are almost entirely devoted to the WZO because they raise in an order of magnitude that can provide a significant share of the WZO annual budget, and the contributions of the State of Israel from the regular government budget. Here the truth is more complex and needs to be told. In recent years, the strength of the dollar and weakness of the economies in the Keren Hayesod countries has led to a decrease in Keren Hayesod contributions in dollar terms, however much the

Keren Hayesod campaigns may still reflect major efforts on the part of the contributors involved. As a result, the Government of Israel has stepped in to provide a substantial sum to the WZO, to make up the difference between the latter's budget and the former's capacity. On one hand, it can be said that the Israeli critics have a case with regard to that transfer, since it means that funds raised from Israeli taxpayers are used for political purposes in the WZO. On the other hand, those political purposes may be entirely legitimate within the Israeli context even if they are not legitimate for the Jewish Agency, which is why they were placed with the WZO in the first place. Moreover, a strong case can be made that the State of Israel does have some obligation to put money into the common treasury of world Jewry for those activities and purposes which relate to the common needs of world Jewry.

POLITICS IN THEIR PLACE

What about the political versus the philanthropic? There is no question that most of what the WZO does is political as distinct from what the Jewish Agency does, which, if not philanthropic, can be described as civic, that is to say, pursuing public, nonpolitical purposes. The WZO is an avowedly political body and has no apologies to make in that respect. Since its activities are legitimately political, if not always necessary or wise, it has at least some legitimate right to seek to influence the workings of the Jewish Agency from the perspective of its constituents as part of the partnership formed under the reconstitution.

It is a conceptual mistake to fail to distinguish between policy-making — who should allocate funds, how much should be allocated, and according to what criteria — and procedural matters, such as the allocations made according to the guidelines and criteria set down by the policy makers. Policy-making is properly political, in the largest sense, albeit not necessarily party political. Indeed, as diaspora community leadership has become more involved in the governance of the Jewish Agency, their politics have been injected into the process, parallel to Zionist politics — no better and no worse.

The real issue is where politics is important and where it is wrong. Much of what the Jewish Agency does should be as apolitical as possible, but even activities which might be assumed to be apolitical in other situations take on a political character in Israel. Take, for example, rural settlement. The Jewish Agency's Rural Settlement Department is one of its most successful ventures. In the 1950s it was responsible for settling new immigrants on the land and at the same time securing the dispersal of population and the establishment of Jewish settlements in strategic areas along the state's peripheries. For the most part, the locational decisions it had to make were nonpolitical (as distinct from the allocation of immigrants to settlement movements), however much the political parties may have been involved in them at the time. Then came the Six-Day War and the issue of Jewish settlements on the other side of the old green line. Two issues were involved: first, the political differences within Israel as to whether settlements across the green line were to be confined to areas that were expected to be Israeli after any future settlement under the terms of the Allon plan, or were to be established throughout the territories so as to make it impossible to repartition them. The second issue was that the United States Internal Revenue Service made it clear that American contributions could not be used across the old green line or the UJA would lose its tax exemption. Both of these were legitimate political issues by any standard.

The first problem remained in abeyance as long as the Labor Party controlled the Israeli Government and with it the WZO and the Jewish Agency, and did not permit more than occasional Gush Emunim settlement outside of the designated areas. After the Likud victory in 1977, that situation changed. The new government policy was to foster settlement in every part of the territories. This led to the need to deal with the second problem. The political solution was to divide the Rural Settlement Department in two: one attached to the Jewish Agency and another to the WZO, with separate heads for the two departments — one from Labor for the Agency's department, and one from the Likud for the WZO's department which was entrusted with settlement building in accordance with government policy, without using Jewish Agency funds.

A similar case could be made for the existence of the two departments of education in the WZO — one for general Jewish education and one for religious Jewish education — given the real differences between the two ideological approaches. But there politics has gone awry, since the two departments not only function separately but bitterly compete with one another to the point where, if one is involved in a project, the other one will not be, even if it is good for the Jewish people to have both cooperating. This is a particularly difficult problem for diaspora Jewry, where there is a religious component in almost all Jewish educational programs, and the separation between religious and other approaches to Jewish education are not as defined as they are in Israel.

Beyond that, a political process is acceptable when it comes to the choice of those who occupy the policy-making positions in the Jewish Agency. Indeed, the diaspora has a politics of its own no less real because it is not expressed through political party competition. It is wrong, however, when it comes to the appointment of the civil servants of the Jewish Agency, other than its most senior members, where competence should be the basic criterion.

CONSTRUCTIVELY CONFRONTING WASTE

Politics, of course, is a major reason for wasteful expenditures in the Jewish Agency. That is not to say that all expenditures for political purposes are wasteful. Far from it. Indeed, the difference between necessary and wasteful expenditures is a matter of some confusion on the part of the Agency's critics. There are, indeed, wasteful expenditures in the Agency as there are in every public institution and in every private bureaucratic one — which includes all large institutions, public and private, in our time. The battle against waste is a perennial one that can never be won, but if relaxed, will only lead to more waste.

Not every expenditure that seems wasteful on the surface necessarily is. For example, there is a tendency on the part of the critics to point to the Jewish Agency's expenditures on travel as wasteful per se, ignoring the fact that the function of the Jewish Agency is to unite, serve, and represent the diaspora, which is farflung. Were there six million Jews in Greece rather than the United States, the travel budget would be far less. Were Argentina and Australia not among the ten largest Jewish communities in the world, there might be less need for Agency officials to go there. Argentina, indeed, is the fifth largest Jewish community in the world and one that is very dependent upon Israel and Israelis for its survival. What are we to do, ignore them? Again, this is not to suggest that there is no wasted travel, but that is a detail to be monitored, which is not when travel itself is made the issue.

More serious questions can be raised about the *shaliach* system, particularly those sent by the parties to youth movements which have virtually no membership and aliyah *shlichim* in the countries of the free world — both WZO responsibilities. The Jewish Agency is involved with two kinds of *shlichim*: aliyah *shlichim*, technically sent under the auspices of the WZO, and community *shlichim*. The latter by all accounts play a useful role in building links between Israel and the diaspora. The question of the former needs to be investigated and, indeed, is being investigated at this time. By now there may be better techniques than the present *shaliach* system: for example, computer terminals in every Jewish institution in the world plugged into a central computer in the Aliyah Department in Jerusalem, with sufficient staff in Israel to maintain updated information which will be far more current than anything that *shlichim* in the field have today. Under such conditions local volunteers can assume many of the responsibilities now performed by *shlichim* or the functions can be integrated into existing communal institutions, such as the local Jewish federations in the United States, who only need to assign a modest amount of staff time to handle the forwarding of papers and such personal contact as would be necessary. One of the biggest criticisms that can be made of the present system is that every department likes to have its own people in the field so that it can claim to have people in the field. That, indeed, is wasteful.

AGENCY'S RAISON D'ETRE

But there are some who argue that the whole system is wasteful, that the kinds of justification for expenditures made in the foregoing paragraphs are predicated on an erroneous assumption, namely, that

the Jewish Agency should continue to exist. That assumption is indeed implicit in the argument in this article. The reasons why the Jewish Agency is necessary should be recognized. The Jewish people as a whole needs some common framework that does not compromise the political sovereignty of the State of Israel or the citizenship ties of diaspora Jews. The Jewish Agency and the institutions connected with it have demonstrated that they can perform that task. Hence, those of us who believe in the unity of the Jewish people as more than a slogan, recognize that for it to be more than a slogan it must be expressed through institutions. Moreover, given the present condition of the Jewish people, these institutions can only function successfully on a partnership basis. Under these conditions, the Jewish Agency becomes very important.

The issue of partnership is key. For many years Israelis took it for granted that diaspora Jews would support Israel no matter what and, indeed, that their only real function was to support Israel. Today it is clear that the second of those assumptions is not accurate. Most diaspora Jews love and need Israel and will bend over backwards to find reasons to support the Jewish state but they want a share of the action, something they cannot have directly with the Government of Israel unless they come here to settle but can find through an instrumentality such as the Jewish Agency. Moreover, Israel needs the diaspora to be more than a source of funds. It needs strong and vital Jewish communities out there. Hence, it needs a vehicle to contribute to the strengthening of Jewish life wherever Jews live. Again, the Jewish Agency and its partners represent the best vehicle for doing just that.

ROOTS OF MISCONSTRUED CRITICISM

If all this is true, why are there such criticisms of the present system? Here it is necessary to understand the most extreme formulations on each side. Classically, Israeli Zionism has tended to look at the Jewish world from a monistic perspective. In this view, Israel as the state of the Jewish people is not only at the center of the Jewish world but should be at the top of the hierarchy of Jewish interests and effort. Indeed, in this view, there should be a hierarchy so that whatever pluralism there is, is contained within the power pyramid.

Expanding on this perspective, there are many Israelis who implicitly assume that the system of government in Israel should be even more monistic than the system establishing unity in the Jewish world. Further, proper government has to have a single power center which can be controlled by whatever political mechanisms are in place but which in turn controls all subsidiary institutions. Here comes the Jewish Agency which functions outside of that pattern, which represents a separate (though not independent) power system in its own right, even if not as powerful as the state, which bridges between politically sovereign and definitely nonsovereign bodies — the Jewish communities of the diaspora, and which is voluntaristic and pluralistic, and hence, must work to a great extent by consensus.

The result is not neat nor does it conform to these preconceived theories. Most Israelis are perfectly content to live with this situation, but there are some who demand — consciously or subconsciously — that realities fit the theories. It is from among their ranks that the Israeli critics are drawn.

In the diaspora, the situation is just the reverse. In the classic diaspora view, Jewish life is apolitical, voluntary, and highly pluralistic as a result. At most, its public faith is one of civic activity, which certainly has a politics of its own but is not one which presents itself in formal political terms. Moreover, being Jewish is strongly associated with Judaism, that is to say, with a religious and spiritual dimension, rather than with Jewish nationality, even among those Jews who feel their Jewishness most keenly. From this perspective, the ideology of support for Israel is basically civic and philanthropic; hence, party political involvement on the Israeli side is seen as tainting the whole process, distorting it, moving it in an unwanted direction, and preventing Jewish goodness from accomplishing what it should.

The diaspora, in this view, is equal to Israel which is, at most, first among equals. The desirable goal, then, is equal partnership among the Jews with no recognition of a difference between a state and a diaspora community. In the diaspora as in Israel, most Jews are not troubled by a reality that is different from their theoretical assumptions and accommodate themselves quite easily to it. But there is that group which — consciously or subconsciously

— cannot; which insists upon the purity of those assumptions, for whatever reasons. It is from among them that the diaspora critics of the Jewish Agency are drawn.

In the last analysis, both groups of critics converge around the same concrete issues, even though they start from radically different premises. That convergence makes their criticisms all the more intense and good 'copy' for the media. But that is not an appropriate response. The Jewish people is confronted with the real issue of how to link a state with a diaspora. We have developed a network of institutions which has made great strides in doing so and has accomplished much along the way. Those who understand that network know all of its weaknesses, but they also understand the importance of the network itself, its true character, and how it needs to be improved, not abandoned or destroyed.

ASSESSING PROGRESS MADE, AND TO BE MADE

By now, we are all agreed that there are things that need improvement in the structure and functioning of the Jewish Agency. What is often overlooked in the rush to reform is what the Agency does do well and how it and its constituent bodies have initiated efforts to confront that which needs improvement. Nor do those advocating drastic change always perceive the degree to which the reform efforts in themselves represent a power struggle for political control of what has proved to be a crucial institution in the contemporary Jewish world, even if they are initiated *l'shem shamayim* (for the sake of heaven; that is, not for personal interest). Hence, a sober approach to improving the Jewish Agency requires that one understand what is good about it as well as what is not; what is being done to improve that which exists, and how well; and what may not be amenable to improvement for reasons beyond anyone's control at this moment.

The principal work of the Jewish Agency is conducted through four functional departments and several specialized funds and programs. The departments include: Rural Settlement, Immigration and Absorption, Youth Aliyah, and Project Renewal. The special funds include the Joint Education Fund, the Israel Education Fund, and the Jewish Agency support programs for institutions of higher education in Israel and Jewish programs in Israel and the diaspora. In addition, there is the Institute for Leadership Development. Finally, there is Jewish Agency support for social welfare services.

RURAL SETTLEMENT

Almost everyone agrees that the Rural Settlement Department has compiled an excellent record of solid accomplishment, so much so that its personnel are in demand for other programs and it has been a source of recruitment for Project Renewal. When the full story of the Jewish Agency is told, the record of the Rural Settlement Department will reflect great achievement in settling the country.

Questions, though, will need to be raised as to whether it is not superfluous to continue to pour in funds in the attempt to shore up settlements whose viability has been demonstrated to be minimal. The problem is that when these settlements were established, they were part of an overall strategy to establish a Jewish presence throughout the territory of the state, and especially in certain strategic areas. While this need has diminished, it has by no means disappeared. Moreover, there are the people who were sent to those settlements as new olim, who, like it or not, have built lives for themselves. A fair amount of this kind of uneconomic but statistically important settlement continues today, along with the ongoing achievements of the department, especially in the Galilee.

A larger problem looms ahead but has yet to be confronted, namely, what to do with the department now that it has essentially accomplished its primary mission, that of rural settlement within the pre-1967 borders of Israel. Its human and material resources should be made available for other deployment. This issue has not been systematically addressed by supporters or critics of the Agency.

PROJECT RENEWAL

Project Renewal, the newest Agency department, also deserves a high rating. Despite all the problems attendant on its beginning, Project Renewal as a whole has proved to be an extraordinarily successful program, and is considered by many to be a model

of the direction in which Agency programs should go in the future. The Project Renewal Department, after a problematic start, has become a major factor in the success of the entire endeavor and is not presently under pressure to be changed.

The main issue confronting it is what the future will bring, as the original neighborhoods are phased out of the Project. How should the diaspora communitites continue the links they have established with their Project Renewal neighborhoods? How can the gains made be preserved? What about those neighborhoods which have not yet benefited? Since there are neighborhoods waiting to be phased in, the solution may be simply to transfer resources from one group of neighborhoods to another, under the department's direction.

YOUTH ALIYAH

Youth Aliyah is still considered to be one of the Agency's most successful programs. Over the years it has rendered great service to the state and the Jewish people, as well as to the individuals who have completed its residential educational programs. Today, however, the question must be asked, whether residential education is needed at all regarding the vast majority of students now recruited by Youth Aliyah, when the task is no longer that of providing a haven for children who have come to the country alone, but of removing children from their families. While Youth Aliyah is to be commended for frequent internal self-studies of student achievement levels, there has been no study made of the larger question: the place of residential education in the Israel of today. Youth Aliyah's own research suggests that, while achievement by the highest and lowest level students in Youth Aliyah centers is greater than that of their counterparts who remain at home, the reverse is true with regard to those in the middle levels. The latter must, perforce, include a major share of the students within the Youth Aliyah system. Thus, any assessment of Youth Aliyah would have to conclude that what they do, they do well, but that it is time for a re-examination of whether they need to do what they do for everyone they seek to include.

ALIYAH

The department which comes in for the most criticism is Immigration and Absorption—the Aliyah Department. For many years, much of that criticism was deserved, at least with regard to aliyah from the Western world. The department suffered from inept staffing in Israel and the diaspora, and a consistent failure of communication, internal and external, in a situation where the communication of information is at the heart of its functioning.

Moreover, there was no evidence that its work in the diaspora of the West had any effect in stimulating aliyah.

More recently there has been a sharp improvement in its performance, a move away from the old patterns which were tied in with Israel's party politics and fettered by preconceptions of how to promote aliyah. Instead, the department has been shifting its emphases to (1) promoting aliyah, by forging links with the mainstream institutions of the diaspora community, such as the Jewish federations and community centers, and (2) maintaining aliyah, by mobilizing successful olim to encourage and help new arrivals from the same communities. Most of these improvements went utterly unnoticed in the controversy surrounding the late Raphael Kotlowitz, the immediate past head of the department, a controversy that had far less to do with the department's functioning than with personality clashes within the Jewish Agency Executive and Board of Governors.

Overlooked, in all the concern for aliyah from the West, were the successes of the department in dealing with rescue aliyah. Perhaps the mass aliyah of the Ethiopian Jews will remind us of how well the Agency can do in difficult situations.

EDUCATION

Education is the least noticed sphere of Jewish Agency success. It has achieved good results, however, particularly in its programs to bring young people to Israel for an Israeli experience, and in its support for teacher training efforts. Israel is an educational resource par excellence, perhaps the most vital single educational tool we have for promoting Jewish identity. Hence, the role of the Jewish Agency in making that experience available to thousands of young people through a wide variety of frameworks is one of its most signal accomplishments. But it is an accomplishment in which the Agency takes a back seat, working through the various education-oriented departments of the WZO and through a myriad of other Jewish organizations, rather than directly. The biggest problem is that the WZO departments are not willing to work together where cooperation is required, a problem that is outside the Agency's jurisdiction.

VIRTUES AND DRAWBACKS OF THE PRESENT SYSTEM

The Jewish Agency's efforts have been criticized as being too diffused, functioning through so many channels. From a managerial point of view that does indeed seem problematic; but as students of administration learn more about how to accomplish things, it becomes more and more clear that cybernetic models, offering a variety of channels to reach the same goal, are usually far better than pyramidal ones, which have neat chains of command and lines of control—but which rarely work in practice the way the organization charts suggest. It is entirely possible that the multiplicity of channels could be a good thing in this case, even if it leads to occasional duplication of effort. Redundancy means that almost every group in the Jewish world can find its point of access, rather than having to meet one single set of criteria before support is available.

What are lacking, in truth, are adequate criteria for determining what is useful redundancy and what is not, which programs should be supported, and proper means to evaluate the various programs. We do not know what can be improved because we hardly understand what is being done now. Useful redundancy should not be an excuse for haphazardness or for departmental 'stonewalling.'

One might ask, "If everything is so good, why is it so bad?" Here we come to the nub of the problem: a legacy which combines excessive party influence on the work of the Agency (particularly in hiring personnel and channeling funds), and excessive influence by the Israeli Government on the entire enterprise. Both exist for historical reasons.

The reconstitution of the Jewish Agency created

the opportunity for changing the situation. Indeed, much was done in the ensuing decade to introduce new leadership and new life into the Agency, to require better budgeting procedures, to limit patronage and introduce merit appointments within the Agency departments, to shift priorities among Agency programs, and to establish new ways of operation, as in the case of Project Renewal.

Many of these accomplishments have been overlooked, even by the people involved in bringing them about, since it is often difficult for those engaged in a task to see the forest for the trees, especially when progress seems so slow. Furthermore, many of the forces opposing change are vociferous at the outset but then adapt to the inevitable.

Most of all, as mentioned at the outset of this article, those not intimately acquainted with the Jewish Agency still do not know that it and the WZO are separate bodies. The WZO is indeed deeply entangled in Zionist politics. This is not unreasonable for a political organization, which is what it is and always has been. However, it often happens that when the WZO acts for political reasons, as in distributing funds, the Jewish Agency is accused of being politicized—even though the action was taken by an independent organization and may have been perfectly legitimate within that context.

On the other hand, when WZO influence within the Jewish Agency leads to unwarranted political involvement, then there is a case for reform. Although this does occur in the distribution of offices and funds, it is mostly a matter left over from the old days.

REFORM MOVEMENTS

It was quite appropriate, as the first decade of the reconstituted Jewish Agency drew to a close, that the Agency Board of Governors should itself initiate a review process, to see what steps should next be taken and to begin to take them. The Caesarea Process, initiated in February 1981, has already borne fruit (see Part III, *The Reconstituted Jewish Agency: Cases and Documents,* for the Commission Reports), not so much in the implementation of formal recommendations, but in the change of atmosphere which it has generated in

the Agency, the new interest it has fostered in the diaspora regarding the Agency and its workings, and the stimulus it has provided for those within the Agency who welcome change to continue their efforts. It has also helped smooth the way for those reluctant to accept changes which strike them as radical departures from a hallowed past — even when such changes serve their needs and and interests — to reconcile themselves with the inevitable. Thus, the report of the Governance Commision, considered the most vital in the effort to reform the Agency, was only partially adopted. At the same time, the Executive and the Board of Governors under the leadership of Leon Dulzin, Jerold Hoffberger, and Max Fisher have implemented some of those reforms, utilizing existing powers to do so. Hence, the objective is attained in a less confrontational manner.

In 1983, the Caesarea Process bore additional fruit in the form of the Herzliya Process, initiated by Leon Dulzin, who holds the dual title of Chairman of the Jewish Agency and the WZO Executives. He convened a representative group of WZO leaders and academics to develop a program for the reform of the WZO.

Although the program was originally thought by many to be only windowdressing, Mr. Dulzin made it clear, at the first meeting of the group in December 1983 and subsequently at the January 1984 meeting of the Zionist General Council, that he was quite serious about its work and the reforms he proposed to introduce. Moreover, in his incisive analysis of the contemporary condition of world Jewry and the role of the WZO on the world Jewish scene, in which he exposed its weaknesses as well as its strengths, he emphasized that the WZO had to become worthy of its partners from diaspora communities.

Dulzin defined his own agenda for change. It included: equal status for non-party members of the WZO; a special plan for Zionists who plan to actually settle in Israel; strengthening the Jerusalem Program, which is the basis of membership in the WZO; and a new basis for individual membership in the Zionist movement. To this agenda was added the exploration of new ways to make the Zionist movement real in Israel, rather than a mere appendage of the Israeli political parties based on the results of the Knesset elections; and a concern with the relationship between the WZO and its Jewish Agency partners, the diaspora communities.

The Herzliya Process is still underway. If it succeeds in fulfilling even part of its potential, it will be a worthy companion to the Caesarea Process, one which could give the world Jewish polity a more effective Zionist organization, able to mobilize Jews to act on behalf of the Jewish people as a whole as well as the State of Israel through common institutions such as the Jewish Agency. Nevertheless, the differences within the group, as within the WZO itself, are real. A major effort will have to be made to reach agreement on which reforms need to be implmented, and then to achieve them.

THE BALANCE TODAY

In sum, the balance sheet of the Jewish Agency shows a result that is neither as bad as some of its critics would suggest nor as good as some of its apologists would wish. The Jewish Agency has come a long way in the past fifteen years towards introducing accountability and more efficient operations. It still has a long way to go, but in that it is not unique. It suffers from the exaggerated weaknesses of the public sector in Israel in terms of overstaffing and underproduction per worker, except perhaps at the highest echelons where the senior staff now consists of people who know how to work. Institutionally, the Agency's machinery remains creaky. The professionalization introduced must compete regularly with pressures to respond to patronage demands. In many ways the Agency remains slow and bureaucratic. In others—the rescue of Ethiopian Jewry, for example—it has shown a real capacity for quick response. There is no reason,

then, for those who would reform the Agency to abate their efforts. On the other hand, there is no reason for them to abandon the field, or to assume that the issue is hopeless and that their efforts do not produce results.

One caveat is in order. As new figures and bodies become influential in the Agency, and put forward their own agendas, they must be watched so that they do not repeat the mistakes of their predecessors. Party politics may be a WZO habit, but Zionists do not have a monopoly on playing politics. There are longstanding recipients of Agency support which do not deserve to draw upon the funds of the Jewish people; but new groups and individuals have their pet projects as well, which are not always the most deserving of support. Some of the old hands at the Agency have often failed to follow proper procedures in the work, but some of the new hands have also begun to fall short in this regard, when their pets are involved. In both cases, continued effort and external vigilance to promote responsibility are called for.

The Jewish Agency, by its very nature, must be the nexus of the institutional network serving the Jewish polity. In order for it to play its proper role, its functioning must be improved. There is much yet to be done. But it can be done only if both Israeli and diaspora Jews change their perceptions of the Agency in two ways. Israelis must stop seeing the Jewish Agency as merely a device controlled by the State of Israel to mobilize diaspora support for Israeli aims. Diaspora Jews must stop looking at the Jewish Agency as principally a philanthropic body designed to help needy Jews who happen to reside in Israel. Beyond that, both must come to recognize where the Jewish Agency has been effective, in order to identify where improvements need to be made.

BEYOND CAESAREA

Even the casual observer of the Jewish scene understands that the establishment of the State of Israel marks a decisive turning point in the constitutional history of the Jewish people, and has brought in its wake both the possibility and the necessity to constitute the Jewish polity. This is not the first time that the Jewish people have entered a period of reconstitution. Indeed, it is only the latest of many such reconstitutions. We all know the reasons why such a reconstitution is necessary: the reemergence of a politically independent Jewish state after two millenia, the massive shift of the Jewish population to new centers, and the entry of all Jewry into a post-emancipation era in which the old rules are being changed.

Knowing that a reconstitution is in the offing is not the same as actually accomplishing the task. Exactly what form the reconstitution will take is not something that is decided around the table in a conference room. Rather, it is a gradual process evolving over several generations.

We have already passed through the first generation since the reestablishment of the State, and have crossed the threshold into the second. During the first generation, several of the cornerstones for the impending reconstitution became visible. First among them was the establishment of the centrality of Israel in the hearts and minds of Jews everywhere coupled with a bipolar division of powers between Israel and the Jewish community of the United States, the two major focal points of the postwar Jewish world. A second was the reemergence of Hebrew as the dominant language of Jewish civilization coupled with the emergence of English as the dominant language of Jewish discourse. A third was the emergence of new or reconstituted institutional structures within the major Jewish communities, the state structures in Israel, and diaspora bodies whose main focus was on fundraising both for Israel and for local needs and whose power flowed from their control over the purse strings. A fourth was extensive Jewish reliance on the new technologies of transportation and communication (in particular the telephone, telex and jet plane) which enable the Jewish people to conduct its day-to-day business on a worldwide basis.

Another factor was the emergence of a number of multi-country functional authorities whose task it became to do the common business of the Jewish people which transcended the boundaries of the individual states in which the Jews found themselves. In effect, these latter replaced the striving for a world Jewish parliament which had been at least a feature of the rhetoric of the previous generation. That idea was rejected by Israel because its leaders could not see the State subordinated to any such voluntary body and by the diaspora Jewish communities because they were uneasy about the image which might be presented by such a body.

The Jewish Agency stands preeminent among these functional authorities. Its evolution over the first generation of the new epoch has made this clear. With the establishment of the State, many of the Agency's original functions and most of its key people were transferred to the new government. For a while, it seemed as if the very existence of the Agency as a separate organization was in doubt. Those who remained with the World Zionist Organization (WZO) wanted to keep it as their vehicle for political participation and the requirements of United States Internal Revenue Service (IRS) laws made a non-governmental vehicle for channeling American funds into Israeli development a necessity.

The result was the 1952 Law of Status between the WZO as the proprietor of the Jewish Agency and the Government of Israel and the subsequent Knesset legislation which established the basis for the relationship between the State of Israel, the WZO, and the Jewish Agency. Under the terms of this covenant, the Jewish Agency was recognized as the third element in the constellation of institutions governing Israel but was decidedly subordinate to the other two. Because it also remained entirely in the hands of the WZO, its position was ambiguous to say the least. According to Zionist theory, the WZO spoke for the Jewish people but in reality Zionist organizations in most diaspora communities were then already in the process of losing power and influence, thus making it impossible for them to speak for their communities. This was particularly true in the United States where the Zionist movement never achieved a power position that came close to the Zionist model, and after 1948 rapidly lost whatever influence it had. Indeed, the Israeli leadership played a leading role in the decline of American Zionism when David Ben-Gurion and his associates decided to embrace the fundraising leadership instead.

For the next fifteen years, this paradoxical situation prevailed. The Agency, rather than diminishing in importance, became rooted-in as part of the system of governance of the Jewish State, while at the same time becoming more and more an arm of the State as its independence diminished. This led, in turn, to the reconstitution of 1969-1971 under the direction of Max Fisher and the late Louis Pincus, who saw the need to overcome the Agency's problematic position and to give it a proper one within the constellation of the world Jewish polity as well as the State of Israel. Their achievement marked the culmination of the postwar chapter in the history of the Jewish Agency.

FIRST FRUITS OF THE RECONSTITUTION

The reconstitution process with its separation of the WZO and Jewish Agency and the restructuring of the governing organs of the latter so that the new representatives of the diaspora communities were included in them in strength, carried the development of the Jewish Agency a stage further. The change was formally marked by a second covenant between the Agency and the State. The new Agency that emerged this time was not simply an instrumentality of the Israeli Government, designed to achieve limited political and institutional ends, but, at least potentially, an instrumentality of the Jewish people and a key element in the reemerging world Jewish polity.

The reorganization of ten years ago, however, must also be understood as part of a much longer process. It marked an intermediate step in the transition from the Jewish Agency as a tool of the State of Israel to what may yet be the Jewish Agency as an instrumentality of the entire Jewish people. The Board of Governors' meeting at Caesarea in February 1981 marked another step in that direction.

The first thing achieved by the reorganization of a decade ago was the emergence of a more broadly-based world Jewish leadership tied into the countrywide and local communities of the diaspora. Obviously, the world Zionist movement had developed a worldwide leadership much earlier, a leadership which continued to exist after the establishment of the State, even if much diminished in power and influence. In fact, the leadership of the Zionist movement never attained the comprehensive scope which it sought. Now, in the reconstituted Jewish Agency, the merging of Zionist and so-called 'non-Zionist' (better: community) leaders, the men and women who speak in the name of the diaspora communities, particularly those of the United States, offered an opportunity for the emergence of a truly comprehensive Jewish leadership. The Jewish Agency provided an arena within which such a leadership could function and the people who entered that arena, on the whole with strong, impressive credentials, were ready to take advantage of the opportunity. If anything, the first decade was a period of some frustration for many of them as the opportunities to function developed more slowly than they would have liked. Nevertheless, in the course of a decade of exposure to one another, that leadership began to take shape.

In that respect, Caesarea represented a synthesis and a leap forward. The highlight of the meeting, by all accounts, was the way in which the Zionist and community leaders got to know one another. After a decade of sitting around the same tables to discuss business, but always on a formal plane with everyone playing his or her role, they actually had an opportunity to learn about one another personally and discover the people behind the roles. This apparently had a decisive effect upon the overwhelming majority of participants at Caesarea and marked a significant advance in the integration of this new Jewish leadership.

In order to understand the wider meaning of all of this, we must go back to the formal reconstitution again to examine:

— the expectations of those involved in it,
— the structures which emerged from it,
— the functions entrusted to the reconstituted Jewish Agency,
— and the relationships which developed between the Agency and its various parts, the new leadership of the State of Israel, and the diaspora communities.

As is inevitably the case in human affairs, there were mixed expectations with regard to what the reconstitution was designed to accomplish. Probably the most minimal expectations were those of many in the Israeli Government and many of the WZO leadership who hoped that the change would be cosmetic and not really alter established patterns. The community leaders, on the other hand, saw the change as an opportunity to:

— raise the level of efficiency in the Agency;
— gain greater accountability over the funds they were raising for Israel;
— and sharpen the Agency's policy focus and functions.

Those who initiated the reconstitution — essentially insiders from within the Jewish Agency — expected to build a more effective instrumentality for the achievement of the Agency's mission in Israel and for the involvement of the diaspora, that is to say, the Jewish people as a whole in that mission.

As the process developed, those who wanted minimal changes found that their expectations would

not be borne out. At the same time, those who expected an easy transition to a new era were also disappointed. Slowly but surely, pressures from the reconstituted governing bodies led to improved Agency budgetary practices, opened up Agency activities for discussion and consideration and in a limited way began to influence the choice of officeholders in senior Agency positions. Each step involved a struggle of its own. On the other hand, with each advance, the Agency acquired greater independence and began truly to function as an arm of the Jewish people. While progress in that direction has been slow, there is every sign that it is steady.

WAGGING THE DOG

A new structure emerged out of the reorganization, in which representation in the two largest governing institutions of the Agency was divided according to a formula balancing Zionist and community leaders on the one hand and Israeli, American and other diaspora representatives on the other. Theoretically, the Jewish Agency Assembly was intended to be the basic policy-making body, the Board of Governors the principal governing body, and the Executive, the body handling day-to-day matters. In fact, as is always the case in such systems, the tail comes to wag the dog. The Executive is the body with the real power. The Board of Governors has been struggling valiantly to find a governance role for itself, given the fact that its members are scattered over much of the world and can assemble only a few times a year for brief periods. The Assembly at best briefly reviews policy matters presented to it, but has not really found an effective role for itself, something which generates a great deal of frustration on the part of many of the diaspora members who want to make their participation in the Assembly meaningful, especially since it comes at substantial personal expense.

It is in matters of governance that the division between Zionist and community leaders seems to be greatest. The community leaders feel far more frustrated about the lack of an appropriate role because their experiences abroad have been those of exercising real leadership and not simply participating in general debate. The top Zionist leadership, on the other hand, tends to be concentrated in Israel, and to sit on the Executive, so that not only are they more accustomed to the general debate, but they can transcend it in their personal power through their day-to-day roles as heads of departments within the Agency. In sum, while on paper the new structure under the reconstitution seems to offer a fair framework for activity, in fact it had become a source of endless frustration and puzzlement on the part of many of the most active and committed participants in the Agency's work.

A NEW DIVISION OF LABOR

While the reconstitution did not, in itself, change the functions of the Jewish Agency, it did in fact set in motion a process which has led to a number of changes in function and which continues to move in the direction of even further changes. Parallel to the reconstitution was the decision on the part of the Israeli Government to assume responsibility for the absorption of immigrants, leaving the Jewish Agency which had previously dealt with both aliyah and absorption only with the former. While matters have not worked out precisely as intended, the Agency's role in absorption has been substantially diminished.

Similarly, at the same time as the reconstitution was being implemented, the role of the Agency in rural settlement was on the decline, mostly because the bulk of the job had already been done. Moreover, the Agency could not directly undertake construction of settlements across the Green Line because of United States IRS constraints. Hence, this task was formally assigned to the WZO. At the same time, the role of the Agency in urban areas began to grow. During the 1970s it continued to grow, culminating in 1977 in the launching of Project Renewal which reversed the previous policy of the Israeli Government, which had prevented the Agency from working directly with municipal governments in common programs, to give the Agency a direct role in urban development. Thus the Agency acquired a new frontier in the 1970s, one whose possibilities and problems are both seemingly unlimited.

Other shifts in Agency functions began to be manifested. The Agency's role in Israeli higher education, once fiscally overwhelming, began to diminish after a struggle between the Agency and the Israeli Government as to whether or not the Agency would have a say in the expenditure of the funds it provided. The Government quashed the Agency's bid for more than token influence and since then the Agency has introduced and implemented a plan to cut back on its share of the total budget for higher education.

There have been shifts in social welfare spending within Israel, with the role of the Jewish Agency being slowly reduced in that sphere. On the other hand, the Agency has begun to take on greater responsibility for Jewish education in the diaspora, a matter of shared concern on the part of all Jewish leaders. All these are matters which are in process and remain to be clarified. All are symptomatic of what some diaspora leaders have suggested as a basic shift in the Agency's mission, from rebuilding the Jewish National Home in Eretz Israel to forging stronger links between Israel and the diaspora.

Reconstitution has brought in its wake a whole set of new relationships within the Agency and between the Agency and other factors in the Jewish polity. Within the Agency, the first new relationship was between the Zionists and the community representatives. Formally, matters were worked out rather quickly. Beyond the formal level, the relationship is still somewhat uncertain and at times uneasy. In this connection there is also the relationship between the Agency and the WZO, which remains quite ambiguous and a subject of much concern on the part of both the new and old leadership within the Agency.

The relationship between the Agency and the Government of Israel, as I suggested above, is slowly moving in the direction of greater independence for the former. This, too, is an issue in flux, with the Government reluctant to encourage or even permit such independence, but increasingly forced to do so by the community representatives. In this respect, too, Project Renewal has been a major step and may prove a decisive factor.

Since the inauguration of Project Renewal, the Agency has been able to develop direct relationships with local government authorities in Israel, something that was prohibited prior to 1977 (although informal relationships developed out of necessity because of the presence of Agency projects within many municipalities). This is a new relationship which is still too new to be evaluated since it comes primarily through Project Renewal, which allows Israeli local government authorities not only to develop ties with the Agency but with their twinned diaspora communities as well. It has not taken long for local leaders to perceive that such ties, especially with the diaspora communities directly, can be invaluable in helping them in their efforts to gain more for their communities from the powers-that-be in the State.

Finally, there is a changing relationship between the Agency and the diaspora communities. Once viewed strictly as a conduit for philanthropic contributions to help Israel's people and as a vehicle for helping diaspora fundraising efforts by the care and feeding of missions to Israel, the Jewish Agency has begun to be perceived as the diaspora's instrumentality within Israel and, for certain purposes outside Israel, to be what it always purported to be, namely a 'national institution' belonging to the entire Jewish nation, which needs to be treated and developed as such, and if necessary, reorganized further.

BEYOND FORMALISM: THE ACHIEVEMENT OF CAESAREA

In the slightly more than ten years between the time of the reconstitution of the Jewish Agency and the meeting at Caesarea, the possibilities which lay within a reconstituted Jewish Agency as potentially the preeminent worldwide functional authority of the Jewish people were clearly exposed. It was demonstrated that there could be a world Jewish leadership drawn from the various elements representing the civic or communal (as distinct from the religious and intellectual) leadership of the Jewish people, what is known in the Jewish political tradition as the *Keter Malkhut* (the crown of civil rule) as distinct from the *Keter Torah* (crown of Torah interpretation) or the *Keter Kehunah* (crown of the priesthood). Much remains to be done, however, to translate that potentiality – or maybe still only a potential potentiality – into reality. First and foremost, it is necessary to break out of the limitations of formalism which have, not surprisingly, accompanied the first decade of the reorganized Agency. That was the principal task of Caesarea.

Thus the principal expectation of the organizers of the Caesarea meeting was integrative; to bring together the leadership of the Jewish Agency and help them understand one another so that they could explore together the goals, purposes and functions of the Jewish Agency with a view toward moving the Agency another step, indeed a major step, along the road toward fulfilling its potential. By most accounts, this integrative expectation was met. This led, in turn, to the establishment of six special commissions of the Board of Governors whose task it was to continue the review process begun at Caesarea, to examine the governance, finances and management of the Agency, its goals and objectives, and its special role in Jewish education and aliyah. Substantively, at least tentative decisions seem to have been taken at Caesarea to shift the Jewish Agency from some of its present functions to emphasize aliyah and Jewish education in the diaspora. This is a momentous decision, because it drastically changes the Agency from an essentially Israel-oriented authority to one that is seeking to play a major role in every part of the Jewish world. Given its implications, it is not a decision that can be taken lightly. The fact that only those two substantive functions were deemed to be worthy of separate commissions is telling.

It is not hard to divine the purposes of each of the six commissions. If the Agency was indeed considering a major shift in its emphasis, a commission of goals and objectives would have to explore that possibility and its implications rather thoroughly. In order to move ahead, the Agency had to extricate itself from its financial situation whereby a quarter of its budget goes to service its debt. That was the major task of the Finance Commission. The problems of management in the Agency seem to be perennial and indeed relate to one of the central purposes of the reconstitution. Hence, there was a commission designed to address them. So too, as we have seen, the question of governance had not been satisfactorily resolved, despite the formal structures instituted as a result of the reconstitution. The task of the Governance Commission was to make another effort to do something about that.

For the next several years the commissions labored, each at its own pace. By 1985, all but the Management Commission had reported and their reports had been adopted in some form or another by the governing bodies of the Agency. While there was no major shift in goals and objectives, the promotion of Jewish education and aliyah was given major priority. The Finance Commission did succeed in stimulating a major effort at debt reduction, with no little success until new financial problems in connection with Project Renewal and the mass aliyah from Ethiopia at least temporarily reversed the trend. The Governance Commission, which had the most difficult task of all since it had to reconcile strongly opposing perspectives, made modest formal gains and stimulated a substantial number of informal changes which led to an increase in the role of the community leadership and an improvement in the functioning of the Board of Governors in the governance process. With the possible exception of debt reduction and Jewish education, one would be hard put to say that the commissions accomplished a great deal. Certainly, the situation with regard to governance and management remains unresolved and efforts are continuing in connection with both.

SINS OF OMISSION NOT ATONED FOR BY COMMISSION

What was entirely left out of the Caesarea process was the question of relationships between the Agency and the rest of the world Jewish polity. It is almost as if the Agency were functioning in a vacuum, accountable only to itself and its leadership.

One thing is certain, the Agency cannot function in a vacuum. Most immediately, its relationships with the Government of Israel are frequently overpowering in their impact on the Agency's work. Certainly this is true in regard to its relationships with the Israeli political party system. The relationship between the WZO and the community leadership stands at the heart of the functioning of the Agency itself.

The relationship between the Agency and the diaspora communities is one that is studded with unresolved issues that did not surface at Caesarea. The organized American Jewish community, for example, has insisted upon stringent limits to Agency activities in the United States and has done so for at least twenty years, making a clear point of its position that the Agency is not to function within the American Jewish framework except in marginal and supplementary ways. French Jewry has taken a similar stance in recent years. Yet the Caesarea meeting has suggested that one of the principal functions of the Agency in the future will be to play a major role in Jewish education in the diaspora. Curiously enough, some of the same people who are responsible for limiting the Agency's scope in their respective diaspora communities are members of the Board of Governors and, in that latter capacity, seem to have ignored this question.

The relationship between the Agency and the American Jewish community has taken on a new dimension with the expansion of the United Israel Appeal and the United Jewish Appeal (UJA) offices in Israel and the reestablishment of an office of the Council of Jewish Federations. This triumvirate of institutions responsible for fundraising for the Agency in the United States has now developed a serious institutional presence in Israel with which the Agency must deal on a regular basis. Their presence has been supplemented by the establishment of Israel offices by local Jewish community federations. Los Angeles and San Francisco federations have done so directly, and several others have done so by expanding the role of their Project Renewal representatives to deal with other matters of concern to them as well, all of which relate closely to the Agency and its departments.

Finally, the relationship between the Agency and the other Jewish multi-country functional authorities will have to be clarified. For example, over the course of the past three decades, the Agency and the American Jewish Joint Distribution Committee (JDC) have been involved in activities in many Jewish communities which have brought them together in a kind of antagonistic cooperation. Each appreciated the necessity of working with the other for common Jewish ends, albeit with perceived goals that are sufficiently different to generate certain tensions from time to time. In my opinion, there is nothing inherent in the goals of the Agency or the JDC as presently defined which demands the perpetuation of such tensions. In the past, before the establishment of the State of Israel, there was a genuine conflict. At that time the JDC was far more interested in assisting Jews to lead productive lives by integration within the diaspora countries of their residence and the Agency was entirely interested in promoting classic Zionist goals. Remembrance of those divisions persists in some circles, and must be taken into account as the Agency moves along new paths, some of which will be competitive with the work of the JDC and others which will demand close cooperation between the two authorities. This is only one example of the question of relationships between the Agency and its sister functional authorities.

CROSSCURRENTS

By creating an arena for a new and more broadly based world Jewish leadership and recruiting key people to participate in that arena, the reconstituted Jewish Agency has done much to create such a leadership, but it is the nature of the arena that, as the leadership forms, it becomes increasingly isolated from the other arenas of Jewish activity. I do not want to overdraw the extent of that isolation; each of the leaders within the Board of Governors wears many hats and has many connections with other arenas of the Jewish world. But as time goes on, their experiences place them at a remove from their peers who have not shared those experiences. This, indeed, has been the fate of other congeries of 'world Jewish leaders,' who have ultimately come to dance only with one another. It may be an inevitable concomitant of the fact that people have only so much time and energy and cannot function in all arenas at once. But it is a problem precisely because of the issues of access, representation, and feedback which accompany all Jewish organizations today.

THREE ARENAS

The Jewish people functions in three arenas: first, an immediately local arena consisting of local Jewish communities around the world of varying sizes, under varying forms of communal organization. Whether we are speaking of Dallas or Chicago, Capetown or Stockholm, Ramat Gan or Afula, the local community remains the basic cell of Jewish communal life, the place where the institutions which serve the Jewish community are organized and function, where Jews, bound by ties of kinship, consent in one way or another to be participants in the Jewish body politic through membership in a congregation, through contributions to the local welfare fund, or whatever.

Beyond the local arena, there is a larger, country-wide arena within which the Jews in particular countries or states organize for common purposes. The organizational expressions of that arena include such phenomena as the State of Israel, the Board of Deputies of British Jewry, and the congeries of 'national' (meaning countrywide) organizations of American Jewry framed by the Council of Jewish Federations. Fundraising for Israel, for example, depends upon work in local communities but is generally organized in this second arena on a country by country basis. Formally, the members of the Jewish Agency Assembly and Board of Governors are designated by bodies serving this second arena, although in the case of the United States the community leaders are designated in tandem with the major local communities.

Beyond the second arena, there is a third, that of the Jewish people as a whole, the *edah,* to use its classic Hebrew name, first applied to the assembled people as a polity in Mosaic times and used regularly throughout Jewish history. It is this arena which was extremely weak for nearly a millenium and which has been given new institutional form within the last century, most particularly in our time. The *edah* is the main focus of the reconstitution of the Jewish people as a whole. It is the arena served by the Jewish Agency and the one in which the Jewish Agency seeks to play a major, if not *the* major role. The Agency will only be able to do so, however, if its leaders appreciate the nature of the arena and its relationships with the other arenas. This should be a major focus of their post-Caesarea efforts. The leadership of the Jewish Agency must come to understand the worldwide Jewish arena, its relationship to other arenas and the place of the Agency within it, in order to design a proper future.

Three crucial issues that must be addressed here are issues of access, representation, and feedback. In other cases of third arena organizations, the tendency has been for the active participants to become isolated — a closed circle in which people increasingly talk to people in their arena alone and have less and less to communicate to the other arenas where the real action is found. One of the perennial questions raised in almost all the arenas, certainly the second and the third, is how representative are those who speak in the name of the Jews. This is an issue frequently confronted by the Jewish Agency.

The WZO members claim to be representatives by virtue of the fact that they are presumably elected by Zionist federations (second arena organizations) or parties. Their claim is countered by questions as to how representative are these federations or parties, especially since there has been only one effort at an election to a Zionist Congress in decades, an effort that was abandoned the next time around in favor of agreed lists — ostensibly on grounds of expense. In fact, even in that election, there were great differences from community to community as to the extent and scope of the Zionist membership and seriousness of their interest. Even then, the Israeli delegates to the WZO Congress were — and continue to be — designated by their respective parties on the basis of the results of the previous Knesset elections with no direct ties to the Israeli public. As a matter of fact, an overwhelming majority of Israelis are unaware of the whole process, much less of the existence of specific people who presumably are speaking in their name.

The members from the communities, on the other hand, claim to be more representative on the grounds that they have been leaders in their respective communities of the first and second arenas, and thus represent broader Jewish constituencies. Questions have been raised, however, as to how they achieved those leadership positions, since elections to them are by and large *pro forma* ratifications of slates presented to the nominating committees, and only people with sufficient resources of time and money are able to offer themselves for leadership roles, especially beyond the first arena. This is particularly blatant since real or nominal responsibility for choosing community representatives is in the hands of the Keren Hayesod and the United Israel Appeal (UIA), the two major bodies responsible for fundraising for Israel, who naturally favor big contributors.

In one sense, another grouping can make a serious claim to being representative. In the diaspora, the lack of bounded polities makes it almost impossible to choose representatives on a popular democratic basis. Indeed, those countries which do have communal elections have registered such low turnouts that their elections are frequently

manipulated by small blocs which, because of the low turnout, can gain disproportionate influence over the electoral process. Thus even for them, the 'democratic elections' argument cannot be said to offer much in the way of an improvement. On the other hand, in Israel, the one bounded polity in the system, where a representative leadership could be chosen, the party system is such that those elected are even less representative of the community than those elected in the diaspora communities.

On another level, however, it can be argued that the leadership is not entirely unrepresentative. Moreover, if it is understood as a reflection of the *Keter Malkhut* which represents only the civil dimension of the Jewish body politic, and not the spiritual, religious or intellectual dimensions, then a case can be made that it is not unduly unrepresentative in comparison with other systems of representation.

What is lacking, however, is proper access and feedback. No channels have been developed to provide Jews with access to their representatives on the Agency governing bodies whether from the Zionist parties or from the communities. Of course, people can always talk to one another and the Jewish world is not so big that Jewish leaders are necessarily isolated, but that is too haphazard a situation for effective access. How does a first arena community in Israel or the diaspora communicate its interests to the Jewish Agency? Today it can only do so on an ad hoc basis. More than that, few local leaders, not to speak of other Jews, follow or are sufficiently aware of the work of the Agency to communicate their concerns. Development of institutionalized channels of access should be high on the priority list of the appropriate post-Caesarea commissions.

Parallel to the question of access is that of feedback. How does the work of the Agency and its various instrumentalities and governing bodies get brought to the attention of the other arenas or, for that matter, to parallel bodies in the third arena? There are few institutionalized channels of feedback, something clearly reflected in the problem of isolation to which I referred earlier. For all intents and purposes, the Agency works in a vacuum, subject only to political pressures when political factors wish to apply such pressures or to complaints and attack when its work is perceived, rightly or wrongly, to be deficient.

Finally, we come to the issue of accountability. The *edah*, the Jewish polity, has always had a democratic grounding, but at the same time, because of its particular circumstances, has tended to be governed by trustees rather than by representatives. The Jewish Agency is another example of a trusteeship institution within that polity. Trusteeship is a useful device given the circumstances, but it is effective only if there is some way to keep it accountable. Accountable to whom? I would suggest that Jewish institutions must be accountable to those Jews who are involved in Jewish life, who have gone beyond their kinship ties to demonstrate their citizenship in the Jewish body politic. The effort to develop better means of accountability must be high on the post-Caesarea agenda.

In many respects, it is the resolution of these problems of expectation, structure and relationship which must precede decisions with regard to changing the functions of the Jewish Agency. At the present time, there is relatively little dispute over *what* the Agency does. Most discussions are confined to *how well* it does what it does. A major shift in emphasis, however — especially in the directions suggested — could lead to serious disputes unless these other problems are addressed and substantial movement is made toward their resolution.

For example, a massive Jewish Agency effort to intervene in Jewish educational matters in various diaspora communities is likely to meet with strong resistance in the larger and better organized ones — and with good reason. (In the smaller communities, Agency intervention is already a serious factor out of perceived necessity.) At the present moment, 'Jewish Agency' means the Israeli leadership of the Jewish Agency. There is nothing to indicate that the Israeli leadership has any better understanding of how to deal with the serious problems of Jewish education than anyone else. Indeed, their frequent lack of understanding of conditions in different diaspora communities may give them even less understanding than the people on the spot.

One thing is clear. The Jewish Agency will either transform itself into a major instrumentality of the third arena within the new generation now upon us and truly become a vital instrumentality of the Jewish people as a whole for whatever tasks it

assumes or are given to it, or it will wither down to become an increasingly useless appendage of the State of Israel, kept alive only as an approved conduit for tax-exempt funds and as a source of patronage for Israeli political parties. In my opinion, the Jewish people needs an effective Jewish Agency as a true national institution. Assuming that the Jewish people is not seeking to establish a Jewish parliament, it still requires national institutions to do its work as an *edah*. There is no other institution in existence which has a better claim to playing a preeminent role than the Jewish Agency, but in order to do so, it must be ready to confront the difficult questions, draw the appropriate conclusions, and make the necessary changes. And it must do so now. Fortunately, the process initiated at Caesarea offers some hope that it will.

WHAT IS TO BE DONE?

If the Jewish Agency is to attain its potential and provide the *edah* with a primary functional authority that could provide a frame for the *edah* as a whole, it can only do so through the constitutionalization of:

1. its status, role and general function within the body politic and vis-a-vis the other institutions. serving the three arenas;
2. its structure and composition, including the way in which the various components are represented in it;
3. its powers or competences, including a listing of exclusive and shared powers; and
4. a process for amending that constitutional framework.

The necessity for a proper constitutional framework cannot be overemphasized. Its importance has already been recognized in the several covenants between the Jewish Agency, the WZO and the State of Israel. Despite Israel's hesitancy to write a single constitutional document for itself, even the Israeli leadership perceived the necessity to establish, in writing, at least the basic terms of the relationship between the Jewish Agency as a Jewish national institution and the State of Israel as the Jewish State.

It is clear, however, at this point, that we must go beyond those covenants. The Agency can never be effective if the Government of Israel is going to decide at every turn what its stated position is on issues or what are to be its functions, or if there is no clear-cut way to enable it to delineate its roles, structure, and powers. The nature of the Jewish polity is such that it is essentially federal in character, functioning through numerous autonomous bodies serving the three arenas described above. At its best, it has been organized as a federation or confederation. That is what is needed now. Relations between the institutions serving different arenas in federal systems must be constitutionalized if the system is to function effectively. As part of its reconstitution, the Jewish people must take that next step.

This is not the place to spell out a draft constitutional plan, which would have to deal with all four elements listed above. Such a plan should be prepared, however, as a starting point for the discussions necessary to move in the direction of constitutionalization.

Subsequent to constitutionalization, the Jewish Agency must develop appropriate means for exercising its powers that will involve those responsible for its governance. One example will suffice at this juncture. If the structure to emerge from the strengthening of the constitutional framework of the Agency were to seek to make the Assembly and the Board of Governors more effective bodies, it could be that each Assembly or Board of Governors member would be assigned to one or more standing or select committees which would deal with policy problems, questions of oversight, or whatever, on a continuing basis during the course of the year. Such committees could be organized so that the location of their members would be appropriate to their function. An oversight committee whose members are drawn from throughout the world would be required to meet in Israel for one week during the course of the year. Particular functional committees, on the other hand, might be drawn primarily from people located on the same continent or perhaps within no more than five hours flying distance from one another so that they might meet periodically during the course of the year. Where communities are broadly based, there could be two subcommittees whose members lived within reasonably short distances of one another, which could meet as subcommittees during the course of the year, with the whole committee coming together once or twice.

Once the powers and functions of the Agency were constitutionally defined, the range of committees would also become more or less self-evident. They could then begin to play a serious role within the Agency structure. Moreover, they could be used to develop and maintain liaisons with other authorities within the *edah* in a systematic and potentially beneficial way.

PART III

The Reconstituted Jewish Agency:

Cases and Documents

THE RECONSTITUTION OF THE JEWISH AGENCY: A POLITICAL ANALYSIS

Ernest Stock

"An event of historic significance in Jewish life" — this is how its organizers and not a few among the participants described the founding assembly of the Reconstituted Jewish Agency, which took place in Jerusalem in June 1971. Only the future can either vindicate this evaluation or consign it to the realm of yesteryear's convention hyperbole. In the meantime, there can be no question but that the Assembly and the work that preceded it represent an ambitious effort to achieve a more balanced relationship than has existed thus far between diaspora Jewry and Israel, at least on the material plane.

For the Jewish Agency is the chief instrument through which the vast sums collected on behalf of Israel by the United Jewish Appeal (UJA) and similar campaigns throughout the world are expended; its reconstitution (actually, that of its governing bodies) is designed to give a meaningful role in that process to those who contribute and 'raise' the funds.

ENLARGED JEWISH AGENCY OF 1929

What lent heightened significance to the Jerusalem proceedings was the fact that a strikingly similar attempt was made more than forty years earlier when, in August of 1929, a meeting of world Jewish leaders called together in Switzerland by Dr. Chaim Weizmann resulted in the creation of what was then called the Enlarged Jewish Agency. It is inevitable that the chances for success of the new attempt should be weighed in the light of the earlier failure. In both instances, the effort aimed at overcoming ideological differences through a complex organizational arrangement in the hope that the structure would permit the ideas held in common to

become the operative ones. Yet, along with the obvious parallels that can be drawn, it is also true that changes in circumstances on both sides since 1929 are so far-reaching as to rule out a simplistic comparison.

The term 'Jewish agency' first appeared in the League of Nations mandate for Palestine, which incorporated Zionist proposals that "an appropriate Jewish agency shall be recognized as a public body for the purpose of advising and cooperating with the Administration of Palestine in such economic, social and other matters as may affect the establishment of the Jewish national home and the interests of the Jewish population in Palestine." The World Zionist Organization (WZO) requested that the British Government recognize it as serving the function, and the mandate, as ratified by the League Council in 1922, explicitly granted this request in article 4.

But it soon became apparent that the WZO, as then constituted, was incapable of raising the funds needed to finance the development of the National Home at a pace commensurate with the vision. The WZO president, Dr. Weizmann, therefore pursued the idea, broached earlier by United States Supreme Court Justice Louis D. Brandeis, of recruiting prominent non-Zionists for the task and making room for them within a wider organizational structure, which would transcend the framework of the financially-limited Zionist circle. It took him six years to accomplish his goal; years spent not only in negotiations with the prospective partners, but also in persuading his Zionist constituency that his policy would not result in non-Zionist hegemony over the new organization.

The Zionist Congress, the governing body of the WZO, finally approved Weizmann's proposal, and the constituent meeting of the Enlarged Jewish Agency took place in Zurich in August 1929. It was a brilliant occasion: "the most spectacular Jewish gathering in centuries," as one participant described it. Louis Marshall, long-term President of the American Jewish Committee (AJC) and representative of the non-Zionist side in the negotiations with Weizmann, more soberly yet with unmistakable pride, characterized the meeting as "coextensive with the Jewish people everywhere." With such luminaries as Albert Einstein, Leon Blum, Lord Samuel and Shalom Asch lending their presence and enthusiastic endorsement, it was difficult not to envisage a bright future for the new body. The Zurich meeting was technically the plenary of the council of the Jewish Agency, which was to have a membership of 224 equally divided between Zionists and non-Zionists. The same principle of parity also governed the composition of the smaller administrative committee and of the executive committee charged with carrying on the Agency's day-to-day affairs.

ZIONISTS BETTER ORGANIZED

In retrospect, it is clear that the parity principle, embodied in the Agency's constitution and at the time widely hailed as a guarantee of an equitable balance of influence, actually contributed to the experiment's failure.[1] For the Zionist half was bound to dominate the institution through its consistent ideology, which enabled it to present a united front regardless of party-political and geographical differences among its members. While the WZO served as an effective coordinating body for its delegates, the non-Zionists functioned as individuals, with no common secretariat. A number of them were prominently associated with such bodies as the AJC, the Anglo-Jewish Association, and the Alliance Israelite Universelle; but none of these groups was ready to involve itself collectively in the work. Also, in the division of the Jewish world into the two groups, Eretz Israel, like the diaspora, was presumed to harbor both, and the non-Zionist component of the Jewish Agency comprised representatives of the Palestine *yishuv* who often saw their real community of interest with the Zionist side. This, too, adversely affected the parity

principle, and among those non-Zionists who viewed it as the heart of the agreement, its infringement (if not in the letter, then in spirit) engendered resentment.

The thrust of the Zionist ideology soon came to be directed toward sovereignty and this was unacceptable to the non-Zionists, whose rationale for joining had been philanthropic rather than political. When, in 1937, the WZO appeared disposed to accept the Peel Commission's partition plan, which would have provided for a Jewish state in a part of Palestine, the non-Zionists went into vehement opposition and all but ceased participation in the joint body. True, there was a readiness to restore the shattered unity in the face of the White Paper of 1939, but the outbreak of war made further joint meetings impracticable.

AGENCY REVERTS TO EXCLUSIVE ZIONIST CONTROL

No effort was made to revive the Enlarged Agency after the war, and the WZO once more found itself acting as the sole custodian of the Jewish Agency concept, as it did before 1929. In the course of time, it came to be taken for granted that the terms World Zionist Organization and Jewish Agency were synonymous, and Israel's Knesset gave official recognition to that proposition when it enacted, in 1952, the WZO-Jewish Agency (Status) Law. Paragraph 3 of the law explicitly provides: "The World Zionist Organization, which is also the Jewish Agency, takes care as before of immigration and directs absorption and settlement projects in the State."

With the attainment of sovereignty, the functions of the WZO-Jewish Agency then had undergone a drastic reorientation. As the Government of Israel understandably insisted on exclusive jurisdiction in the political sphere, the Agency was left in charge of those responsibilities — mainly the reception of immigrants and their resettlement — which the non-Zionist partners all along had seen as their proper concern. But the partnership had gone by default, and the role of the non-Zionists now consisted exclusively of providing the funds for the Jewish Agency to spend.

THE WANING OF NON-ZIONISM

This, in the simplest terms, was the situation which the reconstitution, twenty-three years after the establishment of the State, came to rectify. The new attempt has the advantage of no longer having to contend with the split between Zionists and non-Zionists over the question of sovereignty, which has long since been settled. Not only had the ideological non-Zionist individuals disappeared from the scene, but the American Jewish organizations that had opposed the idea of a Jewish state in the 1920s and 1930s — the AJC and the American Jewish Joint Distribution Committee (JDC) foremost among them — had undergone a profound change as well. It would be an anachronism, therefore, to see the new arrangement as one aiming at parity between Zionists and non-Zionists. At most, one can speak of a 50-50 division between delegates representing the WZO, on the one hand, and those designated by organizations not formally part of the WZO, on the other.

These organizations — the United Israel Appeal (UIA) in the United States and similar drives in other parts of the world — are the ones that raise funds on behalf of the Agency. They are thus not only entirely in accord with the purposes of Zionism, but also provide the money for its projects. While the individuals chosen by these groups to represent them in the Jewish Agency technically may be non-Zionist, it would be wrong to classify the organizations themselves as non-Zionist. Indeed, the campaigns outside the United States are coordinated by the Keren Hayesod central office in Jerusalem, which is the fundraising arm of the Zionist movement.

It is apparent, therefore, that there is little chance of control slipping into the hands of non-Zionists. In sum: rather than underscoring dividing lines between Zionists and non-Zionists, which are delicately balanced by parity, the new plan sets out to attenuate differences, probably with the aim of eventually blurring them altogether. In a sense, it vindicates former Prime Minister David Ben-Gurion's long-held thesis that in the diaspora, "there are no Zionists, only Jews."[2]

The fact that the WZO chose fundraising bodies as its counterpart points to another essential difference from 1929. Then, Dr. Weizmann courted the non-Zionists in order to open up new sources of income to the sorely-pressed Zionist movement. This time, the people who were already providing the resources were being asked to join formally in the body that determines the spending. Whatever immediate material results were expected from the new arrangement, therefore, would not be immediate: the Jews of America, England, and many other countries had for several years been exerting great efforts without formal recognition of their role through participation in the Jewish Agency.

BOTH SIDES SEEK NEW ARRANGEMENT

Still another significant departure from the 1929 pattern has already been alluded to: then, the effort began as a process of unilateral wooing by the Zionist side; this time, the pressure for a new structural arrangement came from the non-Zionist side as well. Looking first at the forces at work within the Zionist movement itself: attempts had been made since the early 1960s to instill new vigor into the Jewish Agency by broadening its base. This took two forms: (1) the opening up of the WZO to 'territorial' (i.e., nonparty) Zionist bodies and to non-Zionist organizations which subscribed to the Zionist program; and (2) through the co-optation of some non-Zionist individuals to the Executive. But neither of these moves had much practical effect. The constitutional dilemma — how non-Zionists could function as part of a body which was totally responsible to the WZO — was not resolved.

What, then, did the WZO-Jewish Agency — which at the time was headed by the late Moshe Sharett, as Jewish Agency Chairman, and by the late Nahum Goldmann, as WZO President — seek to accomplish by these moves? Permitting nonparty-affiliated Zionists to join the WZO had a twofold aim: it was meant to break the stranglehold of the Zionist parties on the movement, dominated as they were by their Israeli branches, and also to give individuals an opportunity to be 'unhyphenated' Zionists, that is, without being at the same time adherents of Mapai, Mapam, or Mizrachi. Goldmann, in particular, had for some time been intent on prying loose the Zionist movement from its traditional tie to the party structure, and thereby from the control of the Israeli power center. Indeed, one gathers from a careful reading of his speeches and policies that one of his goals was the creation of a counterweight to the Israeli establishment, which would be capable of exerting some influence on the shape of Israel's development.[3]

The co-optation of non-Zionist individuals to the Executive had the additional purpose of restoring a more general Jewish complexion to the Jewish Agency Executive than came with being merely the executive arm of the WZO. It was to counteract the impression, widely prevalent in Israel, that the Zionist movement was neither representative of diaspora Jewry numerically, nor primarily responsible for raising the money. This led to a pronounced decline in the prestige of the WZO-Jewish Agency, particularly after the pace of immigration had slackened and questions were being raised as to the function of the organization and its considerable bureaucracy. Goldmann and others were wont to blame Ben-Gurion's vendetta against the Zionist movement for the decline in its prestige. It is more likely that Ben-Gurion was only giving expression to a disenchantment that was quite deeply rooted in public opinion and stemmed from the attrition of the movement's functions in the wake of independence, and the emasculation of its once substantial political role.

Levi Eshkol, who succeeded Ben-Gurion as prime minister in 1963, came in with a more sympathetic attitude toward the Zionist movement and its executive body. (He had for a number of years served concurrently as finance minister in the Government and as Chairman of the Agency's Land Settlement Department.) Nevertheless, it was during his incumbency that the Government decided to establish a new body charged with conducting relations with the diaspora — on the nonmaterial plane. Although officially under the joint auspices of the Government and the WZO-Jewish Agency, the Merkaz laTefutsot (Center for the Diaspora) clearly constituted a bypassing of the latter's area of competence as defined in the Status Law. It was, from the first, unwelcome to the Agency, and it was the Agency's passive resistance, coupled with the Government's subsequent loss of interest, which led to its demise by the end of the decade.

One may conclude, then, that a main consideration for broadening the base of the Zionist movement was to implement the provision of the Status Law, which made it incumbent upon the WZO-Jewish Agency to become more representative of world Jewry as a whole in its relationship with Israel, and thereby to strengthen the Agency's position vis-a-vis the Government. For it had become clear that nonfulfillment of the Agency's mission, as provided for in the law, would lead the Government to seek other channels of contact with diaspora Jewry.

Ben-Gurion himself had opposed the Status Law. In his concept of *mamlakhtiut* (a difficult-to-translate expression signifying the supremacy of the State over factional interests) there was no room for a competing power center that did not derive its influence from factors within the State. There was also a party-political aspect to his coolness toward the WZO: while in Israel the preponderance of the Labor parties was unchallenged, diaspora Zionism had traditionally been dominated by the bourgeois parties. Therefore, control at the source by diaspora Zionists of monies raised for the Jewish Agency could lead to an unwelcome influence in Israel's affairs. Indeed, in a brief contest for key positions in the UJA in the early 1950s, Ben-Gurion had intervened to prevent this from happening.

Thereafter, the Labor Party leadership — including its representatives on the Agency Executive — was content to see the direction of the UJA in the hands of non-Zionist lay leaders and professional executives, rather than of ideologically-committed but party-affiliated Zionists. Since the UJA was, in effect, a contractual arrangement between its two beneficiaries, the UIA representing the needs of the Jewish Agency through the latter's financial arm, Keren Hayesod; and the American JDC, a partnership in which the UIA-Jewish Agency side had the majority 'interest', the Israelis felt assured against any undue interference on that level.

ROLE OF WELFARE FUNDS

But if the UJA itself was not likely to demand a say in the disbursement of funds, where then did the pressure for reconstitution originate on the American side? Behind the UJA in the local communities stood the Jewish federations and welfare funds, and it was here that the mainspring of the drive for greater participation was to be found. It expressed itself in the attempt to bring the operations of the Jewish Agency within the scrutiny of the Large Cities Budgeting Conference (LCBC), an instrumentality of the welfare funds designed to review the budgets of agencies receiving allocations. This attempt was resisted vigorously by the WZO-Jewish Agency leadership, to whom it represented a throwback to an earlier welfare funds initiative called 'national budgeting', which had been abandoned due to opposition by both Zionist and non-Zionist beneficiary agencies. Other unpleasant memories of conflicts between the Zionist fundraising bodies and local philanthropic interests in the 1920s and 1930s also colored the Zionist apperception of the role of the welfare funds which, in the 1950s, continued to be basically negative, approximately as follows:

1. The federations and welfare funds in fact represented the interests of their local institutions, and retained an undue proportion of the funds they collected for distribution locally.
2. Even though these campaigns were being conducted by local welfare funds, most of the giving was motivated by the needs of Israel.
3. Through their nationwide association, the welfare funds were intent on creating a power base from which to standardize the local allocations procedure — a domain which was not legitimately theirs.
4. The welfare fund leadership was concerned only with the 'philanthropic' aspect of aid to Israel, and was opposed to allocating funds to the Zionist side of the Jewish Agency's program, such as Jewish education in the diaspora.

As a result of this analysis and the attitudes it engendered, a relationship which was in essence based on cooperation toward a common goal, namely the maximizing of income from the welfare fund campaigns on behalf of both local causes and UJA, was in actuality shot through with tensions. And it was further complicated by the awareness of the Zionist organizational leadership in the United States of its own marginal role in the fundraising effort, with resulting feelings of frustration and antagonism.

ORIGINS OF UNITED ISRAEL APPEAL

This marginality was the result of a process of mergers and consolidation which had begun in the 1930s, when the various funds active on behalf of the Zionist movement in the United States combined to form the United Palestine Appeal (later United Israel Appeal).[4] With the outbreak of World War II, the United Palestine Appeal and the JDC overcame their long-standing ideological differences and rivalry for the contributor's dollar to join together in the United Jewish Appeal. UJA, in turn, concluded agreements with the federations and welfare funds for a percentage of the campaign proceeds in each community.

As the receipts of the campaigns increased dramatically in response to the growing needs, most of the donors responsible for the increments were non-Zionists, as were the professional personnel in the local and national fundraising bodies. Inevitably, the emphasis in the campaigns was on humanitarianism and rescue work, rather than on Zionist ideology. Simultaneously, the Zionist funds, which had been at the core of the process, became submerged and their identities blurred. Although this produced dismay among Zionist leaders, the financial results made an alternative structure unthinkable.

JEWISH AGENCY FOR ISRAEL, INC.

However, a breakthrough affecting the Zionist-welfare fund relationship occurred in 1960, with a structural reorganization that was the first step leading to the reconstituted Jewish Agency, and to greater harmony. To comply with a new interpretation of United States Government regulations on tax-deductible gifts to charitable organizations, a new body was created in the United States to supervise disbursement in Israel of funds raised by the UJA. The new group, called the Jewish Agency for Israel, Incorporated (JAFI, Inc.), had a twenty-one member Board of Directors (later enlarged to twenty-seven) on which, for the first time since the Enlarged Jewish Agency of 1929, Zionists sat with non-Zionists who were active in fundraising to decide on the use of funds in Israel. The new group designated the Jerusalem Jewish Agency as its agent for implementing the programs for which UJA funds were allocated and to monitor these expenditures it opened a representative office in Jerusalem, with the prominent economist Isador Lubin as consultant.

The Council of Jewish Federations and Welfare Funds enthusiastically endorsed this development. At its 1960 General Assembly, one of the local welfare fund executives summed up the feeling of many delegates with his statement that the "era of the blank check" was at an end; that communities now insisted on detailed information on and participation in the spending of the funds.

However, the actual changes brought about by this new development were not far-reaching. The 'Inc.', as it came to be called, by and large accepted the principles by which the Jewish Agency had been operating and allocating its funds. The composition of the new group ensured that, in case of serious disagreement, the Zionist and pro-Zionist element would be determining. After an initial flurry, in part sustained by the welfare funds, which anticipated innovative approaches within the new structure, public interest in the reorganization declined. The Jewish Agency had insisted that the new body retain the old nomenclature, and the resulting multiplication of agencies bearing similar names was confusing to all but the initiates.

JAFI, INC., INTO UIA, INC.

To the contributor and man-in-the-Jewish-street this meant little more than the addition of still another body to the already arcane roster of organizations; the more so, since the Jewish Agency Executive continued to maintain a branch in the United States known as the Jewish Agency-American Section, Inc., which bore no relationship to the Jewish Agency for Israel, Inc. The UIA, now shorn of meaningful function, continued a somewhat shadowy existence until, in 1966, JAFI, Inc., changed its name to United Israel Appeal, Inc. This somewhat cleared up the semantic confusion by letting the Jewish Agency title revert to its original holders exclusively. It also filled the all but empty shell of the UIA with new content.

The UIA was endowed with a board of trustees of 210 members, of whom one hundred were drawn from names submitted by the federations and welfare funds and one hundred designated by American Zionist organizations (ten were chosen "at large"). The Board of Trustees in turn designated two-thirds of the twenty-seven member Board of Directors, with the remaining one-third appointed by the Jewish Agency-American Section. Severed from the Keren Hayesod, UIA now became an autonomous American body.

The UIA later was given a key function in the Agency's reconstitution, in addition to its role as the group authorized to determine the manner in which UJA funds are spent by the Jewish Agency. Under the Reconstitution Agreement, the UIA designates the 30 percent of the Jewish Agency assembly allotted to non-Zionists from the United States. .[5]

LOUIS PINCUS'S ROLE

Two events gave the needed impetus to progress from the plane of UIA, Inc., to that of the Reconstituted Jewish Agency. One was the selection of Louis Pincus to succeed Moshe Sharett as Chairman of the Executive upon the latter's death in 1965; the other was the June 1967 war.

Pincus, a lawyer from South Africa and former managing director of El Al Airlines, had joined the Jewish Agency as its treasurer in 1960, at about the time the 'Inc.' was brought into being. While his predecessor and others on the Executive had viewed the reorganization as a necessity foisted upon the Agency by the income tax laws of the United States, Pincus took a positive attitude toward the JAFI, Inc., in his role as ex-officio member of its board. Frequent trips to the United States gave him the opportunity to gain a realistic picture of the constellation of forces within the American Jewish community. His conclusions doubtless were similar to those of Weizmann in his day: that much useful energy was being wasted by confrontation, and that co-optation of a wide range of factors in the community would make it possible to harness more resources in Israel's behalf. In the workings of JAFI, Inc., he was able to note that differences with those active in the local welfare funds were marginal rather than substantial, and that the adaptation of the existing machinery could give a sense of participation to all involved.

EFFECTS OF 1967 WAR

But it took the 1967 war and the accompanying upsurge in the diaspora's contributions to Israel to provide the decisive leverage toward reconstitution. Two figures will suffice to mirror the impact in financial terms: in 1966, the net amount made available to the Jewish Agency from worldwide campaigns was $60 million; in 1967, it was $346 million.

Paradoxically, the initial effect of the war was to jeopardize, rather than buttress, Jewish Agency autonomy. Its role in handling the flood of volunteers during the crisis had given rise to dissatisfaction; the fact that most of these young people soon returned to their countries of origin was seen as a wasted opportunity for tapping a ready reservoir of potential immigrants. Once again, it appeared to some Israeli officials that the Government should become more deeply involved in the Agency's policies and operations. Since the early 1960s, the Agency's programs in the area of immigrant absorption, agricultural settlement, etc., already had been closely coordinated with government policy through a joint standing committee. The Ministries of Housing, Health, Education and Welfare had carried much of the responsibility for immigrant integration in their respective fields, with financing from government budgets.

MINISTRY OF IMMIGRANT ABSORPTION

In June of 1968 the Government also decided on the creation of a new Ministry of Immigrant Absorption (*Klitah*) with which the Agency would henceforth have to share its central function. The *modus operandi* provided for continued Jewish Agency responsibility for the staging of immigration abroad, while the new ministry was to deal with most areas of reception and integration within the country. The first incumbent was Yigal Allon, and it was anticipated that his ministry would eventually unite under one roof the 'absorption' functions not only of the Jewish Agency but also of the various government ministries — and do so more effectively. But this was not to be, for two reasons. First, the service ministries affected, having been unwilling to cede any of their functions to the Jewish Agency, were now equally reluctant to turn them over to the Absorption Ministry; and second, the Agency was able to marshal a potent argument in support of its continued independent existence: the fact that contributions of American Jewry (and of some other communities as well) must be disbursed by a non-governmental, voluntary organization in order to enjoy exemption from income taxes. The UJA-UIA leadership in the United States also protested vigorously to the officials involved against any plan to transfer additional responsibilities from the Agency to the Government, arguing that it would jeopardize the fundraising structure in the United States. Their reasoning proved convincing, above all to Minister of Finance Pinhas Sapir, and the integrity of the Agency was maintained.

The Israel Government later transferred some of its own activities to the Agency, rather than the other way round. Among the programs which had previously been financed by the Government and which now became the responsibility of the Jewish Agency was the subsidizing of Israel's institutions of higher learning. Other programs in the fields of health, welfare, immigrant housing, and education, which involve substantial outlays for immigrants, also became the Agency's financial, but not operational, responsibility.

SEPARATION OF WZO FROM JEWISH AGENCY

While the reconstitution thus measurably strengthened the position of the Jewish Agency, it also called for a major concession by the Zionist organization: to separate once and for all the WZO from the Jewish Agency, in both structure and function. Under the Reconstitution Agreement, the WZO was to give up its status of virtual identity with the Jewish Agency, that had been granted legitimacy by the 1952 Status Law, and become once again a limited partner in the Agency.

With the establishment of the Jewish Agency, Inc., in 1960, a *de jure* separation already had taken place on the budgetary level. Since the JAFI, Inc., (later UIA, Inc.) could make allocations only for those activities of the Jewish Agency which were entitled to tax exemption under United States law as interpreted by the Internal Revenue Service (IRS), it was decided to separate out those activities which were ineligible or doubtful from the tax point of view and to group them in a separate WZO budget. These were mainly programs not specifically aimed at new immigrants, some of them for countries other than Israel, such as education in the diaspora, organization and information, and youth work. Together, the cost of these activites amounted to about 10 percent of the Agency's expenditures.

With all JAFI, Inc., funds earmarked for the Jewish Agency proper, the WZO budget was financed by contributions to Keren Hayesod in other countries, as well as by miscellaneous sources of income. Under this arrangement, though the budgets were separate, the same Executive directed the programs of both the Agency and WZO. Thus, for the general public at least, the identity of the two bodies continued as heretofore. But in the negotiations leading to the reconstitution, effective separation of the Jewish Agency from the WZO was a *sine qua non* for many of the leading non-Zionists. The Zionists conceded the point in principle, but were deeply concerned about the funding of the WZO budget. Eventually, a formula was agreed upon whereby the financial needs of the WZO were to be met from funds that did not come under the restrictive provision of tax-exempt gifts in the United States and elsewhere. At the same time, the WZO would not have to conduct a campaign of its own, which would have represented an undesirable interference with fundraising for the Jewish Agency. The fact that the Zionist leadership was able to persuade the non-Zionists to accept this arrangement would indicate that it was able to make a strong case for the legitimacy of Zionist work.

1967 WAR BRINGS CHANGE IN ATTITUDES

No doubt the drastic change in non-Zionist attitudes that occured in the wake of the 1967 war played a role in this. The wave of enthusiasm engulfing everything related to Israel broke down traditional attitudes to the extent that even the notion of aliyah from the United States had become acceptable to many non-Zionists.

During the crisis itself, the results of the campaigns on behalf of Israel had been such that there was enough credit for everyone, and past

organizational rivalries gave way to close cooperation. The much-disputed ratio between local and overseas allocations became a thing of the past as the Israel Emergency Fund tipped the scales overwhelmingly in Israel's favor.[6] There was no quibbling by the welfare funds over the principle that all monies collected over and above the regular campaign proceeds should go to the UJA. Consequently, a Council of Jewish Federations and Welfare Funds delegation, which visited Israel in September 1967, was able to report that:

> We found the warmest of welcomes, based upon new recognition of the extraordinary work our federations and welfare funds had accomplished for the Israel Emergency Fund (in cooperation with the UJA) and, even more fundamentally, a new understanding of the continuing central role of our community organizations in American and worldwide Jewish life.

It was in this atmosphere of mutual good feeling that the plans for the reconstitution of the Jewish Agency gathered support.

THE CONFERENCE ON HUMAN NEEDS

Indicative of the spirit of cooperation seeking an outlet in tangible form even before the new structure was worked out was the Conference on Human Needs (COHN), which took place in Jerusalem in 1969 under joint Government-Agency auspices. The delegates were professional and lay specialists in such fields as housing, agriculture, education, and welfare, who held several days of discussions on Israel's problems and programs in those areas with their Israeli counterparts. The latter apparently came away from the conference convinced that here was a model for future association with diaspora Jewry.

The new symbiotic relationship was perhaps best exemplified by the fact that a single individual, Max M. Fisher of Detroit, was both President of the Council of Jewish Federations and Welfare Funds and Chairman of the UIA. Later, he was also chosen Chairman of the Board of Governors of the Reconstituted Jewish Agency. Finally, Fisher was also Chairman of the Executive Committee of the

AJC, whose leading member in the 1920s was Louis Marshall.

In his speech to the Planning Committee in August 1970, Pincus said that he had "warned Max Fisher that the day will come when I shall call him a Zionist too, when that gap is closed completely, and we will be unable to differentiate in the approach to the problems of Israel between those who come from here or there." But in the same address, Pincus made it clear that the Zionist organization did not intend to take a back seat under the new arrangement:

> We are now entering a joint and equal partnership; fifty-fifty on the organizational basis. In the discussions it was clear to everybody that if we had to count card-carrying Zionists, as it were, versus non-card-carrying Zionists, there is a Zionist majority — that must be in the nature of things. I hope that the fact there is a majority or a minority will play no role beyond what I have just said.

Pincus left no room for doubt that the WZO saw in the separation a necessary evil, and not a *desideratum*, as did some of the non-Zionists. He concluded:

> I also know that nothing will be done by any responsible Jewish leader, in the creation of the expanded Jewish Agency, that will denigrate or derogate, not only from the past of the world Zionist movement, but from its ongoing activities, in the role that it still has to play in Jewish life, and in seeking the realization of our ultimate dream.

THREE TIERS RETAINED IN NEW STRUCTURE

The Planning Committee, which met in Jerusalem in August 1970, initialled the Agreement for the Reconstitution, which was later approved by the Founding Assembly in June 1971. At that time, the Planning Committee itself was named as the Board of Governors of the Agency, the centerpiece in the tier of governing bodies retained from the 1929 structure

(although with somewhat different nomenclature). By all indications, the Board will be the effective policy-making group. The Agreement stipulates that it "shall manage the affairs of the Agency and control its activities." It also is empowered to elect the members of the Executive. Its members are to be elected by the Assembly as follows: 50 percent from among the members of the Assembly, designated by the WZO; 30 percent from among those designated by the UIA, Inc.; 20 percent to be designated outside of Israel and the United States. (An annex to the Agreement specifies that, among the latter, two are to be from England; one each from Canada, Western Europe, and South Africa; two from South America, of whom one is to be from Argentina and the other, in rotation, from one of four other countries.)

The number of members of the Board of Governors was augmented from thirty-eight, as stipulated in the draft agreement, to forty, apparently in order to preserve a delicate balance and also to accommodate more individuals and localities. It is noteworthy that the 50-30-20 ratio is operative as regards Zionist-non-Zionist relationship, as well as geographically. There are, in 1972,[*] twenty Zionists, twelve American non-Zionists, and eight non-Zionists from other countries. But among the Zionists there are also eight Americans, so that the total number of Americans on the board is twenty, as compared to twelve Israelis, and eight from other countries. Without analyzing the Board's composition in detail, the names of the American unit will be of interest. The non-Zionists (some prefer to be called non-WZO members) are Albert Adelman, Milwaukee, Wisc.; Victor Carter, Los Angeles, Calif.; Melvin Dubinsky, St. Louis, Mo.; Max M. Fisher, Detroit, Mich.; Edward Ginsberg, Cleveland, Ohio; Morris Levinson, New York City; Joseph Meyerhoff, Baltimore, Md.; Robert Russell, Miami, Fla.; Louis Stern, Essex County, N.J.; Dewey D. Stone, Brockton, Mass.; Jack Weiler, New York City; and Paul Zuckerman, Detroit, Mich. Those representing Zionist organizations in the United States are Arthur Hertzberg, Englewood,

---

[*] For the 1985 list of members of the Board of Governors see Appendix II.

N.J.; Richard Hirsch, Washington, D.C.; Charlotte Jacobson, New York City; Israel Miller, New York City; Allen Pollack, New York City; Emanuel Rackman, New York City; Kalman Sultanik, New York City; and Jacques Torczyner, New York City.

The Board of Governors is to meet not less than three times a year, one of the meetings to take place in conjunction with the annual meeting of the Assembly.

Aside from appointing the Board of Governors, the functions of the Assembly are described in the Agreement as follows: to receive reports from the Board of Governors and the Executive; to review needs and programs; to determine basic policies; to consider and act upon budgets submitted by the Board of Governors. However, the main purpose of the Assembly would seem to be that of constituting a forum for discussion. The 50-30-20 ratio also applies to the composition of the Assembly, whose 296 members are to be designated by the signatory organizations.

As for the Executive, the Agreement states that it "shall be responsible for the day-to-day operations of the Agency, subject to the control of the board of governors." It further stipulates that the Executive shall consist of persons elected *ad personam* by the Board of Governors, so that the 50-30-20 formula does not apply in this case. Further, according to the Agreement, the Chairman of the Jewish Agency (who also shall be Chairman of the Assembly), as well as the heads of its four major departments and the Chairman of Keren Hayesod, shall be members of the Executive, as are three members of the Board of Governors not designated by the WZO (two of them to be designated by the UIA, Inc.). Since the heads of Agency departments will in all likelihood come from Zionist ranks, this provision would appear to ensure a Zionist preponderance on the Executive. The principal offices of the Executive will be located in Jerusalem, which makes it unlikely that the non-Israeli members will participate in day-to-day business.

The actual makeup of the first Executive shows, however, that four, rather than three, non-Zionists were appointed: Dubinsky, Fisher, and Ginsberg of the United States, and Michael Sacher of Britain. In addition, Gottlieb Hammer, Executive Vice President of the UIA, and Philip Bernstein, Executive Vice President of the Council of Jewish Federations and Welfare Funds, were designated associate members without a vote (the Agreement states that up to three associate members may be appointed).

DECISION-MAKING CONSENSUS

In its actual functioning, the Reconstituted Jewish Agency has borne out the expectation that decisions would be arrived at by consensus, rather than by vote. A mood of comradeship and optimism pervaded the planning sessions in 1970, the Founding Assembly in 1971, and the meeting of the Board of Governors held in London in February 1972. It was a mood shared by all the participants, regardless of the camp to which they belonged. While the non-Zionists showed understanding of the limitations imposed upon their own role as well as on that of the Jewish Agency in the larger institutional structure of Israel, they were nevertheless eager to utilize the opportunities for exerting influence which the new framework offered. The influence — if the present pattern continues — will not flow from the weight of their numerical representation, but rather from their own stature and authority. This will be so even in areas where the Jewish Agency must share control with the Government, as the new structure opens up regular channels of communication with policy-makers in the various ministries. An example is public housing, on which strong (and expert) American views on the applicability of novel construction methods to the conservative Israeli housing industry have already made their impact.

To the extent that the leading non-Zionists succeed in impressing their stamp upon the Jewish Agency, it is inevitable that the future role of the WZO will be put to the test. In the short run, the buttressing of the Agency's position through reconstitution has, by indirection, strengthened the WZO as well. But in the longer term, the WZO will have to evolve a new image for itself, both as far as its relationship to the Agency and its own independent tasks are concerned; it will not be able to maintain its accustomed stance of identity with the Jewish Agency. At the World Zionist Congress, which took place in Jerusalem in February 1972, only perfunctory notice was taken of the new development, and of the WZO's changed status vis-a-vis the Jewish Agency. An observer at the Congress could have gained the impression that the reconstitution was but another in a series of modifications, which left the basic structure unchanged.

This is certainly not the view of most American non-Zionist delegates to the Agency's governing bodies. Through their conscientious approach to the Agency's problems, their vigorous insistence on information, and their incisive questioning, they showed that they take the new structure and their task in it seriously.

NOTES

1. But it was *force majeure* which dogged the new creation by a series of misfortunes, beginning with the Arab rioting, which broke out barely two weeks after the signing of the compact; followed, in September, by the death of Louis Marshall, the central personality on the non-Zionist side; and climaxed by the stock market crash and the worldwide depression.

2. In his address to the preparatory meeting, the Chairman of the Agency Executive, Louis A. Pincus, put it somewhat differently: "Soon all the non-Zionists will also be Zionists."

3. Goldmann's efforts in that direction were not confined to the Zionist movement, of course. They no doubt played a role — as did his unorthodoxy regarding Israel's foreign policy — in the controversial position he occupied among leading Israeli politicians.

4. The principals in the merger were Keren Hayesod (Palestine Foundation Fund, already mentioned as the financial arm of the Jewish Agency), and Keren Kayemet, or Jewish National Fund. Lesser partners were the funds conducted by political parties in Palestine for their so-called "constructive enterprises." These received allocations from the UIA until the early 1960s, when objections to their political complexion brought about their exclusion from the UIA in the United States. It is worth noting that the Labor parties had traditionally conducted their own Histadrut campaign in the United States and were therefore not a partner in the UIA. This ties in with the earlier preponderance of the 'bourgeois' Zionist element in the UJA leadership, discussed above.

5. To ensure broad representation among those prominent in fundraising, both on the community and national levels, the UIA made up the list in close consultation with the Council of Jewish Federations and Welfare Funds.

6. The welfare funds raised $145 million in 1967 through their regular campaigns, of which UJA received about 50 percent. An additional $173 million in pledges was raised through the Emergency Fund, all of which was earmarked for UJA. In 1968 the respective amounts were $153 and $80 million. (Figures from the *American Jewish Year Book* 71 (1970): 182.)

MEMORANDUM ON RECONSTITUTION AGREEMENT*

Eli Likhovski

In the paper which I previously submitted to the Caesarea meeting, I outlined the legal history of the World Zionist Organization (WZO) and the Jewish Agency up to the present day.

The object of this paper is to examine the historical and legal nature of the Reconstituted Jewish Agency as reflected in the Agreement for the Reconstitution of the Jewish Agency signed on 21 June 1971. The two papers should be read together. (See "Highlights of the Legal Status of the World Zionist Organization (WZO) and the Jewish Agency for Israel (JA)" in Part I).

It is a known principle of universal jurisprudence that artificial legal persons are either the creation of international law, or of a given municipal system of law. In my first paper, I pointed out the fact that the Jewish Agency was established as a legal person pursuant to international law (article 4 of the Mandate for Palestine, and see *Mavromatis Concession, Case, P.C.I.J.,* Series A, No. 2, 12). The WZO (which was known at the time as the Zionist Organization) was recognized by the Mandatory Courts as a "public body" and was accorded legal personality in Palestinian Municipal Law (see the *Zionist Executive v. Appenzeller,* 4 C.O.J., 1451). It will be recalled that until 1929, the Jewish Agency was, in effect, the WZO.

The 1929 Agreement did not create or constitute a new legal person; it merely provided for the enlargement of the existing Jewish Agency by adding to it on the principle of parity with the Zionist Organization of Jews "not affiliated with the Zionist Organization."

The Jewish Agency, as enlarged, was to be

known as "the Enlarged Jewish Agency." The substance of the Agreement is a partnership Agreement providing for the establishment, composition and working arrangements, and the operation of the enlarged Jewish Agency. That partnership was recognized by the Mandatory Government and by the League of Nations as the Jewish Agency, the international legal personality created by the Mandate for Palestine. The Enlarged Jewish Agency continued to have the legal personality of the Jewish Agency created by the Mandate, so long as that recognition was not withdrawn.

It is my submission that the termination of the Mandate for Palestine and the establishment of the State of Israel on 15 May 1948 did not change the legal nature of the personality of the Jewish Agency and it continued, in effect and in law, to enjoy that personality under international law. On the other hand, the 1929 Agreement which brought into being the partnership between the WZO and the non-Zionists, enlarging the basis of the Jewish Agency, became obsolete after that date. Thereafter, the WZO was again recognized both by the international community and by the State of Israel which replaced the Mandatory power as constituting the Jewish Agency.

The Law of Status expressly recognized that choice and gave it effect in the domestic law of Israel.

In my first paper, I described the status of the Agency during the period between the establishment of the State of Israel and the Reconstitution of the Jewish Agency consequent to the signing of the Reconstitution Agreement on 21 June 1971. There is no need to recapitulate here. I will, therefore, pass directly to the description, analysis, and discussion of

---

* Circulated to members of Governance Commission, 10 August 1981.

the Reconstitution Agreement.

THE RECONSTITUTION AGREEMENT

There are certain underlying assumptions.

1. The Reconstitution Agreement is predicated on the Law of Status.

2. The Agreement is based on a partnership between the WZO and the fundraising organizations.

In pursuance of Section 6, the Law of Status provides as follows:

> The State of Israel expects efforts on the part of the World Zionist Organization for achieving this unity; if, to this end, the Zionist Organization, with the consent of the government and the approval of the Knesset, should decide to broaden its basis, the enlarged body will enjoy the status conferred upon the World Zionist Organization in the State of Israel.

The WZO invited the fundraising organizations to reconstitute the Jewish Agency. Article no. 8 of the Preamble to the Reconstitution Agreement provides as follows:

> The WZO has invited the organizations signatory to this Agreement to join with it, and with each other, in the reconstruction of the Jewish Agency for Israel on a broader basis for the purpose of continuing the tasks referred to above, and for the mobilization of the resources required in connection therewith.

Section 2A of the Law of Status as amended, as detailed below, states clearly:

> The Jewish Agency for Israel is an independent voluntary association consisting of the World Zionist Organization and other organizations and bodies. . .

3. No new legal personality is to be created by the Reconstitution Agreement. Section 1A merely describes the Reconstituted Agency as the Jewish Agency. No new legal person is created by the Reconstituted Agreement. The amendment to the Law of Status, passed on 1 January 1976 retroactive

to the date of 21 June 1971, recognized the Reconstituted Jewish Agency for the purposes of the domestic laws of Israel (see Section 2A and 12 of the Law).

4. The Reconstituted Jewish Agency was to be limited in its objectives as set out in full in Section 1C and 1D of the Reconstitution Agreement:

> C. Except with respect to activities and facilities which the Government of Israel is by law obliged to furnish, the Agency will undertake the following functions:
>   1. Immigration to and absorption of immigrants in Israel.
>   2. Social welfare services in connection with immigration and absorption.
>   3. Health services in connection with immigration and absorption.
>   4. Education.
>   5. Institutions of higher learning and research.
>   6. Youth care and training.
>   7. Absorption in agricultural settlement.
>   8. Immigrant housing.
>   9. Such other functions and tasks as the Agency may deem necessary or advisable.
> D. The functions and tasks and programs administered by the Agency or to which it may contribute funds, shall be only such as may be carried on by tax-exempt organizations.

The Law of Status, as amended, Section 2A, recognizes the power of the Reconstituted Agency to operate:

> . . . in the State of Israel in fields chosen by it, with the consent of the Government (of Israel).

THE COMPOSITION AND WORKING ARRANGEMENTS OF THE JEWISH AGENCY FOR ISRAEL

Part II of the partnership agreement in the Agreement for the Reconstitution of the Jewish Agency provides a set of bylaws as Articles of

Association describing the Governing Bodies of the Agency, namely, the Assembly, the Board of Governors and the Executive. The representatives to these bodies are selected on a parity basis by the two parties to the Agreement.

AMENDMENT

Part IIIC of the Reconstitution Agreement provides as follows: "This Agreement may be amended at any time only by the consent of two-thirds of all the members of the Assembly at the time of such amendment."

CONCLUSIONS

The Compositions and Working Arrangements, that is, the bylaws contained in Part II of the Agreement, could be changed by an amendment for which the consent of two-thirds of the members of the Assembly voting at the time of the Assembly would be needed. However, changes in the structure of the Jewish Agency and/or the WZO would need not only the consent of the parties involved, but also the agreement of the Government of Israel and the Knesset.

It should be borne in mind that the Agreement is only the reflection of the understanding between the partners. Therefore, there is no reason to change this Agreement unless the understanding between the partners has changed.

It should also be remembered that the built-in flexibility in the wording of the Agreement was purposeful at the time, in order to allow the parties to find *working* solutions to problems that might arise.

These are some legal guidelines which must be taken into account by the Committee on Governance in its deliberations.

FLEXING THEIR MUSCLES

Charles Hoffman

SHARON VS. THE CONFEDERATION

Minister without Portfolio Ariel Sharon is a general with a reputation as a tough fighter and a brilliant field commander. He led Israel's thrust across the Suez Canal into Egypt in 1973, and smashed the Syrian armor and air-defense in Lebanon in 1982. But the 'unstoppable Arik' finally met his match recently in Jerusalem when he was beaten back by a group of Hadassah women in his bid for the chairmanship of the Aliyah Department of the Jewish Agency.

Sharon and his backers in the ruling Herut Party failed to 'read' correctly the array of forces on the field of battle where Sharon went down to defeat. This was the General Council of the World Zionist Organization (WZO), which would have been the first step on his way to the Aliya portfolio. The delegates from the Zionist Confederation, which is composed mainly of Hadassah leaders, held the balance of power in the council voting between the confirmed pro-Sharon and anti-Sharon blocs.

The Confederation delegates heard appeals by Prime Minister Yitzhak Shamir and Defense Minister Moshe Arens to support their party colleague, but were unmoved. They felt that the divisive and pugnacious Sharon was the wrong man for the wrong job, and that's the way they voted.

Frustrated Herut leaders and supporters cried foul. They blasted what they called illegitimate diaspora interference in Israeli political affairs.

NEW DIASPORA ASSERTIVENESS

This thunderous Herut denunciation was a bit late and out of date. The new wave of diaspora assertiveness in Israeli affairs had already hit them as recently as last October. At that time, the Agency Board of Governors, under the leadership of Chairman Jerold Hoffberger of Baltimore, voted to oust the previous Herut incumbent in the aliyah post, Raphael Kotlowitz, who was considered unfit after several years on the job.

In the latest tangle over the aliyah post, Shamir asked Hoffberger to support Sharon's candidacy. Hoffberger's 'no' reverberated throughout the Israeli media and was a factor in stopping Sharon.

These two incidents provided Israelis, who usually do not pay much attention to Jewish Agency/WZO affairs, with vivid illustrations that diaspora passivity is a thing of the past — at least in areas where their 'advice and consent' is actively sought.

While most Israelis would deny an active role to diaspora Jews in determining life and death matters such as security policy, many Israelis are getting used to the idea that diaspora Jews should have a voice in determining how their contributions to Israel are spent and who does the spending.

JEWISH AGENCY AS ARENA

The main arena today for diaspora participation in Israeli affairs is the Jewish Agency, which, since the establishment of Israel in 1948, has spent over $7 billion on bringing immigrants to Israel and providing the settlements, schools, social and health services intended to ensure their successful absorption. In the 1970s, with the mass immigration of the 1950s well behind it, the Agency turned its attention to helping the disadvantaged sectors of the population catch up with the more established groups.

Diaspora Jewry's contribution to the building of Israeli society through the Agency is clearly reflected in the figures. Two-thirds of the $7 billion spent by the Agency since 1948 has come from the United Jewish Appeal (UJA) and the Keren Hayesod. Of the $424 million collected in 1982/83 for the Agency, some $324 million came from the UJA and $97 million from the Keren Hayesod.

For most of the Agency's fifty-five year history, however, diaspora participation in policy-making and supervision has lagged far behind their monetary contributions. The Zionist political parties and their Israeli counterparts have continued to control most of the funds and administrative apparatus of the Agency and the WZO.

The WZO, which last year had a budget of close to $100 million, is a legally distinct entity from the Agency, although they have some joint functions and overlapping governing bodies. The WZO's budget comes mainly from the Israeli Government and the Keren Hayesod, with some funds provided by the Agency.

FROM PHILANTHROPY TO PARTNERSHIP

Since the reconstitution of the Agency in 1971, the relation between the Israeli and diaspora components of the Agency has been officially based on the principle of partnership. This principle has been implemented in some areas, but in others it remains no more than an attractive slogan.

In political matters such as the recent flap over Sharon, partnership means that the Israeli political parties and their counterparts in the WZO have the right to nominate candidates for executive posts in the Agency, but they must first gain the approval of a majority of the Zionist parties, many of whom represent the diaspora. Once this hurdle is passed, the candidates must be approved by the Agency Board of Governors.

Partnership also extends to policy-making and to the supervision of Agency operations and budgets, which is carried out by the Board of Governors.

The Jewish Agency for Palestine, as it was first called, was the brainchild of the long-time president of the WZO, Dr. Chaim Weizmann. Established in 1929, it was intended to provide a framework for wealthy and prominent 'non-Zionist' Jews around the world to support the Zionist aims of building a 'national home for the Jewish People in Palestine,' without requiring them to formally identify as Zionists.

As it was later humorously expressed, the Agency enabled 'one Jew to give money to a second Jew so that a third Jew could immigrate and settle in Palestine.'

A framework separate from but interrelated with the WZO was considered necessary in those days because many diaspora Jewish supporters of Zionist goals shied away from the label of Zionist. Before 1948, and in some quarters well afterwards too, the Zionist label raised the specter of dual loyalty and put Jews under suspicion of being 'Zionist agents' in their home countries.

The separate framework of the Agency also proved eminently suitable for American tax regulations, which allowed deductions for contributions to philanthropic organizations but prohibited them for expressly political bodies such as the WZO or for foreign governments.

The non-Zionists in the Agency played only a minor role in its operations in the 1930s and 1940s. Then and after 1948 the Agency and the WZO were for all practical purposes one organization controlled by the Israeli political establishment. The attitude of the Israeli leaders was in effect: "Give us your money and keep your advice to yourselves." At that time the Agency was highly politicized and some of its funds were diverted to party institutions. To the public at large, the Agency became a byword for inefficiency, featherbedding, and political corruption.

The Six-Day War of 1967, which proved to be a watershed for Israel-diaspora relations in many spheres, was also the catalyst leading to the transformation of the diaspora role in the Agency. Israeli leaders such as the late Louis Pincus, who was then Agency Chairman, and diaspora leaders such as Max Fisher, then Chairman of the Council of Jewish Federations, understood the need for greater mutual involvement and responsibility in running the Agency. They used the outpouring of concern, identification – and money – for Israel during that critical time as an opportunity to press for change.

The result was the reconstituted Jewish Agency founded in 1971, which gave the diaspora fund-raisers half of the delegates on the Agency policy-making bodies, but confined them to minority status on the Executive.

THE NEW GENERATION

Many of the diaspora leaders who entered the reconstituted Agency were much less constricted by the approach of sentimental philanthropy that characterized the previous generation. They were not automatically in awe of everything Israeli, nor did they feel a sense of overwhelming inferiority in relation to the new generation of Israeli leaders as their predecessors had to Ben-Gurion and his colleagues. They were less emotional and more critical and businesslike.

At the same time, a different Israel was revealed to them in the 1970s, an Israel more aware of its own shortcomings and — let it be said — failures. The plight of a large segment of the Sephardi population still living in poor conditions and with restricted opportunities blew up as a major social issue in the early 1970s. The trauma of the Yom Kippur War exposed the inadequacies of the long-time Labor Party leadership. Israelis also became more self-critical and less tolerant of past excuses for inefficiency and political corruption.

The second half of the 1970s witnessed a deepening diaspora involvement in Israel's problems and a greater willingness to resolve differences of opinion with Israel leaders out in the open instead of behind closed doors.

Project Renewal — the comprehensive slum rehabilitation program launched in 1977 — opened a new perspective on Israel. For the first time it offered diaspora fund-raisers and professionals direct involvement in wrestling with the problems of closing the social and cultural gap between the established and disadvantaged segments of Israeli society.

The experience in Project Renewal of working directly at the grass roots with the residents of disadvantaged areas and government officials had an especially critical impact on the newest generation of diaspora fund-raisers and federation professionals in their 30s and early 40s. It made them even less tolerant of the confusion and inefficiency in Israeli bureaucracy and more determined to assert a closer control over the disposition of diaspora funds in Israel.

PARTNERSHIP TESTED

The rise to power of the Likud in 1977 prepared the ground for open confrontations between diaspora and Israeli leaders, such as the recent spectacle of Sharon's defeat. The leading party in the Likud, Herut, never adjusted ideologically to the reconstituted Agency and the active role in Israeli affairs it conferred on diaspora Jews.

In particular, it resisted the principle laid down in black and white in the Agency's bylaws that the diaspora representatives in the WZO and the Agency could have a say in the selection of top Agency officials. Thus, instead of quietly seeking diaspora consent to its candidates for these posts, Herut has on several occasions tried to ram them down the throats of the diaspora delegates, even when it was known that they were unacceptable. Each time such attempts have backfired for Herut, causing it much embarrassment and further entrenching the fact of diaspora influence that they so sorely resent.

DIFFICULTIES OF LONG DISTANCE MANAGEMENT

The diaspora leaders in the Agency, or at least the top segment in this group of several hundred men and women, have recently tried to forge better organizational tools for supervising Agency activities and the all-important task of determining its annual budget.

Long-distance management has proven to be inherently problematic, they now realize, especially as the Board of Governors convenes only twice a year for a brief period. Furthermore, these leaders do not always have a firm grasp of how Agency programs complement or conflict with social and educational activities carried out directly by the Government. Finally, in evaluating the performance of Agency departments, they have to rely mainly on what the Agency bureaucrats tell them.

Some of the worst instances of waste, duplication and politicization in the Agency have been done away with since the early 1970s, but there is still room for considerable improvement. Yet it should be noted that some of these changes would have come about even if the Agency administrators did not have diaspora leaders looking over their shoulders.

'NEW ZIONISTS'

Over the years there has been an ideological rapprochement with diaspora Jewry that would have been unthinkable under someone like Ben-Gurion, who stoutly asserted that only someone who makes aliyah can be considered a Zionist. Today, leaders like Max Fisher, the Board of Governors Chairman from 1971 to 1983, have embraced the term 'new Zionist' to describe their outlook.

This term refers to any Jew who upholds the centrality of the State of Israel in Jewish life; endorses the importance of aliyah, even if not making a personal commitment to come to Israel; and seeks to strengthen Jewish values and identity through Jewish education.

Although some Israelis sneer at this as a watered-down Zionist commitment, these ideas have recently received some practical expression that would have been unheard of ten or fifteen years ago. One is a growing interest at the top levels of the Agency in greatly expanding its Jewish education programs for the diaspora, which are today mainly the preserve of the WZO. The other is the formation of programs in local Jewish federations to provide material and moral support for members of the local community who decide to take the plunge and settle in Israel.

The open discussion and encouragement of aliyah has broken down the taboo on the subject that was imposed by the previous generation of Israeli and diaspora leaders. Their unwritten pact put the diaspora Jews in a morally inferior position, since they had declined to give up their material comforts for the rigors of practical Zionism. The diaspora Jews forked over their contributions as a sort of 'guilt tax' and the Israelis for their part agreed not to raise the touchy subject of aliyah.

Nowadays, with tens of thousands of Israeli *yordim* headed towards Babylon-on-the-Hudson and a growing Israeli appreciation of the importance of a strong, vibrant American Jewish community, the mutual complexes on both sides have abated somewhat. This has made communication and cooperation easier on both sides.

FURTHER DEVELOPMENT

Although the Zionist parties have lost   most of the influence they once had among world Jewry, they continue to control most of the funds and positions in the Agency and WZO. Lately these anachronistic arrangements have come under attack from two directions.

No less a personage than Agency/WZO Chairman Arye Dulzin recently blasted the structure of the WZO as outmoded and unrepresentative. He proposed that Jewish defense and community organizations such as the American Jewish Congress and B'nai B'rith be incorporated into the WZO, following the lead taken by other non-political groups such as the Reform and Conservative movements. He also said that these non-party organizations should be given more power in the WZO.

From the other direction, some diaspora leaders such as Max Fisher have talked about extending the representation and control of the diaspora fund-raisers into the WZO.

The thrust of these proposals would be to enhance world Jewry's role in the Agency and WZO at the expense of the depleted and outmoded Zionist parties. They also imply reshaping these two bodies into Israel-based service organizations for the Jewish people that are run on a professional basis with as little politics as possible.

The growing involvement of diaspora and especially American Jews in the Agency over the last decade has led some leaders such as Fisher to envision it with a new structure and purpose. Others, more skeptical of the possibility of rooting out the politics, have recently broached the heretical idea of bypassing the Agency altogether by taking UJA funds from the federations and contributing them directly to worthy causes in Israel. Still others, aware that Israel is more able now to provide for its social needs than it was thirty years ago, have started talking about using a greater share of UJA money for community needs or for strengthening Jewish life in other countries.

Wherever these ideas for the future of the Agency ultimately lead, it is clear by now that an increasing number of informed and active diaspora Jews will be influencing the process that takes it there.

COVENANT BETWEEN THE GOVERNMENT OF ISRAEL

AND THE JEWISH AGENCY FOR ISRAEL

Entered into pursuant to the World Zionist Organization and Jewish Agency for Israel (Status) Law, 5713-1952 (hereinafter referred to as the "Law of Status")

BETWEEN

The Government of Israel (hereinafter referred to as "the Government")

AND

The Jewish Agency for Israel (hereinafter referred to as "the Jewish Agency")

WHEREAS
The Government is desirous to enhance the activities of the Jewish Agency and the Jewish Agency desires to cooperate and to act in full coordination with the State of Israel and its Government, in accordance with the laws of the State

NOW THEREFORE this Covenant is hereby entered into:

1. FUNCTIONS OF THE JEWISH AGENCY The functions of the Jewish Agency are as follows:
a. The organization of immigration abroad and the transfer of immigrants and their property to Israel.
b. Participation in immigrants' housing and in their absorption in agriculture, industry, trades and professions.
c. Health services in connection with immigration and absorption, and to the underprivileged.
d. Youth Aliya and youth care and training.
e. Maintenance and support of cultural, educational, scientific, religious, sports and social service institutions and activities therein.
f. Maintenance and support of institutions of higher education and research institutes.
g. The care of aged, disabled, handicapped and other persons in need of assistance and social services.
h. Generally to engage, by itself or in cooperation with other institutions, in any activities designed to help immigrants and needy persons to become integrated in the life of the community in Israel.
2. ACTIVITIES ACCORDING TO LAW Any activity carried out in Israel by or on behalf of the Jewish Agency for the purpose of performing all or any of the aforementioned functions shall be carried out in accordance with the laws of the State of Israel applicable from time to time, including administrative directives in force from time to time with regard to the governmental authorities whose jurisdiction includes or is relevant to the activity in question.
3. IMMIGRATION In the organization of immigration and the handling of immigrants, the Jewish Agency shall act on the basis of plans agreed upon in advance with the Government or recommended by the Coordinating Committee defined hereinafter.
4. COORDINATION BETWEEN INSTITUTIONS The Jewish Agency shall, in agreement with the Government, coordinate the activities in Israel of Jewish institutions and organizations operating with public funds within the sphere of the functions of the Jewish Agency.
5. TRANSFER OF FUNCTIONS The Jewish Agency may carry out any of its functions through its own departments and institutions under its control, and it may enlist in its activities the cooperation of other institutions, provided that it shall not delegate any of its functions or rights hereunder and shall not authorize any body or institution to carry out its

functions, wholly or partly, without the prior written consent of the Government.

6. MOBILIZATION OF RESOURCES The Jewish Agency shall be responsible for the mobilization of financial and material resources required for the execution of its functions and mainly derived from contributions, donations, grants and bequests from communities all over the world, from the income of investments and from loans.

7. LEGISLATION The Government shall consult with the Jewish Agency in regard to legislation specifically affecting the functions of the Jewish Agency before such legislation is submitted to the Knesset.

8. COORDINATING COMMITTEE There is hereby established a Coordinating Committee (hereinafter referred to as "the Committee") for the purpose of coordinating activities between the Government and the Jewish Agency in all fields covered by this Covenant.

The Committee shall consist of an even number of members, not less than four (4), half of whom shall be members of and appointed by the Government and half of whom shall be members of and appointed by the Executive of the Jewish Agency. The Government and the Jewish Agency shall be entitled from time to time to replace members of the Committee appointed by them respectively and to appoint others in their stead, provided that the new members shall be members of the Government or of the Executive of the Jewish Agency, as the case may be.

9. COMMITTEE'S RULES OF PROCEDURE The Committee shall meet at least once a month and shall have power to appoint sub-committees consisting of its own members and/or of other persons. The Committee shall from time to time submit to the Government and to the Jewish Agency reports of its deliberations and recommendations. Subject to the foregoing provisions, the Committee shall determine its own rules of procedure.

10. PERMITS AND FACILITIES The Government undertakes to see to it that its ministries and competent authorities provide the Jewish Agency and its Funds and other Institutions defined in the Annex hereto with all permits and facilities required by law for the carrying out of the activities specified herein.

11. TAX-EXEMPTION All contributions, gifts, donations and bequests to the Jewish Agency or to any of its Funds and other Institutions defined in the Annex hereto shall be exempt from all taxes and compulsory charges.

Furthermore the Jewish Agency and its aforementioned Funds and other Institutions shall be exempt from all taxes and other compulsory government charges specified in the Annex hereto, subject to the limitations and conditions stated in the said Annex.

12. ALTERATIONS Any proposed change or amendment to this Covenant or its Annex, or any addition thereto, shall be made in writing and shall require the consent of the Government and the Jewish Agency.

13. REPEAL The Covenant between the Government of Israel and the Zionist Executive called also the Executive of the Jewish Agency for Israel, entered into in 1954, is hereby repealed.

14. DATE OF COMING TO FORCE This Covenant shall be deemed to be in force and effect as of the 28th of Sivan 5731 (June 21, 1971).

Done and signed in Jerusalem
(the 28th day of June 1979)

THE GOVERNMENT OF ISRAEL   THE JEWISH AGENCY FOR ISRAEL

by   by   by
Menachem Begin   Chairman of the   Chairman of the
Prime Minister   Board of Governors   Executive
                                            Max M. Fisher   *Arye Dulzin*

ANNEX
To the Covenant between the Government of Israel and the Jewish Agency for Israel

1. In this Annex:

"the Jewish Agency" includes its Funds and other Institutions.

"the Funds and other Institutions of the Jewish Agency" means —

a. the United Jewish Appeal, Inc.;

b. the United Jewish Appeal of Greater New York, Inc.;

c. the United Israel Appeal, Inc.;

d. the United Israel Appeal of Canada - Hamagbit Hameuchedet Le Israel B'Canada Inc.;

e. the Joint Israel Appeal of Great Britain;

f. companies for the benefit of the public under the Charitable Trusts Ordinance exclusively controlled by the Jewish Agency;

g. any corporation wholly owned and controlled by the Jewish Agency, and/or by any of the Funds and other Institutions mentioned above, which is non-profit-making or whose activities and/or properties are exclusively devoted to the achievement of the purposes of the Jewish Agency and/or of the said Funds and Institutions; provided that in the event of the winding up of any such corporation all its residual assets shall be transferred to the Jewish Agency or to any such Fund or Institution as aforesaid;

In this sub-clause —

"corporation" means any company, association or other legal entity exclusively controlled by the Jewish Agency or by all or any of the aforementioned Funds and Institutions.

2. Subject to the undermentioned limitations and conditions, the Jewish Agency shall be exempt from the following taxes and compulsory government charges imposed by or in accordance with the undermentioned enactments:

a. property tax and compensations fund, under the Property Tax and Compensation Fund Law, 1961, on those of its properties serving its purposes which bear no income or which bear income wholly devoted to the achievement of its purposes;

b. fees under the Land (Fees) Regulations, 1975;

c. land appreciation tax and additional tax under the Land Appreciation Tax Law, 1963;

d. compulsory loans imposed by law;

e. income tax and capital gains tax under the Income Tax Ordinance and any other tax imposed on income; provided that the exemption shall not apply to dividend or interest on debentures paid to the Jewish Agency by a company engaged in any commerce, trade or business, unless such company is so engaged for the purpose of the settlement of Israel or the absorption of immigrants;

f. fees under the Companies (Fees and Forms) Regulations, 1976, clauses 1, 2(a), 2(b), 2(d), 3, 5, 6, 8, and 9 of the First Schedule, provided that the exemption shall only apply —

(1) in the case of a company with a share capital — in the proportion of the part of the Jewish Agency and its Funds and other Institutions in such share capital;

(2) in the case of a company without a share capital — in the proportion of the part of the Jewish Agency and its Funds and other Institutions in the membership of the company;

g. stamp duty under the Stamp Duty On Documents Law, 1961, on the following:

(1) debentures issued by the Jewish Agency, the redemption of which is guaranteed by the State of Israel;

(2) the transfer or assignment to the Jewish Agency of shares in a company controlled by not more than 5 persons and mainly concerned with the acquisition and holding of land;

(3) guarantees of debts of the Jewish Agency and guarantees by the Jewish Agency of debts of bodies in whose budgets the Jewish Agency participates;

h. license fees under the Traffic Ordinance for vehicles other than private motor vehicles, of the Jewish Agency and its Funds and other Institutions.

3. The exemptions specified in this Annex are in addition to and not in derogation of exemptions under any law.

AGREEMENT FOR THE RECONSTITUTION OF THE
JEWISH AGENCY FOR ISRAEL

AS AMENDED BY THE JEWISH AGENCY ASSEMBLY—JUNE 1985

PREAMBLE

WHEREAS:

1. In accordance with the World Zionist Organization-Jewish Agency (Status) Law, 5713-1952, and the Covenant entered into thereunder between the Government of Israel and the Executive of the Jewish Agency for Israel dated July 26, 1954, the World Zionist Organization (WZO) has undertaken certain tasks set forth therein, and more particularly the responsibility for bringing Jewish immigrants and refugees into Israel and for their resettlement, rehabilitation and absorption into the country.

2. The WZO has for many years acted also as The Jewish Agency for Israel.

3. Jewish communities throughout the free world have with great devotion and selfless dedication evidenced their deep concern for the welfare of their fellow Jews everywhere and have contributed generously large financial means in order to meet the urgent and continuing needs of immigration, resettlement and absorption.

4. The historic task of repatriating to the State of Israel all homeless, persecuted Jews seeking refuge in their historic Home, and their resettlement therein as free and self-supporting human beings, will continue to require ever-increasing efforts on the part of Jewish communities throughout the world.

5. The organizations signatory to this Agreement, which in the past served as the principal instruments through which the financial participation of Jewish communities outside of Israel for the work of rescue, relief and rehabilitation and their resettlement in Israel was channeled, are determined to intensify their service and to secure ever-increasing cooperation on the part of all Jews throughout the world who share a sense of dedication to these tasks.

6. The WZO seeks to obtain the active participation of Jews throughout the world in the work of rescue, rehabilitation, resettlement and reconstruction in Israel and to share with them the responsibility for the planning and the execution of these great tasks.

7. In the firm belief that sharing of responsibility of planning and implementing the aforesaid tasks will strengthen the bonds existing between the Jewish people in Israel and the Jewish communities everywhere and will serve the best interests of all concerned.

8. The WZO has invited the organizations signatory to this Agreement to join with it, and each other, in the reconstruction of The Jewish Agency for Israel on a broader basis for the purpose of continuing the tasks referred to above, and for the mobilization of the resources required in connection herewith.

THEREFORE,

The World Zionist Organization and the organizations signatory hereto have agreed as follows:

I. THE WORLD ZIONIST ORGANIZATION AND THE JEWISH AGENCY FOR ISRAEL

    A. The WZO agrees to the reconstitution of The Jewish Agency for Israel (Agency) in the manner herein provided. From the effective date of this Agreement as herein provided, "The Jewish Agency for Israel" shall mean the body reconstituted in accordance with the provisions of this Agreement, and is the body which enjoys the Status under the provisions of the World Zionist Organization and The Jewish Agency for Israel (Status) Law, 5713-1952 which became effective on the 1st of January 1976, retroactively from the 21st of June 1971. *(Amendment July 1976)*

    B. The WZO and its institutions will continue as the organs of the Zionist Movement for the fulfillment of Zionist programs and ideals. *(Amendment July 1976)*

C. Except with respect to activities and facilities which the Government of Israel is by law obliged to furnish, the Agency will undertake the following functions:
  1. Immigration to and absorption of immigrants in Israel.
  2. Social welfare services in connection with immigration and absorption.
  3. Health services in connection with immigration and absorption.
  4. Education.
  5. Institutions of higher learning and research.
  6. Youth care and training.
  7. Absorption in agricultural settlement.
  8. Immigrant housing.
  9. Such other functions and tasks as the Agency may deem necessary or advisable.
D. The functions and tasks and programs administered by the Agency, or to which it may contribute funds, shall be only such as may be carried on by tax-exempt organizations.
E. As of the effective date of this Agreement, the WZO and the Agency shall each have their own governing bodies.

II. THE RECONSTITUTED JEWISH AGENCY FOR ISRAEL

A. The Agency, as reconstituted in pursuance of this Agreement, shall consist of the designees of the following:
  1. The World Zionist Organization.
  2. The organizations signatory to this Agreement.
  3. Such other organizations, as referred to in paragraph 5 of the Preamble, as may from time to time be given the right by the Assembly to appoint designees.
B. The governing bodies of the Agency shall be the Assembly, the Board of Governors, and the Executive.
C. THE ASSEMBLY
  1. (a)　　The Assembly shall be designated as follows:
     (i)　　50% of the total number of members shall be designated by the WZO on behalf of itself and the Jewish people in Israel;
     (ii)　　30% of the total number of members shall be designated by the United Israel Appeal, Inc., New York, as representing the Jewish Community in the United States;
     (iii)　　20% of the total number of members to represent Jewish communities in countries and areas other than Israel and the United States, to be designated in accordance with the distribution set forth in Annex A attached hereto and made a part hereof. *(Amendment July 1980)*
     (b)　　The First Assembly shall consist of not more than 296 members, designated as follows:
     (i)　　50% of the total number of members, namely 148 persons, shall be designated by the WZO;
     (ii)　　30% of the total number of members, namely 89 persons, shall be designated by, or under the authority of, the Board of Trustees of the United Israel Appeal, Inc.;
     (iii)　　20% of the total number of members, namely 59 persons, to represent Jewish communities in countries other than Israel and the United States, shall be designated in accordance with the distribution set forth in Annex A attached hereto and made a part hereof.
     (c) (i)　　The presence of 30% of each of the groups referred to in sub-sections (a) (i) and (ii) and (iii) of this paragraph shall be required to constitute a quorum of the Assembly.
     (ii)　　For purposes of the First Assembly a quorum shall consist of 44 members of the group referred to in sub-section (b) (i), 27 members of the group referred to in sub-section (b) (ii) and 18 members of the group referred to in sub-section (b) (iii), respectively of this paragraph.
     (d)　　The Board of Governors shall establish the total number of members of the Assembly, which shall always be an even number, to be designated in accordance with the provisions of Article II C1(a) of the Agreement for the Reconstitution of the Jewish Agency. This action shall be taken by the Board of Governors not less than three (3) months prior to the meeting of the Assembly. If the Board of Governors fails to take such action in any one year, the numerical composition of the ensuing Assembly shall be the same as the last Assembly. *(Amendment June 1979)*
  2. (a)　　Each member of the Assembly, designated as above, shall have one vote, shall serve for a period of one year or until the next annual meeting of the Assembly, and shall serve without compensation. A member of the Assembly is eligible for redesignation to serve succeeding terms.
     (b)　　Between meetings of the Assembly, the designating organization shall have the right to fill a vacancy in membership of the Assembly created by death, resignation, or inability to serve. *(Amendment July 1976)*
  3. Each designating organization shall submit the list of its designees to the Secretary of the Agency at least two

months prior to the date set for the ensuing meeting of the Assembly. *(Amendment July 1976)*

4. (a)   The Assembly shall meet once a year at a time and place determined by the Board of Governors.

    (b)   A special meeting of the Assembly may be convened for such purposes and at such time and place as the Board of Governors shall determine. The Chairman of the Assembly and the Chairman of the Board of Governors, acting jointly, may convene a special meeting of the Assembly at such time and place as they shall determine.

    (c) (i)   Twenty-five percent (25%) of the members of the Assmebly shall have the right to cause a special session of the Assembly to be convened by giving ten (10) days written notice of their intention to the Secretary of the Assembly, setting forth the specific subjects which shall be on the agenda of such special session.

    (ii)   A special session shall thereupon be convened within forty-five (45) days from the date of such notice to deal with the specific items suggested in the request for the special session.

5. The fuctions of the Assembly shall be *(Amendment June 1984):*

    (a)   To receive and review reports from the Board of Governors;

    (b)   To make recommendations on major issues;

    (c)   To determine basic policies and goals of the Agency;

    (d)   To advise on major trends in the budget, including long-range perspectives;

    (e)   To consider and act upon budgets submitted by the Board of Governors;

    (f)   To adopt resolutions on the above;

    (g)   To elect the Board of Governors.

6. The officers elected by the Assembly from among its members shall be its Chairman, the Treasurer, and such additional officers as the Assembly may determine from time to time. A committee on nominations, composed in the same proportion as the Assembly, shall be appointed to recommend candidates for the office of the Chairman, Treasurer, and such other offices as the Assembly may determine.

7. The Assembly shall establish its own rules of procedure.

D. THE BOARD OF GOVERNORS *(Amendment June 1984)*

1. (a)   The Board of Governors determines the policy of the Jewish Agency for Israel and manages, supervises, controls and directs its operations and activities.

    All bodies (other than the Assembly), officers and officials of the Jewish Agency shall act within the policies set by the Assembly and Board of Governors and are accountable to the Board of Governors.

    Between meetings of the Assembly, the Board of Governors shall have full power to act for the Agency and may fix policy, provided that its acts and decisions are not inconsistent with previous decisions or instructions of the Assembly.

    (b)   The Board of Governors shall have the power to appoint a Standing Budget and Finance Committee.

    (c)   The Board of Governors approves and determines the Annual Budget of the Jewish Agency for Israel in accordance with the provisions of Clause II.F.2 hereinafter.

    (d)   The Board of Governors elects Members of the Executive in accordance with the provisions of Clause II.E. hereinafter.

    (e)   The Board of Governors receives and considers Reports of the Executive.

2. (a)   The Board of Governors consists of persons elected by the Assembly from among its members as follows:

    (i)   50% from among Members of the Assembly designated by the WZO;

    (ii)   30% from among Members of the Assembly designated by the United Israel Appeal, Inc. ('the UIA');

    (iii)   20% from among Members of the Assembly designated by organizations other than the WZO and the UIA, substantially in the manner set forth in Annex B attached hereto and made a part hereof.

    (b)   In accordance with the ratios determined in subsection (a) above, the Board of Governors is composed of 74 Governors as follows: *(Amendment June 1985)*

    (i)   37 Governors, from among Members of the Assembly designated by WZO;

    (ii)   22 Governors, from among Members of the Assembly designated by UIA;

    (iii)   15 Governors, from among Members of the Assembly designated by organizations other than the WZO and the UIA.

    (c)   The Board of Governors shall appoint a Nomination Committee, from among its Members and other Assembly Members, composed in the same proportion as the Assembly, to recommend to the Assembly, candidates for Board membership.

3 (a)   The Governors referred to in section 2(b)(i) and (ii) above shall be elected by the Assembly to serve for

a period of four years or until their successors are elected.

(b)   The Governors referred to in section 2(b)(iii) above shall be elected by the Assembly to serve for a period of two years, so that the principle of rotation may be applied as equitably as possible with respect to Governors so elected, or until their successors are elected.

(c)   Elections pursuant to subsections (a) and (b) shall take place on a date to be determined by the Chairman of the Assembly during the Assembly session at which they are to be held.

(d)   The Governors shall retire from office on the day on which new Governors are elected in accordance with the provisions of subsection (c).

4. (a)   The Board of Governors shall, at its first session held after the election of all its Members, elect its Chairman from among the Governors referred to in section 2(b)(ii) and (iii).

A nominating committee selected by the Board of Governors for this purpose shall make recommendations for the office of the Chairman.

The Chairman of the Board of Governors, or in his absence, the Chairman of the Budget and Finance Committee of the Board of Governors, shall preside at every meeting of the Board of Governors.

(b)   The Chairman of the Board of Governors shall serve for a four-year term.

(c)   Until the Chairman of the Board of Governors is elected, the retiring Chairman of the Board of Governors shall act as Acting Chairman and shall convene the first session of the Board of Governors to be held after election of its Members has taken place.

(d)   In the event that the office of the Chairman of the Board of Governors becomes vacant by reason of death, resignation, incapacity or inability to serve, the Board of Governors shall elect from among members of the Assembly designated by the Organization which had designated the Chairman whose office became vacant — a Chairman who shall serve for the unexpired term of office mentioned in subsection (b) above.

5. (a)   The Board of Governors shall hold not less than four regular sessions in each calendar year, at such times and places as shall be determined by the Chairman of the Board of Governors; provided that one of such regular sessions shall be held during, or in immediate proximity to, every Assembly session and provided further that not less than three regular sessions are held in Israel.

(b)   The Chairman of the Board of Governors may convene, whenever he thinks fit, an extraordinary meeting of the Board of Governors for such purpose and at such time and place as he shall determine.

The Chairman of the Board of Governors shall convene an extraordinary meeting of the Board of Governors upon the requisition in writing of not less than 20% of the total Members of the Board of Governors. Any such requisition shall express the object of the meeting proposed to be called and shall be left at the office of the Secretary-General of the Jewish Agency for Israel.

6. (a)   40% of the Governors, referred to in section 2(b)(i), together with 40% of the Governors, referred to in sections 2(b)(ii) and (iii), present in person, shall be a quorum at any meeting of the Board of Governors, whether held during a regular session or held as an extraordinary meeting.

(b)   If within 30 minutes from the time appointed for any meeting, a quorum is not present, the Chairman of the Board of Governors shall adjourn the meeting for not less than 48 hours. If at the adjourned meeting a quorum is not present within 15 minutes from the time appointed for such adjourned meeting, 30% of each of the three groups mentioned in section 2(b) above, shall be a quorum and in such cases, notwithstanding the provisions of section 7 hereinafter, action shall be taken by an affirmative vote of at least 75% of those present and voting.

7. (a)   Actions of the Board of Governors shall be taken by a majority of those present and voting. In counting the votes, only votes for or against a resolution shall be taken in consideration and abstentions shall be disregarded.

(b)   A resolution put to the vote of any meeting of the Board of Governors shall be decided on a show of hands or voice vote, unless a poll is demanded by the Chairman of the Board of Governors or by not less than 20% of the Governors present.

(c)   Unless a poll is so demanded, a declaration by the Chairman of the Board of Governors that a resolution has been carried or lost, and an entry to that effect in the minutes of the meeting, shall be conclusive evidence of the fact.

(d)   If a poll is demanded it shall be taken in such a manner as the Chairman of the Board of Governors shall direct and the result of the poll shall be deemed to be the resolution of the meeting at which the poll was demanded.

8. The Governors shall not be compensated for their services as such.

9. (a) The Chairman of the Board of Governors, in consultation with the Chairman of the Executive, shall have the power to appoint, from time to time, Standing or Ad-hoc Committees from among the Governors and other Assembly Members, and shall determine the scope of their functions.

   (b) Each Committee Chairman shall report to the Board of Governors, at such times as shall be determined by the Board of Governors, of his Committee's findings, conclusions, and recommendations.

10. The Board of Governors shall elect the Comptroller of the Jewish Agency and determine the scope of his activities.

11. The Board of Governors may from time to time make such general Regulations for the conduct of the affairs of the Jewish Agency and the administration of its activities (to be termed 'the By-laws of the Jewish Agency for Israel') as it may deem necessary.

12. Any vacancy occurring in the Board of Governors by reason of death, resignation, incapacity or inability to serve or by reason of a Governor ceasing to be a Member of the Assembly, may be filled by the other Governors, from among Members of the Assembly designated by the Organization which had designated the Governor whose place became vacant.

    The person elected to fill any vacancy shall serve for the unexpired term created by such vacancy.

13. The Board of Governors shall act, notwithstanding any vacancy occurring in its Members, and shall continue so to act and discharge its functions and exercise its powers in accordance with the provisions hereof.

14. If by reason of war or of any other unexpected or unusual situation beyond the control of the Board of Governors (hereinafter 'the State of Emergency') it shall be necessary, in the opinion of both the Chairman of the Assembly and the Chairman of the Board of Governors (in this section 'the Chairmen') to deviate from the provisions of this Agreement, the following provisions shall apply:

    (a) The said opinion shall be signed, or approved by letter, telegram or telex, by both Chairmen, and may consist of two separate documents.

    (b) As long as the State of Emergency shall continue, or as long as it will not be possible, in the opinion of the Chairmen, to convene the Governing Bodies of the Jewish Agency in accordance with the provisions of this Agreement, the Members of the Executive present in Israel shall constitute the Executive (in this section 'the Executive in Israel').

    (c) All the powers, authorities and functions vested in the Board of Governors and the Executive, by virtue of this Agreement, shall vest in the Executive in Israel.

    (d) The Executive in Israel shall from time to time, fix the quorum at its meetings, the required majority and the method of voting thereat.

    (e) Every Member of any of the Governing bodies of the Jewish Agency shall continue to serve as such until proper elections shall take place, in accordance with the provisions of this Agreement.

    (f) A statement in writing of both Chairmen that the State of Emergency has come to an end shall be conclusive evidence of the fact, and shall be effective as of the date stipulated in said statement.

    (g) At the termination of the State of Emergency as aforesaid, the Chairmen shall take all necessary steps for the reconvening of the Governing Bodies of the Jewish Agency in accordance with the provisions of this Agreement, and, if necessary, for the election of the Members of the Board of Governors and Members of the Executive.

15. The Board of Governors shall establish its own Rules of Procedure.

E. THE EXECUTIVE *(Amendment June 1984)*

1. The Executive shall administer the operations of the Jewish Agency, subject to the control of the Board of Governors.

   Policies adopted by the Assembly and the Board of Governors shall be implemented by the Executive and the Departments under the direction of the Chairman of the Executive.

   The Executive shall act as a collective body with collective responsibility.

2. (a) The Executive shall be composed of Members ex officio and of Members elected by the Board of Governors.

   (b) Members of the Executive shall serve as such only as long as they are Members of the Board of Governors.

3. (a) The following holders of offices or positions shall be Members ex officio of the Executive while holding such offices or positions:

   (i) the Chairman of the Assembly, who shall also serve as Chairman of the Executive;

   (ii) the Chairman of the Board of Governors;

   (iii) the Founding Chairman of the Board of Governors, who shall serve as a life Member of the Executive;

    (iv) the Treasurer;

    (v) the Chairman of the Board of Governors Committee on Budget and Finance;

    (vi) the Chairman of the UIA, Inc.;

    (vii) the National Chairman of the UJA;

    (viii) the Chairman of the Board of Trustees of the UJA;

    (ix) the President of the Council of Jewish Federations (U.S.A),

    (x) the Chairman of the Board of Trustees of Keren Hayesod;

    (xi) the World Chairman of Keren Hayesod.

(b)   The following Governors shall be Members ex officio of the Executive:

    (i) two Members, to be appointed by the WZO, from among the Governors referred to in Clause II.D.2(b)i;

    (ii) two Members to be appointed by Organizations other than the WZO and the UIA, and who serve as Appeal Trustees on the World Board of Trustees of Keren Hayesod.

(c)   The Chairman of the Assembly and the Treasurer shall serve for a period of four years, or until their successors are elected.

4. The Board of Governors shall elect to the Executive and as Heads of Departments:-

(a)   one Member, from among Members of the Assembly designated by the WZO, to serve as Head of the Immigration and Absorption Department.

(b)   two Members, from among Members of the Assembly designated by the WZO, to serve as Co-Heads of the Agricultural Settlement Department.

(c)   one member, from among Members of the Assembly designated by the WZO, to serve as Head of the Youth Aliyah Department.

5. (a)   Elections pursuant to section 4 shall take place on a date to be determined by the Chairman of the Board of Governors during the Board of Governors session held during, or in immediate proximity to the Assembly session at which the Chairman of the Assembly and the Treasurer are to be elected.

(b)   Heads of Departments elected as aforesaid shall:

    (i) serve for a period ending on the Board of Governors session held during, or in immediate proximity to, the Assembly session at which the Chairman of the Assembly and the Treasurer shall retire.

    (ii) retire from office on the day at which elections of new Heads of Departments are to be held in accordance with subsection (a) above.

6. (a)   Notwithstanding any provision hereinbefore mentioned, the Board of Governors may, at the meeting at which Heads of Departments retire in manner aforesaid in section 5 above, resolve not to elect one or more of the persons mentioned in section 4 and not to fill any vacated office of Head of Department, and in such case the provisions of section 12 hereinafter shall apply.

(b)   Should a Head of Department not be elected as aforesaid:-

    (i) The WZO shall have the power to appoint to the Executive one Member, from among the Governors referred to in Clause II.D.2(b)(i), who shall serve as a Member ex officio until a new Head of Department is elected pursuant to the provisions of section 7.

    (ii) The Chairman of the Executive shall assume, and with the consent of the Chairman of the Board of Governors, may delegate to a Member of the Executive, the functions of the Head of such Department until a new Head of Department is elected pursuant to the provisions of section 7.

7. In the event that one or more of the persons mentioned in section 4 above are not elected to the Executive, the Chairman of the Board of Governors shall, by mutual consent with the Chairman of the Executive, set a date for election and in case any person is so elected, he shall serve as Head of Department for the unexpired term of office mentioned in section 5.

8. Members of the Executive may be compensated for their services as such, in such manner as may be determined by the Board of Governors from time to time.

9. The Board of Governors may, in its discretion, appoint Associate Members of the Executive, who shall serve on such terms and for such periods of time, and perform such duties and functions as the Board of Governors may from time to time determine. No more than three Associate Members shall serve at any time.

Associate Members shall have the right to attend all meetings of the Executive, but they shall not be entitled to vote.

10 (a)   The Executive shall meet not less than once each month at such dates and places, either in Israel or abroad, as the Chairman of the Executive shall determine.

(b)   The Board of Governors shall from time to time, by resolution, fix the quorum at the meetings of the

Executive, the required majority and the method of voting thereat.

11. In the event that the office of the Chairman of the Executive, the Treasurer, or any Head of Department becomes vacant, the Board of Governors may elect an Acting Successor who shall serve in that capacity until a new successor is elected in accordance with the provisions hereof.

Such Acting Successor and successor shall be from among the Governors referred to in Clause II.D.2(b)(i).

12. The Executive shall act, notwithstanding any vacancy occurring in its Members, and shall continue so to act and discharge its functions and exercise its powers in accordance with the provisions hereof.

13. (a) The Executive is empowered to exercise all the powers of the Agency to enter into contracts; to borrow money, to issue evidences of indebtedness, debentures, guarantees and other securities; to acquire, and dispose of, any property; to execute any document in respect of any matter whatsoever concerning the Jewish Agency and generally to represent the Agency and to act in its name and on its behalf.

(b) The Executive may delegate any of its powers to one or more of its Members.

(c) The Board of Governors may, by resolution, authorize from time to time the Executive or any Member thereof to delegate, with the power to sub-delegate, to any person who is not a Member of the Executive, the power to act on behalf of the Agency in such manner and extent as the Board of Governors shall deem fit.

14. The principal Office of the Executive shall be located in Jerusalem. The Executive may, with the approval of the Board of Governors, establish and maintain offices in other parts of the world, as may be required for the efficient conduct of the affairs of the Agency.

15. Subject to the provisions of section 10(b) the Executive shall prescribe and determine its own rules of procedure.

F FINANCES, BUDGETS AND CONTRACTUAL COMMITMENTS

1. The financial resources at the disposal of the Agency for the conduct of affairs shall be derived from allocations made to its programs and functions by the parties to this Agreement, from fund-raising activities for the benefit of its programs and functions by Keren Hayesod and others, from income on investments, from collection of debts, from grants by the Government of Israel, from borrowings, and from such other funds as it may receive by grant or otherwise from other sources.

2. All expenditures by and on behalf of the Agency shall be in pursuance of budget, which shall be determined in the following manner:

(a) The Executive shall each year prepare and submit to the Board of Governors the following:
 (i) an estimate of receipts from all sources for the ensuing fiscal year;
 (ii) a 'budget of needs' for the ensuing fiscal year;
 (iii) a detailed budget of recommended expenditures during the ensuing fiscal year.

(b) The Board of Governors shall review, examine and, if it sees fit, change or amend the estimate of receipts and the budget of expenditures submitted by the Executive, and shall determine the budget for the ensuing fiscal year, subject only to such changes and amendments as may be recommended by the Assembly at its next ensuing meeting.

(c) The Board of Governors may, between meetings of the Assembly, increase, reduce, change and amend any budget previously fixed as circumstances, in its judgement, may necessitate, and report to the Assembly the reasons for any such action.

3. The Jewish Agency for Israel, as reconstituted in pursuance of this Agreement, shall be an independent body whose membership consists solely of the persons designated to serve as members of the Assembly in the manner hereinabove set forth. The organizations signatory hereto are not, as such, members of the Jewish Agency for Israel. This Agreement does not create or imply the existence of any relationship of principal and agent between any of the signatories to this Agreement. To the extent that the Agency is designated as the Operating Agent for any of the signatories hereto such designation shall be made by separate agreements between the parties concerned.

III. A. This Agreement shall go into effect and become operative on the 21st day of June, 1971.

B. This Agreement may be executed in several counterparts, each of which shall be deemed to be an original, and such counterparts together shall constitute a single instrument binding upon all signatories.

C. This Agreement may be amended by a two-thirds majority of those present and voting at the Assembly. Notification of proposed amendments shall be sent to all the Members of the Assembly, not less than 60 days prior to the Assembly meeting. *(Amendment June 1984)*

DONE AND SIGNED IN JERUSALEM: THE CAPITAL OF ISRAEL ON 28 SIVAN 5731, 21 JUNE 1971.
The Weizmann Hall, the Jewish Agency for Israel.

ADDENDUM
To the Agreement for the Reconstitution of the Jewish Agency for Israel

1. This addendum is of equal validity and is an integral part of the Agreement for the Reconstitution of the Jewish Agency for Israel (hereinafter referred to as the "Agreement") dated as of the date hereof, as though fully set forth therein.
2. With reference to sub-section II D (6) of the Agreement, it is agreed that two of the meetings of the Board of Governors referred to in the said sub-section shall be held each year in Israel and one meeting of the Board of Governors shall be held each year in a country other than Israel at such time and place as will be determined by the Board of Governors.
3. It is understood that the Chairman of the WZO shall serve as the Chairman of the Assembly and the Executive of the Agency.
4. It is agreed that only members of the Board of Governors designated by an organization other than the World Zionist Organization may serve as Chairman of the Board of Governors.

Signed in Jerusalem this 27th day of August 1970

The World Zionist Organization
by (sgd) L.A. Pincus

The United Israel Appeal, Inc.,
by (sgd) Max M. Fisher

ANNEX "A" (As amended July 1980)

Distribution of members of the Assembly from countries other than Israel and the United States.[*]

Committee	No. of Delegates and Votes	Committee	No. of Delegates and Votes
1. Argentina	6	15. Mexico	3
2. Austria	3	16. Peru	1
3. Australia	1	17. South Africa	5
4. Belgium	3	18. Spain	1
5. Brazil	3	19. Sweden	1
6. Canada	7	20. Switzerland	3
7. Central America	1	21. Uruguay	2
8. Chile	2	22. Venezuela	1
9. Colombia	1	23. West Germany	2
10. Denmark	1	24. Hong Kong	1
11. France	7	25. To be designated by Keren Hayesod Board of Trustees	3
12. Great Britain	7		
13. Holland	1		
14. Italy	2	TOTAL	68

The Chairman of the Board of Governors, and the Chairman of the Executive may, jointly, permit an increase in the number of the members of the Assembly designated from any country, provided that the aggregate number of votes allocated to any such country, as set forth above, shall not be changed by reason of any such increase.

[*] Currently being updated to conform with the increase in number of Assembly Members representing fund-raising bodies affiliated with Keren Hayesod (80).

ANNEX "B" (As amended July 1980)

Distribution of Members of the Board of Governors*

A. United States	18	
		18
B. English-speaking communities (excluding the US)		
Great Britain	2	
Canada	2	
Australia	1	
South Africa	1	
		6
C. Europe**		
France	1	
Switzerland	1	
Europe (rotating)	1	
		3
D. Latin America**		
Argentina	1	
Latin America (rotating)	2	
		3
E. To be designated by Keren Hayesod Board of Trustees	1	
		31

* Currently being updated to conform with the increase in number of Members on the Board of Governors.

** As required by changing conditions and considerations, Keren Hayesod may make appointments to the Board from other countries, and in such cases, the membership listing shall be transferred from B, C, or D to E (to be designated by Keren Hayesod Board of Trustees).

CAESAREA COMMISSION REPORTS*

THE JEWISH AGENCY FOR ISRAEL
COMMISSION ON GOALS AND OBJECTIVES
Report and Recommendations to the Board of Governors, October 1982,
as Amended by the Board of Governors, March 1, 1983

CHAIRMAN: Raanan Weitz

I. PRINCIPLES

A. The Jewish Agency continues to view the upbuilding of the Land of Israel as its primary task.

B. The decade of activity since the reconstitution of the Jewish Agency has steadily underlined and increased its role in strengthening the Jewish people and links between Israel and the diaspora.

C. These principles are expressed in The Jerusalem Program (1968) adopted by the 27th World Zionist Congress, which states the aims of Zionism to be:

The unity of the Jewish people and the centrality of Israel in Jewish life;

The ingathering of the Jewish people in its historic homeland, Eretz Israel, through aliyah from all countries;

The strengthening of the State of Israel, which is based on the prophetic vision of justice and peace;

The preservation of the identity of the Jewish people through the fostering of Jewish and Hebrew education and of Jewish spiritual and cultural values;

The protection of Jewish rights everywhere.

II. PRIORITIES

A. From its very establishment, the Jewish Agency viewed *Aliyah* and *Rural Settlement* as integral to its functions. These activities continue to be essential to the needs of Israel and the quality of Israel's society, albeit with changes in emphasis and content.

B. Jewish communities throughout the world recognize the fundamental role of Jewish education in maintaining Jewish identity and continuity. In recent years, in conjunction with the World Zionist Organization departments dealing with *Jewish Education,* both formal and informal, the Jewish Agency initiated and supported activities in this field. The needs of the Jewish communities in the diaspora and the struggle against assimilation demand substantially increased concern with this crucial work.

C. The Jewish Agency is deeply concerned with the quality of life in Israel and, therefore, looks forward to seeding new programs in this field on a time-limited basis, such as Project Renewal.

III. CRITERIA

A. Jewish programs shall be undertaken in accordance with the above priorities, subject to the Jewish Agency's ability to effectively manage them.

B. Jewish Agency programs shall be based on projects of specific duration, and shall be so designated. The periods involved can be one of the following:

a. Long-term: likely to extend beyond ten years;

b. Intermediate: five to ten years;

c. Short-term: less than five years, consisting primarily of projects of limited duration or specific purpose which are self-liquidating.

---

* At the time this publication went to press, the work of the Management Commission was still in progress and its final report not yet completed.

C. All programs must have specific achievement targets. This is a prerequisite for *new* undertakings while ongoing projects should also be reviewed for specific goals.

D. Where possible, services should be obtained on a contract basis to avoid creating new permanent structures. Subventions to organizations shall be limited to those which meet the Jewish Agency's criteria and will be accountable to the Jewish Agency.

E. The vital activities of the Jewish Agency in the past have resulted in a burdensome accumulated debt. A debt reduction program should receive special attention and high priority. To this end, concentration on fewer programs of maximum impact should be considered on the way to a balanced budget.

IV. PROPOSED PROGRAMS AND PROJECTS

A. General

a. Jewish Agency Israel-centered programs require clear separation into categories delineating Government and Agency responsibility, as well as areas of cooperation. While cooperating with Government, the Jewish Agency will assume full responsibility and accountability for those activities which it undertakes.

b. Similarly, the increasing cooperation between the Jewish Agency and the World Zionist Organization on programs relating to the diaspora require definition of responsibility and implementation.

B. Aliyah and Absorption

a. These two fields should be separated in terms of primary responsibility and implementation. While general overall policy is the function of Government, the Jewish Agency and the World Zionist Organization have been charged by the Knesset and by tradition with the responsibility of encouraging and organizing aliyah.

b. Jewish Agency activities in *Absorption* should be limited both in time and in function. This requires close cooperation with Government agencies, particularly in housing, employment, education and other public services, so that the responsibility to the *oleh* is clear cut. The Jewish Agency should limit its responsibility to not more than six months, including Hebrew language ulpan, temporary housing and immigrant advocacy.

c. The encouragement of *Aliyah* will require closer cooperation between the World Zionist Organization and the Jewish Agency and more precise definition of functions.

C. Rural Settlement

a. The establishment of new settlements, particularly in areas of sparse population, is a continuing function of the Jewish Agency. Its responsibility is to bring such settlements to self-sufficiency as soon as possible, including the need to encourage and develop industry.

b. It is recommended that the name of the department responsible for this activity be changed to Rural Development Department.

D. Jewish Education

a. Recognizing the basic responsibility of local Jewish communities for the all- important task of Jewish education, the emphasis in all Jewish Agency—World Zionist Organization sponsored educational programs shall be on Hebrew, Israel and Zionist content and orientation.

b. The Jewish Agency—World Zionist Organization sponsored programs should seek to increase substantially the numbers of Jews and particularly Jewish youth who spend a period in programs of various lengths and intensity (summer, semester, university, kibbutz ulpan—work and similar programs). Beyond such short-term programs, the educational experience and facilities of the Jewish Agency departments should be utilized for long-range study, including full high school programs.

c. In cooperation with the various World Zionist Organization departments, special efforts should be expended in involving diaspora communal bodies in encouraging Jewish identity and aliyah through education programs in the schools, in informal settings (community centers, camps), and by programs in Israel. Attention should also be given to increasing adult education programs.

E. Youth Aliyah

a. The Youth Aliyah Department should give priority to dealing with children of newcomers. As the process of receiving new children is a gradual one, and currently a slow one, the Youth Aliyah Department should continue its services to disadvantaged Israeli youth. It is noted that this service corresponds to the three priorities listed by the Goals and Objectives Commission, namely, aliyah, Jewish education and improvement of the quality of life in Israel. Finally, the Commission has recommended that projects be of specific duration; the Youth Aliyah Department should consider some feasible limitation on duration of its services.

F. Project Renewal

The significance of this project lies in its positive impact on the inhabitants of the neighborhoods, as well as its role in strengthening the relationship between the people of Israel and the communities in the diaspora. While these programs separately will be done on a time-limited basis, they should be extended to include all the neighborhoods which have been designated for renewal.

V. FOLLOW-UP

A. Jewish Agency programs shall be reviewed regularly – annually – as part of the budgetary process, and periodically (three years) according to overall goals and objectives, placed in the perspective of changing social and political developments, as well as their impact on fundraising.

B. In view of the Jewish Agency's responsibility to its widespread constituencies, the Board of Governors should establish a broadly representative standing committee to evaluate its programs and priorities, including contracted programs, and their degree of responsiveness to the criteria noted above. The Board of Governors, after considering the reports of this committee, will communicate its recommendations to its constituencies in all countries.

C. The organizational structure of the Jewish Agency should be examined every five years in order to assure the active involvement of the members of its governing bodies, overseas as well as in Israel, in the decision-making process and the development of overall policy.

D. The Jewish Agency has over the years built competent professional staff. In order to achieve increasing success, the professional staff of the Jewish Agency must be continually enhanced by emphasizing merit and experience as the principal factors in selection of personnel.

VI. GENERAL COMMENTS

A. The availability of special expertise in the diaspora which would enhance Jewish Agency programs and activities provides an important field for additional Jewish involvement in Israel.

B. Departmental facilities shall be available and utilized for any and all Jewish Agency programs whenever needed.

C. The Jewish Agency shall phase out its functions in housing, health and welfare, recognizing the responsibility of Government in these fields.

GOVERNANCE COMMISSION OF THE CAESAREA PROCESS AND SPECIAL COMMITTEE OF THE BOARD OF GOVERNORS OF THE JEWISH AGENCY FOR ISRAEL
Summary Report, June 1984

CHAIRMAN: Raymond Epstein
COCHAIRMAN: Kalman Sultanik

The mandate to the Commission called for an effort to improve the decision making process and for a definition of the role of the governing bodies. The structure of the Agency was carefully examined in order to establish clearly the functions and responsibilities of its various components. A Special Committee was charged with the task of preparing the recommendations on Governance for presentation to the Board of Governors and the Assembly.

What follows is a precis of the Committee's work, emphasizing the recommendations that reflect consensus, clarifications and change in the Agency.

A. THE BOARD OF GOVERNORS

1. The Board of Governors is the primary governing instrument of the Jewish Agency. Therefore, the following shall be added to the Reconstitution Agreement: "All bodies (other than the Assembly) and officers and officials of the Jewish Agency shall act within the policies set by the Assembly and the Board of Governors and are accountable to the Board of Governors."

2. A Nominating Committee of the Board of Governors shall be appointed to present a slate of nominees designated by the constituent organizations (UIA, Keren Hayesod, WZO) for election by the Assembly to the Board of Governors.

3. The Board of Governors shall meet at least four times a year and consideration should be given to holding one meeting in the diaspora.

4. In the absence of a quorum, the Reconstitution Agreement allows for the Chairman to reconvene the Board after 48 hours. The quorum requirement therefore should be increased to 30 percent participation from each constituent organization. Action can then be taken by an affirmative vote by at least 75 percent of such a quorum.

5. Members of the Board of Governors may place items on the agenda through the Chairman. (The specified number of members required shall be determined by the Implementation Committee.)

6. Committees:

　　a. Standing and ad hoc committees are appointed by the Chairman of the Board of Governors with the prior advice to the Chairman of the Executive, and in consultation with him.

b. Committees are an essential part of the Jewish Agency structure. The process is designed to seek a more informed leadership, able to advise, monitor and guide the departmental operations according to the policies set by the Board of Governors.

c. Committees and their chairmen are not the operating supervisors of the Department Heads and Directors-General. Nevertheless, the planning and programming of departmental operations will have Committee participation and the actual carrying out of the operations will be reviewed, evaluated and reported upon by the Committee.

d. Departmental budgets should be discussed and reviewed by the appropriate Committee prior to presentation to the Budget and Finance Committee. The Department Head and Committee Chairman shall be invited to the meeting of the Budget and Finance Committee during which the Department's budget is presented.

e. Board of Governors Members will serve on at least one Committee and Committee assignments shall be limited to a reasonable number. Additional Committee members shall be drawn from the Assembly and others may be invited to serve in an advisory capacity.

f. Meetings of Departmental Committees take place at the time of Board of Governors meetings or more frequently, if necessary. Adequate time shall be reserved in the schedule for such meetings.

g. Each Committee will report to the Board of Governors at regular intervals.

h. The Secretary-General serves the Committees as part of his responsibilities to the Board of Governors. He shall make available qualified staff drawn where possible from the appropriate Departments.

7. Relations with the Israel Government shall be conducted through the Coordinating Committee, in accordance with the policies determined by the Board of Governors.

8. The Board of Governors recognizes the practice of Advise and Consent as part of the procedure of electing Jewish Agency Heads of Departments. Refer to Page 16 of the Board of Governors Minutes of October 26 and 27, 1983.

B. THE EXECUTIVE

1. The Executive of the Jewish Agency shall be expanded to eighteen members (from the current twelve) in conformance with the ratio specified in the Agreement and as detailed in the resolution of the Board of Governors of October 1983.[*]

2. The Executive will meet monthly. At least two members from the diaspora should participate in each meeting. Quorum requirements, however, shall permit the meeting to take place when diaspora members are not able to attend.

3. The Executive may take emergency action on behalf of the Board of Governors as required. In such cases, there shall be telephone consultation of diaspora members if possible, and all such actions will be reported to the Board of Governors.

4. The responsibilities of the Chairman of the Executive are in the context of the Executive's collective responsibility and he is accountable to the Board of Governors. The Chairman of the Executive can bring to the Executive any matter which he believes requires its attention. The Board of Governors looks to the Chairman to see that decisions of the Executive are carried out.

C. THE ASSEMBLY

1. The functions of the Assembly shall be to:
    a. Receive and review reports from the Board of Governors;
    b. Make recommendations on major issues;
    c. To determine basic policies and goals of the Agency;
    d. Advise on major trends in the budget, including long-range perspectives;
    e. Consider and act upon budgets submitted by the Board of Governors;
    f. Adopt resolutions on the above;
    g. Elect the Board of Governors.

2. The Assembly elects officers from among its members, including Assembly Chairman, Treasurer, and additional officials as may be determined. In accordance with the addendum to the Reconstitution Agreement, the Chairman of the World Zionist Organization shall be the Chairman of the Assembly.

D. ROTATION AND TENURE

1. The principle of rotation and the limitation of tenure, in order to provide for broad and renewed representation in the governing bodies of the Agency, is recognized by all. Since the election procedures and terms of office of the constituent organizations vary, it is recommended that these organizations review their bylaws in this regard so that they arrive at common or agreed upon procedures. The World Zionist Organization has undertaken to consider this subject in its Constitution Committee with the intent of presenting its recommendations at the next World Zionist Organization

---

[*] As amended to the Reconstitution Agreement in June 1984, there are currently nineteen members on the Executive.

Congress. The recommended guidelines are as follows:

    a. The Chairman of the Board of Governors shall serve a maximum of one four-year term.

    b. Members of the Board of Governors shall serve a maximum of two four-year terms.

    c. Members of the Executive, elected by virtue of their office, shall serve during their terms of office. Those elected ad personam will serve a maximum of two four-year terms.

    d. Members of the Assembly shall be appointed for two years and shall serve a maximum of four successive terms.

2. A process for termination of services of elected officials of the Jewish Agency is deemed necessary. Legal Counsel is requested to recommend a process for such termination, the process to be subject to consideration by the World Zionist Organization within a specified period of time. Legal Counsel is requested to recommend appropriate language for such process.

3. In the event that the Chairman of the Board of Governors or the Chairman of the Executive is unable to serve temporarily, the Chairman of the Budget and Finance Committee will serve as Acting Chairman of the Board of Governors and the Treasurer will serve as the Acting Chairman of the Executive respectively.

    In the event of the Board of Governors Chairman's death or his inability to serve and complete his term of office, the procedure regarding temporary placement shall be followed and a Nominating Committee then appointed followed by the election of an interim successor who is eligible for election to a full term.

E. OTHER OFFICIALS

1. Senior staff members (Director-General, Secretary-General, and Directors-General of Departments) shall be appointed by the Board following a formal search process based on a written job description. Heads of Departments and Chairmen of Department Committees shall be involved in the selection for their respective Departments.

    The principle underlying the appointment of senior staff is to ensure excellence in carrying out the responsibilities involved.

2. The Director-General of the Jewish Agency is responsible to the Chairman of the Executive. He supervises and coordinates the ongoing operations of the staff and shall be responsible for general administrative operations (manpower, training, administrative departments, etc.).

3. The Secretary-General shall be responsible for serving and staffing the governing bodies of the Jewish Agency, the Assembly, the Board of Governors and its Committees and the Executive. He shall be responsible to the Chairman of the Board of Governors and the Chairman of the Executive.

F. AGREEMENT REVISIONS

1. The Reconstitution Agreement shall be revised and bylaws shall be adopted where appropriate to codify changes recommended in this report and approved by the Board of Governors.

2. In the future, such changes will be adopted by a two-thirds majority of those present and voting at the Assembly. Notification of proposed changes or amendments shall be sent to all delegates 60 days prior to the Assembly meeting.

3. All recommendations approved by the Board of Governors not requiring such change or amendments shall be transmitted for action to the Implementation Committee.

THE JEWISH AGENCY FOR ISRAEL
COMMISSION ON ALIYAH
Report and Recommendations to the Board of Governors, October 1982

                                   CHAIRMAN: Irwin S. Field
                             COCHAIRMAN: Yoske Shapira

The Commission on Aliyah was asked to recommend strategies which would increase Jewish Agency/WZO effectiveness in promoting aliyah. The Commission determined its role was not to evaluate existing programs, but to make specific recommendations for improving the working relationship between the Jewish Agency and WZO as well as other bodies which might have the potential for, or were involved in, contributing to the aliyah process.

    The Commission first discussed its aims and goals. They were presented to the Tenth Jewish Agency Assembly and expressed the Commission's desire to elevate the concern about and commitment to aliyah among all Jewish communities worldwide; to delineate more clearly lines of communication, action and responsibility within and between all organizations and institutions presently and potentially concerned with aliyah; to deal with operating principles and long-range concerns which transcend the day-to-day operations related to aliyah; to encourage the development of more effective and efficient ways of operating in the diaspora to the end that duplication of effort is minimized and cooperation is maximized among all concerned; to encourage the continued contact of communities of origin with olim in their absorption process.

With the presentation of these aims and goals, the Commission also expressed its concern about certain conditions in Israel. Namely, difficulties in employment and housing, social problems, lessening of idealism, bureaucratic obstacles and lack of public acceptance of some aspects of religious expression. While the Commission understood these factors were beyond its mandate, it nevertheless felt compelled to voice its concern about the significant impact they have on the decisions of potential immigrants.

North America was viewed as a first priority among free communities with people in a position to take up residence in Israel. Immigration from North America, to date, was never a significant factor, amounting to only a small percentage of total immigration since the inception of the state.

With the decline of total immigration in recent years, and with the large potential source of immigration from North America, the Commission felt it essential to focus its attention on the adoption of approaches consistent with conditions in Israel and the United States and Canada in the 1980s.

After several meetings, two miniplenums at Agency gatherings, listening to a diverse group of individuals and conducting a survey on the literature on aliyah from the United States, the Commission adopted the following basic principles. They reflect a consensus of thought among the members.

I. Increasing the population of Israel as a result of movement of people in-migration from free countries is of equal importance to individuals, diaspora Jewish communities, and Israel. The challenge must be viewed as the responsibility of the Jewish people everywhere and not only the responsibility of the WZO, Jewish Agency and/or the State of Israel alone.

II. Every Jew who comes to live in Israel is considered to have made aliyah. The motivation to live in Israel may stem from either ideological or non-ideological influences. The motivations and decision criteria, as well as procedures attached to each, must be better understood in order for both processes to add significant numbers of newcomers to the population of Israel in the years to come.

III. The movement of a large number of people from free countries needs a wider consensus among the people in Israel; which must be expressed in visible efforts to promote and create investment, employment, settlement and housing opportunities which are both available and affordable throughout the country.

IV. The Government of Israel and the Jewish Agency/WZO should organize and mobilize their respective resources to create conditions for aliyah which will result in the introduction of the prospect of living in Israel to more people and add significantly to the decision to settle in the country.

Specific recommendations, also reflecting a consensus among members of the Commission, relating to the above principles:

1. Diaspora community involvement is essential to the creation of a greater awareness about aliyah among Jewish communities in free countries. In the United States, this means involving federations. In other countries, there must be some link to the central community organization. The nature of aliyah activities in each community will depend on local organizations and agencies and the roles they assume in the process. Programs should be developed in conjunction with local community organizations to conform to local situations, capabilities and capacity. Great flexibility will be needed to accommodate local variations between geographical areas and within individual countries.

A series of demonstration models should be developed utilizing differing approaches to encourage aliyah. Community leadership must be involved with the Jewish Agency in the early phases of development of programs and processes.

The Commission noted some initial progress in this development by special representatives of the Aliyah Department in North America. Their experience should be continued, reviewed and modified as conditions warrant. The Aliyah Department should continue to provide guidance and encouragement to local efforts, disseminate ideas and information, as well as providing national exposure for successful models.

Community involvement must be a continuing process. Therefore, it is also recommended that the North American Association of Americans and Canadians in Israel be shifted from the WZO to the Jewish Agency, since all communities now deal directly with the Jewish Agency.

2. Communication about opportunities for living in Israel must become a part of the program of all organizations whose principal membership is in the diaspora.

3. All members of Government and Jewish Agency officials should view themselves as important promoters of opportunities for living in Israel. Such individuals should include in their itinerary of travel a special effort to meet with

national organizations and local communities as well as organizations specifically concerned with aliyah.

4. All *shlichim* in the employ of the Jewish Agency/WZO should see the promotion of aliyah as an essential part of their role in addition to their primary function. This may entail special orientation seminars, as well as in-service seminars.

The Commission took note of the changes in the institute for training *shlichim* whereby a more comprehensive approach to preparation for *shlichut* is now the standard program. However, this recommendation specifically highlights the importance of the aliyah portion of a *shaliach's* activity.

5. Program opportunities on a large scale for potential olim of all age levels, of varied intensity and time periods, must be established to create a broadened base of interest. Such programs may involve government agencies, the Jewish Agency or WZO — either individually or in cooperation. Some programs should be tailored to meet the local needs of various communities and should be developed in consultation with community organizations on the basis of joint responsibility for planning and execution.

6. An interdepartmental committee on aliyah within the Jewish Agency should be established to raise the status of aliyah. This committee should be at the department head level and hold regularly scheduled meetings. It should provide a basis for exchanging ideas, new concepts and plans with other department heads on all aspects of aliyah and absorption. It should also serve as a forum for solving specific problems with the ability to call on the diverse resources of the Agency to provide solutions.

7. The Board of Governors is urged to recommend to the Government the creation of an interministerial commission on immigration and absorption. Such a commission would facilitate the exchange of information and ideas between ministers, and set the stage for more effective means of dealing with problems connected with immigration and absorption.

8. The Commission recommends that the Government station a customs official in the United States with the authority to grant binding judgments, so as to reduce confusion, misinformation and frustration among potential or actual immigrants and olim.

9. The Board of Governors to recommend to the Jewish Agency members of the Coordinating Committee to place aliyah and immigration on the agenda each time they meet with Government.

10. With due consideration to the present division of activities between the Jewish Agency and WZO, the Commission recommends the Assembly and Board of Governors be given greater involvement, of a practical nature, with aliyah from free countries.

While many of the above recommendations relate to specific circumstances or conditions in the United States and Canada, the Commission nevertheless feels they involve conceptual approaches adaptable to other countries or regions of the world.

The Commission has completed its current mandate. The Board of Governors is asked to determine the appropriate means of implementing the principles and recommendations as brought forth above.

THE JEWISH AGENCY FOR ISRAEL
COMMISSION ON EDUCATION
Report and Recommendations to the Board of Governors, October 1982

CHAIRMAN: Avraham Katz
COCHAIRMAN: Martin E. Citrin

Presented herein is a summary report of the Commission on Education including: (1) the charge to the Commission; (2) the central issues dealt with; and (3), the conclusions and recommendations.

CHARGE TO THE COMMISSION

As enunciated at the special conference in Caesarea of the Jewish Agency Board of Directors, the charge to the Commission on Education was: *To review the structures and functions of the Jewish Agency/WZO as an effective central world resource in the field of formal and informal Jewish education.*

In elaboration of the charge, the mandates of the Commission were to:

a. Consider ways of strengthening the Jewish Agency/WZO framework for conducting the Jewish educational programs and activities sponsored by the WZO and the Jewish Agency.

b. Identify areas of Jewish/Zionist education that are weak and require special attention.

c. Develop appropriate strategies for the heightening of Israeli and Zionist content of diaspora Jewish education.

CENTRAL ISSUES

In its consideration of the factors that impacted most directly on these concerns, the Commission identified three central issues:

a. *Improved Communication*– Can inter-communication between Israel and the diaspora be more effectively developed to achieve a shared understanding of Jewish/Zionist education goals, needs, priorities and respective and mutual tasks?

b. *Setting Priorities* – How can we assure the most effective use and deployment of Jewish Agency/WZO educational resources to meet the priority needs of the various diaspora countries and communities in order to achieve the Jewish Agency/WZO educational objectives?

c. *Improving Organization Effectiveness* – How can organizational effectiveness be enhanced within and between the Jewish Agency and WZO structures to achieve clearer definition of tasks, effective coordination, and improved procedures for planning, budgeting, and evaluation of educational services and programs?

CONCLUSIONS AND RECOMMENDATIONS

These issues were pursued diligently at the meetings of the Commission and resulted in specific conclusions and recommendations. The Commission had the benefit of background documents and working papers prepared at the direction of the Chairman and CoChairman by groups of Israeli and diaspora formal and informal Jewish educators and by the staff aides to the Commission. The Commission also found most helpful the input of the members of the Jewish Agency Board whose views on the issues were invited and were fully considered. The Chairman and Cochairman met periodically to plan the agendas. In turn, the members of the Commission demonstrated by the quality of their participation their profound conviction that effective Jewish/Zionist education is essential to assuring a Jewish future invigorated with a sharing of Jewish purpose and destiny.

Accordingly, the following conclusions and specific recommendations were reached by consensus:

A. Assuring Effective Inter-Communication Between Israel and the Diaspora on Jewish/Zionist Education Goals and Services

Conclusions: The Jewish Agency/WZO is the major central means of inter-communication and dialogue between Israel and the diaspora on Jewish/Zionist education concerns. As the principal instruments for carrying out this essential function, the various WZO departments involved with educational services and programs have developed and provided these in consultation with the diaspora community organizations they serve. The Commission concludes that the present needs of world Jewry require an intensification of such inter-communication and dialogue; that the objective should be to build the educational bridge more firmly between Israel and the diaspora to assure the mutuality of understanding between two true partners – Israel and the various diaspora communities – in regard to Jewish/Zionist education goals, the various lacks and needs to be met in view of the challenges to Jewish survival in different lands, the respective and mutual ways and responsibilities in meeting these needs.

Recommendations on Improving Israel/Diaspora Inter-Communications: The Commission recommends that the following principles and specific measures be adopted to deepen the common understanding between Israel and diaspora areas on Jewish/Zionist education goals, needs, service and program priorities, and mutual and respective responsibilities:

a. The communication process must be a two-way, continuous approach.

b. Dialogue, to be effective, must involve top national and communal leadership and leaders of other appropriate bodies in Jewish/Zionist education.

c. Dialogue must take into account the significant differences in the Jewish condition in the various lands where Jews live.

d. A central mechanism must be established to develop specific means to ensure improved and strengthened dialogue and inter-communication between Israel and the diaspora, including means of implementation.

B. Setting Sound Priorities

Conclusions: In order to carry out its Jewish and Zionist education mission most effectively and efficiently, it is essential that the Jewish Agency/WZO maintain a systematic priority-setting capacity in three vital areas:

1. *Age groups* which should be the targets of its attention;

2. *Types and quality of services and programs* which can most readily meet educational goals and the needs of diaspora communities; and

3. Most effective use of its *financial and manpower resources.* Jewish Agency/WZO should concentrate on tasks that are most urgently needed to assure maximum use of its limited resources.

Recommendations on Priorities: Based on these conclusions, the Commission makes the following recommendations in order to ensure that proper emphasis is placed on objectives and programs relevant to current Jewish Agency/WZO goals and diaspora needs oriented to Zionism, Israel, peoplehood and continuity:

a. The principal target population for Jewish Agency/WZO educational efforts should be from kindergarten up to and inclusive of teenagers and young adults of student age. This includes reaching out to young people who are unaffiliated with Jewish life and untouched by Jewish education.

b. Based upon the dialogue on the needs of each community, programs and services addressed to the target population should include:

(1) In-service training for educators — formal and informal — working with the young persons referred to above;

(2) Formal and informal educational programs in Israel (both short-term programs of up to three months and long-term programs of six months to two years) for such groups as diaspora students in universities, in yeshivot and high schools, youth movements, Jewish organizations, etc.;

(3) Preparation of new study aids and materials on Israel, Zionism, Judaism, Hebrew and related topics. This should include surveying other available materials to avoid duplication;

(4) Providing qualified and well-trained Israeli teachers and *shlichim* where needed in the diaspora;

(5) Organizing family educational experiences in Israel;

(6) Encouraging local follow-up with returnees from all Israel programs.

c. Among these priorities, the Jewish Agency/WZO should concentrate on tasks that are most urgently needed, to assure maximum use of limited resources.

C. Enhancing Organization Effectiveness

Conclusions: The Commission gave careful consideration to the charge "to review the structures and functions of the Jewish Agency/WZO as an effective central world resource in the field of formal and informal Jewish education." Its deliberations were based on the recognition that, as is the case within all types of complex organizational systems, *it is indeed essential that the Jewish Agency/WZO undertake periodic updating of its organizational structures and functions to assure effectiveness and efficiency.* It concluded that the aspects of operation that would benefit from such a review included:

a. Planning, producing, delivering and evaluating services;

b. Means of assuring effective coordination among departments; and

c. Clarifying the respective and mutual functions of the Jewish Agency and the WZO in respect to Jewish and Zionist education.

Recommendations on Improving Organizational Effectiveness: In keeping with the Caesarea mandate with regard to improving organizational and operational effectiveness, the Commission makes the following recommendations:

a. A permanent mechanism must be established by the Jewish Agency/WZO to secure more effective coordination and cooperation between and within the Jewish Agency/WZO systems. This mechanism should be responsible for clarifying the relationship of the Jewish Agency and WZO with respect to planning, budgetary operations, evaluation and follow-up.

b. It is proposed that mechanisms be established for improving inter-departmental communication, planning and collaboration in addressing services to diaspora areas and to facilitate cooperative working relationships among the educational departments, the foundations, the JDC, the several North American Jewish education agencies, the Fonds Social and similar bodies in other countries.

c. We propose the establishment of a special follow-up committee composed of appropriate members of the Jewish Agency/WZO involved in Jewish education to carry forward the recommendations presented herein.

REPORT OF THE BOARD OF GOVERNORS
COMMISSION ON FINANCES AND FISCAL POLICY
May 24, 1983

CHAIRMAN: Arthur Levine
COCHAIRMAN: Philip Granovsky

INTRODUCTION

The Commission on Finances and Fiscal Policy was created by the Board of Governors of the Jewish Agency. The Commission is one of six that were created to review the activities of the Agency since its reconstitution in 1971. The Commission was asked to consider a number of policies and processes affecting the Agency's financial planning.

Since its first meeting on February 19, 1981, the Commission has concentrated its efforts on several areas identified as most essential to the fiscal well-being of the Agency including:

— How can the Agency debt be liquidated? What should the borrowing policies of the Agency be? What is the possible exposure to further debt as a result of commitments to such programs as Project Renewal?

— By what means can the Agency increase its income? What sources are available in addition to the campaigns?

— How should the Agency manage its assets? What policies should be followed for acquisitions or liquidation of existing assets?

— How should the Agency administer the financial planning and budgeting process?

The initial efforts of this Commission were well received and the Commission's recommendations were accepted. A debt retirement policy was adopted by the Board of Governors and the fund-raising communities. That Board of Governor's resolution was followed by the adoption of the first balanced budget (for the year ending March 31, 1983). Moreover, the Special Campaign reflects the Commission's recommendation that the Agency limit its responsibility for programs and services to the amount of funds available.

JEWISH AGENCY DEBT RETIREMENT

The magnitude of the Agency global debt — approximately $600,000,000 — and the annual cost of servicing these loan obligations is the most important fiscal matter confronting the Jewish Agency. Included in the Agency's figure is a $150,000,000 debt ceiling of United Israel Appeal, Inc. Since the inception of this Commission, the total has been reduced by $50,000,000. During the past five years, the interest expense of the Agency (including that of UIA) has doubled, reflecting substantially higher levels of interest throughout the world. Today, debt service is the largest expense of the Agency's operating budget. The debt burden is causing serious cutbacks in programs and services which could greatly affect the Agency's credibility.

The Commission does not question the causes which led the Agency to its present fiscal situation. However, it is clear that, until recently, the Board of Governors had not given sufficient attention to the Agency's debt. The first step taken in correcting the Agency's casual attitude toward its debt was the establishment of a debt ceiling three years ago. This was followed by several policy decisions announced at the Board of Governors' meetings in February 1982. The announcement of a debt retirement program and the adoption of a balanced budget for the year ending March 31, 1982, each reflected recommendations made by this Commission.

Reduction of the current outstanding indebtedness is the Agency's most important fiscal objective. But the Agency cannot be expected to achieve that goal by itself. This is the responsibility of the entire Jewish community. The announcement of the debt retirement program and a balanced budget are but two steps to be taken. Increasing the Agency's income, reducing operating expenses and the selling of assets must also take place. The success of the debt retirement program will depend upon the Agency's demonstrating its seriousness of purpose.

The Commission recommends that the Treasurer provide regular, ongoing reports of the progress of the debt retirement program. Further recommendations are discussed in the following sections.

JEWISH AGENCY DEBT RETIREMENT — SOURCES OF INCOME: SALE OF ASSETS

The Jewish Agency's assets — subsidiary companies, investments and accounts receivable — are the result of the Agency's operating activities over the past fifty years. The value of these assets is difficult to determine in view of the fact some assets, such as housing units, have a limited market for their sale. The Treasurer has estimated that the value of these assets is between $25 million and $30 million.

Housing units represent the largest asset of the Agency. The 30,000 units owned by the Agency and UIA are administered by Amigour and are roughly one-third of the number of units owned by the Government of Israel. The Agency depends upon the Government to set housing policy with regard to occupancy, rent income and terms of sale. There must be a consistency between the Agency's policy and that of the Government. In general, there are two possible buyers for these properties: the Government and the occupants. Considering the Government's current economic and fiscal situation, it is not likely that it would consider purchasing the housing units. The sale of the apartments to the occupants also may not be feasible. Tenants of these dwellings are generally poor, receive rent subsidies and, therefore, there is little economic incentive for them to purchase their homes. Any sale to these individuals would be for a token value and the Agency would then have to provide long-term mortgages. There is some consideration being given to a possible third category of purchaser: private developers.

Over the course of time, the Agency has created companies to fulfill certain program and service needs. Housing construction firms and furniture-making factories are two examples. The continuance of these companies as wholly-owned subsidiaries is no longer justified. Wherever possible, the companies should be sold to private investors. The Jewish Agency should rely upon the private sector to provide necessary services. The Agency should not own or operate any company that is not an essential part of providing services to the Agency's clients.

The Agency holds securities in various companies, including Bank Leumi L'Israel (Founders' shares) and El Al Airlines. These securities may not have any real market value because the stockholder may not have voting rights in the company or share in the corporate profits. Those securities that have a market value should be sold.

The Agency's receivables from immigrants and settlers have a nominal value. Earlier loans were made to individuals for the purchase of basic necessities. The loans were denominated in Israel pounds, unlinked to an inflation index, with only a nominal rate of interest. In recent years, the lending policies of the Agency have been changed to provide shorter terms of repayment, reasonable rate of interest, and the principal amount is linked to the consumer price index.

The value of the Agency's assets, and those of United Israel Appeal, Inc., are unrelated to the amount of the Agency's indebtedness. The sale of these assets is a potential source of funds or may be a means of reducing the Agency's operating expenses.

The Agency should accelerate its efforts to divest itself of its assets. Professional expertise from the diaspora and from Israel should be called upon to assist in the assessment of these properties and to identify potential purchasers. The net income (or loss) of each Agency asset should be calculated. Those assets which are not required by the Agency to fulfill its activities should be sold. It is also recommended that the role of the Assets and Liabilities Committee be determined at this time.

JEWISH AGENCY DEBT RETIREMENT – SOURCES OF INCOME: CAMPAIGN INCOME

The American Jewish community has provided approximately two-thirds of the Agency's income since 1967. During these past fifteen years, the level of giving to federation campaigns in the U.S. has increased from less than $200 million to nearly $600 million annually. In spite of the fact that the levels of giving increased as a direct response to Israel emergencies, the communities' allocations of funds to National UJA have declined from two-thirds of every dollar to slightly more than 50 cents. United Israel Appeal's income from the UJA regular and emergency campaigns has remained relatively constant, in absolute dollars, since 1973. Those same dollars, adjusted for increases in the Consumer Price Index, have a purchasing power less than the value of dollars received in 1969.

The outstanding community allocations (receivables of UJA) are estimated at $250 to $400 million. UJA is currently attempting to establish the exact amount due on a community-by-community basis. These receivables represent unpaid pledges for campaigns back to 1970. The largest portion represents the current year's campaign allocations. The community allocations are based on anticipated revenues; the receivables are outstanding obligations of the communities and not just unpaid pledges of the individual contributors.

United Jewish Appeal has embarked on a campaign to increase the community allocations for overseas needs and accelerate the cash flow from the federations. UJA has emphasized the importance of the *partnership* which depends upon an equal sharing of the funds available. Community federations, having funded local needs on a priority basis, have placed the burden of the outstanding, unpaid pledges on the Jewish Agency. The needs of the communities are clearly recognized. It is therefore essential that the level of the total campaign be increased so that the local agencies and the overseas agencies can both benefit.

The decline in the amounts allocated to National UJA is considered a more serious financial threat to the Agency than the large sum of uncollected pledges. The large outstanding receivable of UJA reflects the failure to emphasize the importance of cash collections. In the absence of a sharing of campaign income with UJA on an ongoing basis, there is little incentive for the communities to stress cash collections when local needs are taken care of first. There is some feeling that the basis for community allocations must be changed to *cash* from estimates of campaign pledges. The assignment of community pledge receivables to National UJA and UIA is inequitable and unrealistic. The change would lead to an accelerated cash flow, thus reducing the Agency's need for borrowed funds to meet current operating needs on a daily basis.

The debt retirement programs begun in the United States and Canada must not be allowed to falter. They are a priority; in fact, they are an emergency campaign. The awareness of the communities' total obligations to UJA will encourage greater efforts to collect outstanding pledges. It will also foster changes in the community allocation process for campaign pledges as well as cash. Communities must be encouraged to support UJA's efforts to increase allocations for National UJA, debt retirement and accelerated cash remittances to UJA.

The Agency's debt was partially undertaken in anticipation of the campaign allocations made to National UJA and UIA for programs and services in Israel. Determining the approximate amount due to UJA, and the amount that may be anticipated from the communities in settling these accounts, will assist the Agency in its financial planning.

The campaign reporting of National UJA at the Board of Governors' meetings can be misleading. It is urged that UJA speak in terms of amounts that the organization will receive, instead of the National campaign figures which include amounts that will be allocated for local needs. While the strength of the larger figure is imposing, it is deceptive and leads to misunderstandings as to the financial resources available to the Agency.

THE BUDGETING PROCESS

The development of the Jewish Agency's financial plans is a joint effort between the Agency Treasury Department and the Board of Governors' Budget and Finance Committee. The existing budgeting process is cumbersome and complex and does not permit the Budget and Finance Committee to make a viable contribution.

There is agreement among the Commission members, Chairman of the Budget and Finance Committee and the Agency Treasury that the budgeting process can and should be amended to permit a more effective means of financial planning. This recommendation has been made to the Board of Governors and the proposed changes will be implemented.

A first step to simplify the process was taken by the Budget and Finance Committee when it appointed a sub-committee to work with the Treasurer in developing a preliminary budget for the year ended March 31, 1983. This small group was able to establish a framework for the Budget and Finance Committee's review. Their success demonstrated the effectiveness of a small group.

Agency budgets are too complex to permit Committee members to become familiar with the myriad details and properly review ongoing activities. The Committee should be divided into smaller sub-committees with the responsibility for reviewing, in detail, the budget presented by each of the Agency's three departments. A fourth sub-committee would be responsible for other Agency expenses, including debt service and Project Renewal. Each sub-committee would also be responsible for reviewing interim financial statements provided by the Agency Treasury Department. The full Budget and Finance Committee would be responsible for reviewing the findings and recommendations of each sub-committee.

Budgeting is a continuous process. The Budget and Finance Committee should meet at least twice each year, first to review and recommend the budget, and during the year, to review actual performance as compared with the budget. To be effective, the Treasurer must provide continuous, timely reports to permit a comparison of expenditures against the financial plan, a step that is essential both to control current year activities as well as provide a basis for future year plans.

The Agency has adopted the principle of a balanced budget. Effective budgeting would therefore require a close examination of income projections as well as expenses. The Agency Treasury has been successful in the past in estimating income from its various sources. A sub-committee, focusing on income, is deemed necessary. For example, reviewing the Keren Hayesod and United Jewish Appeal estimates of income with the campaign leadership may provide for an exchange of ideas that have an effect on the Agency. Specifically, attention should be given to the earmarking of gifts for special projects which limits the amount of funds available for general programs of the Agency. The role of this sub-committee would be limited to campaign income projections and not to a discussion of the conduct of the campaigns. The sub-committee should include in its review campaign income earmarked for special campaigns, Project Renewal and debt retirement.

The proposed changes in the Budget and Finance Committee should be implemented immediately.

The Agency Executive, when adopting the budgetary framework, must first establish the Agency's goals and objectives. To be meaningful, the budget must reflect those Agency priorities.

SUMMARY STATEMENT

The successful implementation of the Finances and Fiscal Policy Commission's recommendations will be affected by other Commissions. The establishment of goals and objectives will enable the financial planning process to provide budgets which reflect the priorities of the Agency. The Governance Commission's recommendations regarding the administration of the Agency will set responsibilities and authority.

The minutes of the meetings of this Commission identify numerous opportunities for the Agency to introduce better methods for financial planning and the setting of fiscal policies. The size of the Agency's annual operating budget, and the enormity of its assets and liabilities, underscore the need for more attention to financial matters by the Board of Governors.

The Commission has had the opportunity to make a number of interim recommendations to the Board of Governors for their prompt action. The implementation of a debt retirement program, a balanced budget during the year ended March 31, 1983 (the first such budget during a non-emergency campaign year), and the formulation of the Special Campaign budget all reflected policies expressed by this Commission. But each of the steps taken requires further supportive action by the Board of Governors, as expressed in the body of this report.

The Commission members wish to express their appreciation to Akiva Lewinsky, Treasurer, and Dr. Shimon Ravid, Director General Finance, and their respective staffs, for providing the Commission with the background information essential to its deliberations.

PART IV

Appendixes

APPENDIX I

STRUCTURE AND BUDGET OF THE WORLD ZIONIST ORGANIZATION

STRUCTURE*

The Zionist Congress

The Zionist Congress is the supreme governing body of the World Zionist Organization (WZO). It convenes once every four years. Sixty-two percent of the delegates to the Congress are representatives of Zionist organizations outside of Israel. Israel's 38 percent of the delegates represents Zionist parties in proportion to their numbers in the Knesset. Since the 29th Zionist Congress in 1978, five world Jewish bodies that have accepted the Jerusalem Program and encourage their members to formally join the Zionist movement have been represented by fifteen delegates each. They are the World Union for Progressive Judaism (Reform movement); the World Council of Synagogues (Conservative movement); the Conference of Kehillot and Organizations (Orthodox movement); World Maccabi Union; and the World Sephardi Federation. WIZO, the Women's International Zionist Organization, has been represented at the Congress since 1965 through a special arrangement allocating their world body representation with voting rights, but they may not submit nomination lists or candidates for election in the various countries.

A Zionist world union is a Zionist organization which represents a special ideological point of view within the WZO, has branches in at least five countries, and is represented at the Congress. The following is a list of the Zionist World Unions:

> World Union of Herut Hatzohar
> World Union of General Zionists
> World Confederation of United Zionists
> Labor Zionist Movement
> World Mizrachi and Hapoel Hamizrachi
> World Union of Mapam
> Artzeinu, World Reform Zionists

The Congress elects, *inter alia*, two governing bodies: the Zionist Executive, whose task it is to manage the affairs of the WZO in Israel and the diaspora; and the Zionist General Council (Va'ad HaPoel), to which the Executive is responsible and which meets annually to determine the policy and budget of the WZO between Congresses.

---

* See Table 1 on pages 14-15.

The Executive

The Executive is composed of thirty-six members, twenty-four of whom live in Israel. The twelve who reside in the United States make up the American Section of the Zionist Executive representing the WZO among American Jewry. Approximately twenty members of the Executive represent Zionist organizations affiliated with Israeli political parties. The various portfolios are assigned among the Executive's members, with some serving without portfolio. The portfolios are:

Development and Services	Settlement
Education and Culture	Spiritual Services
External Relations	Student
Immigration and Absorption	Torah Education
Information	Treasury
Organization	Young Leadership
Sephardi Communities	Youth and Hechalutz

Five associate members of the Executive have no voting rights.

The thirty-six members of the Executive serve as members of the WZO component of the Jewish Agency Board of Governors. In this capacity, the members of the Executive make recommendations to the Jewish Agency Board of Governors regarding leadership of the various Agency departments. By common agreement (and to avoid the necessity of a 'close vote' in the Board), the WZO has agreed to the principle of "consent by the partners" in choosing nominees for Jewish Agency posts.

By agreement, the Chairman of the Zionist Executive also serves as Chairman of the Jewish Agency Executive.

The Zionist General Council

The Zionist General Council consists of 144 members with full voting rights, of whom 113 are representatives of the various Zionist movements represented in the Congress; the rest are representatives of the affiliated world Jewish organizations. The Council oversees the activities of the Zionist Executive by means of its various committees, the most important of which is the Permanent Budget and Finance Committee.

Treasurer

The Treasurer of the WZO is elected by the Jewish Agency Assembly and traditionally is the same individual serving as the Treasurer of the Jewish Agency.

Comptroller

The Comptroller scrutinizes the programs and finances of every functional unit of both the WZO and the Jewish Agency, and investigates all complaints. The post is non-political, and the Comptroller serves as independent auditor, inspector-general and guarantor of rigid enforcement of proper financial controls and operations. The post has an independent budget and a staff of accountants and attorneys. The Comptroller reports to the Zionist General Council and Congress and to the Jewish Agency Board of Governors and Assembly. The published reports are available to the public, and contain findings, responses and descriptions of corrective actions taken.

BUDGET

Funding for WZO programs comes from Keren Hayesod and the Government of Israel. Since the Agreement for the Reconstitution of the Jewish Agency for Israel came into force in June 1971, no funds are allocated to the WZO budget from monies raised by the United Jewish Appeal (UJA).

The programs of the WZO, which are implemented in the framework of the regular budget, cover various fields of activity and are carried out in different countries in the free world:

— Promotion of immigration from the free countries and assistance to new immigrants from those countries in their aliyah to Israel and certain aspects of their absorption.
— Activities with Jewish students and youth from the diaspora (abroad and in Israel) and support for the pioneering Zionist youth movements.
— Educational and cultural activities with diaspora communities and especially for Jewish schools abroad.
— Religious education and cultural activities for diaspora Jewry and particularly with religious educational institutions.
— Organization work in the Zionist movement throughout the world and with the local Zionist federations.
— Information activities throughout the world.
— Development of a young Zionist leadership.
— Fostering relations between non-Jewish organizations and Zionism and Israel.
— Spiritual services to isolated communities in the diaspora.
— Collection and storage of documentary material on the Zionist movement.
— Enhancement of Zionist values among the Israeli public through the work of the Zionist Council in Israel.
— Zionist and social activities among Sephardi and Oriental Jewish communities.
— Publication of books and articles of importance to Jewish culture and Zionism.

TABLE 8: WZO BUDGET SUMMARY

SUMMARY		1984/5 $1000		1985/6 $1000/M Shekel	
		%	59,000.0	59,000.0	%
	TOTAL				
9310	IMMIGRATION AND ABSORPTION	30.26	17,850.0	17,000.0	28.81
9331	EDUCATION AND CULTURE	6.41	3,783.6	3,650.0	6.18
9332	TORAH EDUCATION AND CULTURE	6.41	3,783.6	3,650.0	6.18
9340	YOUTH AND HE'CHALUTZ	19.65	11,591.0	11,350.0	19.24
9341	STUDENT DIVISION	0.83	495.0	480.0	0.81
9342	ZIONIST FULFILLMENT	0.33	200.0	185.0	0.31
9345	INFORMATION	2.73	1,600.0	1,575.0	2.67
9350	ORGANIZATION	6.66	3.927.4	3,818.2	6.48
9351	YOUNG LEADERSHIP	1.15	684.0	660.1	1.12
9352	EXTERNAL RELATIONS	1.06	629.0	610.0	1.03
9354	SPIRITUAL SERVICES	0.77	454.0	445.0	0.76
9357	ZIONIST COUNCIL IN ISRAEL	0.66	390.0	380.0	0.65
9358	SEPHARDI COMMUNITIES	0.90	532.3	515.0	0.87
9359	DEVELOPMENT AND SERVICES	1.00	590.0	570.0	0.96
9360-89	OTHER FUNCTIONS	13.70	8.080.9	7,681.8	13.04
9390-97	FINANCE & ADMINISTRATION	5.15	3,040.0	3,036.0	5.15
9398	RESERVE	2.33	1,369.2	2,394.0	4.05
	SPECIAL RESERVE – NEW ACTIVITIES			1.000.0	1.69
INCOME			59,000.0	59,000.0	

COMPARISON BY YEARS	($)		
EXPENDITURE	1983/4	1982/3	1981/2
TOTAL	64,904,623	53,057,644	56,666,112

APPENDIX II

THE JEWISH AGENCY FOR ISRAEL
BOARD OF GOVERNORS

as of October 1985

Note: * indicates Member of Executive

*1. Mr. Jerold C. Hoffberger,
     Chairman, Board of Governors
     Baltimore, Maryland, USA   UIA

*2. Mr. Max M. Fisher
     Founding Chairman
     Chairman, Committee on
     Long Range Planning
     Chairman, Pincus Fund
     Committee
     Detroit, Michigan, USA   UIA

*3. Mr. Arye Leon Dulzin
     Chairman, Executive
     Chairman, Coordinating
     Committee of Jewish Agency/
     Government
     Chairman, Committee on Joint
     Programs for Jewish Education
     Jerusalem, ISRAEL   WZO

4.   Mr. Joe Ain
     Montreal, Quebec, CANADA   KH

*5. Mr. Chaim Aron
     Head, Immigration and
     Absorption Department
     Jewish Agency
     Jerusalem, ISRAEL   WZO

6.   Mr. Eli Artzi
     Rehovot, ISRAEL   WZO

7.   Mr. David Avayou
     Head Department of
     Sephardic Communities
     World Zionist Organization
     Jerusalem, ISRAEL   WZO

*8. Dr. Avraham Avi-hai
     World Chairman, Keren Hayesod
     Jerusalem, ISRAEL   WZO

9.   Mr. Irving Bernstein
     New York, New York, USA   UIA

10. Rabbi Louis Bernstein
     Bayside, New York, USA   WZO

11. Mr. Herschel W. Blumberg
     Hyattsville, Maryland, USA   UIA

12. Mr. Morris Borsuk
     Herzlia Pituach, ISRAEL   WZO

13. Mr. Morton Brownstein
     St. Laurent, Quebec, CANADA   KH

14. Mr. Joel Breslau
     Chevy Chase, Maryland, USA   UIA

*15. Ms. Shoshana Cardin
     New York, New York, USA   UIA

16. Mr. Trevor Chinn
     London, ENGLAND   KH

17. Mr. Martin E. Citrin
Romulus, Michigan, USA   UIA

18. Mr. Ben Cohen
New York, New York   WZO

*19. Mr. Matityahu Droblas
Head, Rural Settlement Department
Jewish Agency
Jerusalem, ISRAEL   WZO

*20. Mr. Raymond Epstein
Chairman, Committee on
Budget and Finance
Chicago, Illinois, USA   UIA

21. Mr. Misha Feldman
Mexico City, MEXICO   KH

*22. Mr. Irwin S. Field
Norwalk, California, USA   UIA

23. Dr. Hertzl Fishman
Jerusalem, ISRAEL   WZO

24. Dr. Nessim Gaon
Geneva, SWITZERLAND   KH

*25. Mr. Uri Gordon
Head, Youth Aliyah Department
Jewish Agency
Jerusalem, ISRAEL   WZO

26. Mr. Osias G. Goren
Chairman, Committee on
Project Renewal
Beverly Hills, California, USA   UIA

*27. Mr. Philip Granovsky
Scarborough, Ontario, CANADA   KH

*28. Mr. Alex Grass
Harrisburg, Pennsylvania, USA   UIA

29. Mrs. Sylvia Hassenfeld
Chairman, Committee on Rural Settlement
Palm Beach, Florida
New York, New York, USA   UIA

30. Mr. Mauricio Hatchwell
Madrid, SPAIN   KH

31. Rabbi Richard Hirsch
Jerusalem, ISRAEL   WZO

32. Mr. Harold Jacobs
Laurence, New York, USA   WZO

33. Dr. Maurice A. Jaffe
Jerusalem, ISRAEL   WZO

34. Mrs. Raya Jaglom
Tel Aviv, ISRAEL   WZO

*35. Mr. Mendel Kaplan
Braamfontein
TVL, SOUTH AFRICA   KH

36. Mr. Avraham Katz
Head, Youth and Hechalutz Department
World Zionist Organization
Jerusalem, ISRAEL   WZO

37. Rabbi Charles Kroloff
Westfield, New Jersey, USA   WZO

38. Mr. Arthur Levine
New York, New York, USA   WZO

39. Mr. H. Irwin Levy
Chairman Committee on Housing
Palm Beach, Florida, USA   UIA

*40. Mr. Akiva Lewinsky
Treasurer, The Jewish Agency
Jerusalem, ISRAEL   WZO

41. Mr. Norman Lipoff
Chairman,
Bylaws Committee
Miami, Florida, USA   UIA

*42. Mr. Robert E. Loup
Denver, Colorado, USA   UIA

43. Mr. William J. Lowenberg
San Francisco, California, USA   UIA

*44. Mr. Isador Magid
Chairman, Committee on
Immigration and Absorption
Mulgrave, Victoria, AUSTRALIA   KH

45. Mr. Morton L. Mandel
Chairman, Committee on Jewish Education
Cleveland, Ohio, USA   UIA

*46. Mr. Yitzhak Mayer
Head, Torah Education Department
World Zionist Organization
Jerusalem, ISRAEL   WZO

47. Mr. Uzi Narkiss
Head, Information Department
World Zionist Organization
Jerusalem, ISRAEL   WZO

48. Mr. Asher Ohayon
Director-General
Ministry of Labor
Jerusalem, ISRAEL   WZO

49. Dr. Israel Peled
Paris, FRANCE   WZO

50. Mr. Moshe Rivlin
Chairman, Jewish
National Fund
Jerusalem, ISRAEL   WZO

51. Mr. David de Rothschild
Paris, FRANCE   KH

52. Mr. Michael M. Sacher
Chairman, Committee on
Controllers Reports
London, ENGLAND   KH

53. Mr. Jose Sasson
Buenos Aires, ARGENTINA   KH

54. Mr. Avraham Schenker
Head, Development and
Services Department
World Zionist Organization
Jerusalem, ISRAEL   WZO

55. Rabbi Alexander M. Schindler
New York, New York, USA   WZO

56. Mr. Irving Schneider
Chairman, Committee on Assets
and Liabilities
New York, New York, USA   UIA

57. Mr. Stephen Shalom
New York, New York, USA   WZO

58. Mr. Eliezer Sheffer,
Head, Department of Young
Leadership Division
World Zionist Organization
Jerusalem, ISRAEL   WZO

59. Mrs. Jane Sherman
Birmingham, Michigan, USA   UIA

60. Mr. Stanley L. Sloane
New York, New York, USA   UIA

61. Mr. Kalman Sultanik
New York, New York, USA   WZO

62. Mrs. Phyllis Sutker
Skokie, Illinois, USA   WZO

*63. Mrs. Bernice Tannenbaum
New York, New York, USA   WZO

64. Mr. Henry Taub
Roseland, New Jersey, USA   UIA

65. Mr. Harry Taubenfeld
Cedarhurst, New York, USA   WZO

66. Dr. Yaacov Eliezer Tavin
Head, Education and Culture
in the Diaspora Deparment
World Zionist Organization
Jerusalem, ISRAEL   WZO

67. Mr. Melech Topiol
Paris, FRANCE   KH

68. Mr. Jacques Torczyner
    New York, New York, USA   WZO

69. Mr. Arye Tzimuki
    Jerusalem, ISRAEL   WZO

70. Mr. Izak Warszawski
    Head, Organization Department
    World Zionist Organization
    Jerusalem, ISRAEL   WZO

71. Mr. Julius Weinstein
    Chairman, Committee on
    Youth Services
    Birdhaven, Johannesburg,
    SOUTH AFRICA   KH

72. Mr. Paul Zuckerman
    Chairman, Committee on
    Institute for
    Leadership Development
    Livonia, Michigan, USA   UIA

*73. Mr. Nissim Zvili
    Head, Rural Settlement Department
    The Jewish Agency
    Jerusalem, ISRAEL   WZO

74. (To be filled.)   KH

ASSOCIATE MEMBERS OF THE EXECUTIVE

Mr. Irving Kessler,
Executive-Vice Chairman
United Israel Appeal, Inc.
New York, New York, USA

Dr. Shimon Ravid
Director-General
Finance Department
The Jewish Agency
Jerusalem, ISRAEL

Mr. Carmi Schwartz
Executive Vice President
Council of Jewish Federations
New York, New York, USA

COMPTROLLER
Mrs. Renana Gutman
The Jewish Agency
Jerusalem, ISRAEL

COUNSEL
Dr. Eli Likhovski
The Jewish Agency
Jerusalem, ISRAEL

DIRECTOR-GENERAL
Mr. Shlomo Gazit
The Jewish Agency
Jerusalem, ISRAEL

SECRETARY-GENERAL AND SECRETARY
Mr. Harry M. Rosen*
The Jewish Agency
Jerusalem, ISRAEL

Mr. Howard Weisband*
Baltimore, Maryland, USA

Mrs. Tsila Blum-Rosen
The Jewish Agency
Jerusalem, ISRAEL

---

* Mr. Rosen retired from the post of Secretary-General at the end of October. Mr. Weisband is his successor in the post.

A NOTE ON THE SOURCES

"The Jewish Agency — An Instrument of the World Jewish Polity" and "The Growth of Diaspora Influence," formerly titled "The Jewish Agency and World Jewry" and "The Jewish Agency Since the Reconstitution: The Growth of Diaspora Influence," are from: *Annual of Bar-Ilan University Studies in Judaica and the Humanities* XVI-XVII. Ramat Gan: Bar-Ilan University, 1979. They also appear as Jerusalem Center reprint IC8A, Elazar, Daniel J., "Israel, American Jewry and the Re-emergence of a World Jewish Polity." Jerusalem: Jerusalem Center for Public Affairs, 1979.

———"Beyond Caesarea," formerly titled "The Jewish Agency and the Jewish People After Caesarea," *Forum* 42/43 (Fall/Winter 1981). Also, reprint IC12. Jerusalem: Jerusalem Center for Public Affairs, 1981.

Hoffman, Charles, "Flexing Their Muscles," *Baltimore Jewish Times,* 17 February 1984. Permission to reprint granted by the *Baltimore Jewish Times.*

Stock, Ernest, "The Reconstitution of the Jewish Agency: A Political Analysis," *American Jewish Year Book, 1972* 73. New York and Philadelphia: The American Jewish Committee and the Jewish Publication Society of America, 1972. Also, reprint IC2. Jerusalem: Jerusalem Center for Public Affairs, 1972.

All other materials published in this handbook are based on sources provided by the Jewish Agency for Israel and the World Zionist Organization in Jerusalem.

FOR FURTHER READING

Books and Articles on the Jewish Agency published by the Jerusalem Center for Public Affairs

A Common Agenda: the Reconstitution of the Jewish Agency for Israel by Zelig Chinitz. A companion to *Understanding the Jewish Agency: A Handbook,* this work is one of the only other books published on the Jewish Agency since its founding in 1929. This volume serves as an introduction to the history of the Jewish Agency's reconstitution through the first decade of its implementation. It is an insider's account of how diaspora and Israeli leaders engaged in a partnership to revitalize the Agency so that it could become the nexus of the emerging world Jewish polity. 1985, 128 pages, Hardcover $15.00, Softcover $10.00.

The Jewish Agency: A Balance Sheet, by Daniel J. Elazar. An assessment of the functioning of Jewish Agency departments—what they do well and how they and their constituent bodies have initiated efforts to confront that which needs improvement. *Jerusalem Letter* no. 78, March 18, 1985.

Does the Diaspora Influence Israel? The Case of the Reconstituted Jewish Agency, by Charles S. Liebman. An examination of the role of diaspora Jewry in bringing about the reconstitution of the Jewish Agency in 1971. Reprinted from *Forum,* 1975, 13 pages, $1.50, IC6.

In Search of Status: The Israeli Government and the Zionist Movement, by Charles S. Liebman. An enlightening account of the battle between Ben Gurion, the WZO, the Jewish Agency, and the American Jewish Committee for footholds of power in the new State of Israel. Reprinted from *Forum,* 1978, 19 pages, $1.50, IC10.

THE JERUSALEM CENTER FOR PUBLIC AFFAIRS is an independent, non-profit institute for policy research and education serving Israel and the Jewish people. The Center is governed by a Board of Fellows consisting of leading academic figures in Israel and the diaspora, as well as a distinguished Board of Overseers, all leaders of the Jewish world. It is able, therefore, to maintain its integrity of action, as well as its freedom to draw upon a wide variety of resources in Israel and abroad.

The Center undertakes multi-disciplinary policy-oriented research and educational projects and is distinguished from other such institutes by virtue of its independence, its organic ties with scholars drawn from Israel and throughout the world, its linking of both Israeli and general Jewish problems through the perspective of the Jewish political tradition with its covenantal or federalist emphasis.

The Jerusalem Center for Public Affairs incorporates two institutes: The Center for Jewish Community Studies and the Jerusalem Institute for Federal Studies. It has offices in Jerusalem, Philadelphia, Montreal, Canada and Montpellier/Paris, France.